# THE ARMIES AND WARS OF THE SUN KING 1643–1715

Volume 2: The Infantry of Louis XIV

**René Chartrand**

'This is the Century of the Soldier', Fulvio Testi, Poet, 1641

Helion & Company

Helion & Company Limited
Unit 8 Amherst Business Centre
Budbrooke Road
Warwick
CV34 5WE
England
Tel. 01926 499 619
Email: info@helion.co.uk
Website: www.helion.co.uk
Twitter: @helionbooks

Published by Helion & Company 2020
Designed and typeset by Serena Jones
Cover designed by Paul Hewitt, Battlefield Design (www.battlefield-design.co.uk)
Printed by Henry Ling Limited, Dorchester, Dorset

Text © René Chartrand 2020
Photographs and illustrations © as individually credited
Colour plates 1–5 by Ed Dovey © Helion & Company 2020
Cover: French Infantry at an assault, late seventeenth century. A grenadier has lit his grenade to throw it at the enemy while a sergeant of the Provence Regiment charges. Print after Marbot. Canadian War Museum, Ottawa. Author's photo.

Every reasonable effort has been made to trace copyright holders and to obtain their permission for the use of copyright material. The author and publisher apologise for any errors or omissions in this work, and would be grateful if notified of any corrections that should be incorporated in future reprints or editions of this book.

ISBN 978-1-912866-54-0

British Library Cataloguing-in-Publication Data.
A catalogue record for this book is available from the British Library.

All rights reserved. No part of this publication may be reproduced, stored in a retrieval system, or transmitted, in any form, or by any means, electronic, mechanical, photocopying, recording or otherwise, without the express written consent of Helion & Company Limited.

For details of other military history titles published by Helion & Company
Limited, contact the above address, or visit our website: http://www.helion.co.uk

We always welcome receiving book proposals from prospective authors.

# Contents

| | |
|---|---|
| Preface | 7 |
| 1. The Netherlands | 9 |
|    Insult and Retribution | 11 |
|    The Strength of the Army | 13 |
|    Command Crisis in France | 15 |
| 2. 1672: Invading the Netherlands | 18 |
|    *Blitzkrieg* on the Dutch | 18 |
|    Political Revolution in Amsterdam | 25 |
|    Aardenburg | 27 |
|    The Bishop's Invasion | 29 |
|    The *Blitzkrieg* Ends | 32 |
|    A "Rape and Pillage" Reputation | 34 |
|    Dutch Resistance | 36 |
| 3. 1673–1674: The War Expands | 39 |
|    1673 and Maastricht | 39 |
|    1674: Franche-Comté, Rhineland and Senef | 45 |
| 4. 1675–1678: Movements and Sieges | 52 |
|    1675: the Rhineland and the Moselle | 52 |
|    Tax Revolts in France | 59 |
|    1676: the *Pré carré*, Flanders, Rhineland, Roussillon | 60 |
|    1677 | 63 |
|    1678 | 66 |
| 5. The Sicilian Adventure | 69 |
| 6. 1678–1684: Peace, Expansion and Ottomans | 78 |
|    Peacetime Military Activities | 78 |
|    Ottoman Invasion, Ottoman Equation | 82 |
| 7. The Business of War | 88 |
|    Money and Armies in the 1660s and 1670s | 88 |
|    War as a Profitable Venture | 92 |
|    The Sun King's Military-Industrial Complex | 92 |
|    Infantry Pay | 95 |
| 8. French Line Infantry | 97 |
|    Raising Standards by Central Authority | 97 |
|    Organisation | 97 |
|    Standardised Infantry Discipline | 102 |
|    Regimental Composition | 103 |

| | |
|---|---:|
| Regimental Officers and Enlisted Ranks | 108 |
| 9. Foreign Mercenary Troops | 122 |
| 10. Infantry Weapons | 134 |
|     Swords | 134 |
|     Polearms | 136 |
|     Muskets | 142 |
|     Bayonets | 145 |
|     Infantry Musket Production | 145 |
|     Arms Drill | 147 |
|     Battle Lines | 149 |
|     Firepower | 150 |
|     Accoutrements | 151 |
|     Weapons Into a New Century | 155 |
| 11. Uniforms, Colours and Music | 157 |
|     Uniforming the Infantry | 157 |
|     Colours | 164 |
|     Military Music and Early Infantry Bands | 167 |
| 12. Camping on Campaign | 172 |
|     The Sun King and his Army on Campaign | 172 |
|     The Infantry's Lodging | 175 |
|     Rations | 179 |
| | |
| Appendix I: Length Measures and Currency in France in the Reign of Louis XIV | 181 |
| Appendix II: Infantry Regiments 1643–1715 | 183 |
| Appendix III: Uniforms | 227 |
| Appendix IV: The Dutch Army | 240 |
| | |
| Colour Plate Commentaries | 244 |

**Note**

Describing the heraldry-inspired colours of the French infantry requires a few notions on heraldry. We have borrowed a plate from Clark's *An Introduction to Heraldry* (London: H. Washbourne, 1840) to guide the reader insofar as basic hues are concerned. From the seventeenth century, engravers sometimes resorted to points and thin lines to indicate the hue of a coat of arms and colours, as was the case with Dutch plates of captured French regimental colours in the early eighteenth century, many of which are reproduced in this book.

The heraldic colour code. Since the Middle Ages (and before colour printing), this simple code has been used by printers. Lines, be they vertical, horizontal, slanted or criss-crossed denote a colour of many of the early eighteenth century Dutch prints showing regimental colours, many of which are reproduced in these pages. Plate from Hugh Clark's *An Introduction to Heraldry*, 1840. (Author's photo)

Colour descriptions. Most infantry colours had a white cross with four quarters that are generally numbered as shown, and that we use in this work to describe them. (Author's photo)

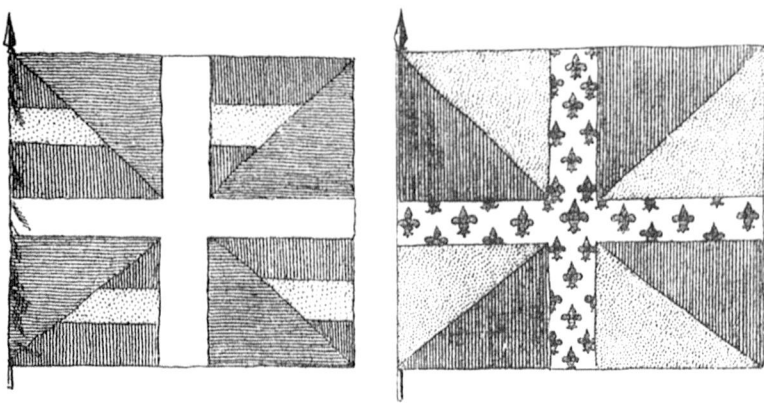

Regimental colours of the Laonnois and Royal-Italien regiments, early eighteenth century. Red, yellow and blue for Laonnois; brown and red with gold lilies on the white cross for Royal-Italien. (Courtesy Rijksmuseum, Amsterdam. RP-P-OB-84.205)

# Preface

*Songs are of Kings, but battles are of men;*
*the creatures of the field and by-lanes …*
From: "The Forgotten" in *Thorn Kings* by Clare Mulley, Poet at the Battlefield Trust, by kind permission.

This second volume continues our survey of the troops and wars of Louis XIV. The narrative of the events goes from the end of the War of Devolution in 1668 to 1684, which shows that it was not a good idea to mock someone like Louis XIV whose French army was the largest and most modern in Europe. The smug Dutch did and, in 1672, Louis made another *Blitzkrieg* on the Netherlands, but that brought forth young William of Orange who saved his nation by letting the sea flood it, and became the Sun King's most bitter and persistent enemy. The French evacuated the Netherlands, but war then spread to include other countries, so the campaigns were fought on four fronts and went on until 1678–1679, the French army raising its strength to unseen levels. A large standing army was kept in peacetime that was sometime used to convince recalcitrant neighbours. We end the narrative with a geo-strategic glance at the "ghost in Europe's closet" –the great Ottoman Empire. We also look at the "business of war", quite literally showing that there were good economic reasons to have wars.

The main part of this volume is devoted to the line infantry. There were a lot of infantrymen that served in over seven hundred regiments during the reign of Louis XIV. We delve on their organisation, their lifestyle, their weapons and their uniforms–these last having then-revolutionary developments like standard calibre and all soldiers wearing coats of the same colour in their regiment. Uniforms are of interest to many nowadays, but there are relatively few descriptions of the period so far know and we have translated just about all we have seen to form several appendices. The regiments are listed with a few of the battles in which they fought in a rather large appendix.

The illustrations show many plans, battles, weapons, colours and soldiers in uniform. Some are from contemporary sources, others from more or less forgotten artists and Mr. Dovey's plates reconstructs dress that has mostly never been before illustrated.

RC

# THE ARMIES AND WARS OF THE SUN KING 1643–1715 VOLUME 2

Louis XIV, 1677. The King is shown as supreme commander wearing gilded armour, red ribbons, white sash with gold fringes, blue coat skirts sprinkled with gold lilies, scarlet and gold housings, gold laced hat with white and red plumes. One of the King's tents at right is blue with gold lilies and lace. Detail of a mural by Jacques Friquet de Vauroze made in 1678 on the wall of the dining hall at Les Invalides in Paris. (Author's photo)

# 1

# The Netherlands

In 1668, western Europe knew that its largest state, the kingdom of France, was in a vigorous period under its autocratic young king. With a state-of-the-art army led by the finest generals, part of Spanish Flanders and all of Franche-Comté had been invaded and occupied the year before in record time comparable to the twentieth-century *Blitzkrieg*. It joined other relatively recent annexations following previous battlefield successes of the French armies. The 1648 treaties of Westphalia turned over to France nearly all of Alsace except the Republic of Strasbourg, which was a "free Imperial city" of the Holy Roman Empire although supposedly independent and neutral. This had been followed in the 1659 treaty with Spain by western Artois and, in the south, the cession of Roussillon to France thus extending the French border into the Pyrenees. The Duchy of Lorraine was still theoretically a province of the Holy Roman Empire, but was in fact under French influence, especially as its territory was sprinkled with various enclaves that were part of France. France too had certain small enclaves resulting from ancient and peculiar privileges. There were for instance the principalities of Dombes, of the Comtats and of Orange, the duchies of Nevers and of Penthièvre, the counties of Charolais, of Turenne and the republic of Mulhouse. All these small fiefdoms, although submitted to France, did not make much sense to the Sun King. He had already bought Dunkirk from Great Britain and would eventually incorporate in one way or another these other rather wayward territories.

France was thus slowly but surely expanding, but not as much as the King would have wished. The Netherlands, which had been France's naval ally during

Overleaf: Map of Europe in the mid seventeenth century. Louis XIV's France was the hub of western Europe and had the largest population and army. The Germanic Holy Roman Empire covering the centre was a myriad of independent cities and states with its imperial capital being Vienna in Austria, the most powerful of the Empire's states. Spain's reach extended to Italy. Northwards were Great Britain, the Scandinavian kingdoms, Poland and Russia further east. The mysterious and powerful Ottoman Turk Empire went from southern Hungary to the reaches of Persia and North Africa. These were the main players in the geostrategic game of those times. The French army campaigned in most of them in the days of the Sun King. (Author's photo)

# THE ARMIES AND WARS OF THE SUN KING 1643–1715 VOLUME 2

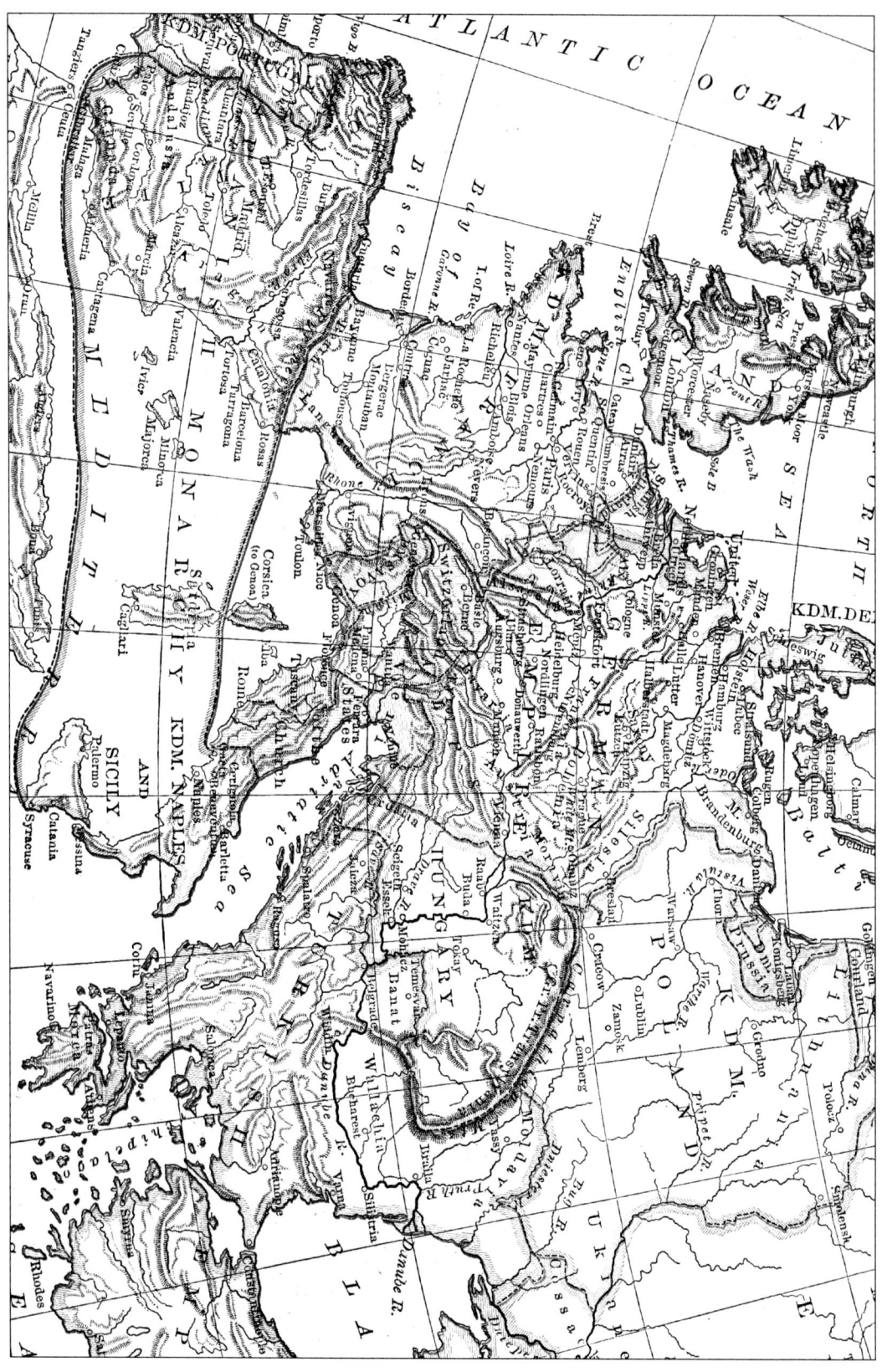

the War of Devolution, had become suspicious and fearful of the remarkable feats of the French army during that war. Almost overnight, it turned from ally to potential opponent. Its actions were seen as treasonous by the King of France and a lot of his subjects.

## Insult and Retribution

The peace treaty of Aix-la-Chapelle signed on 2 May 1668 left a bitter feeling in Louis XIV's heart and soul. In spite of his successful *Blitzkrieg* at the head of Europe's finest army, his lofty objectives had been frustrated by the diplomacy of the Netherlands. A Triple Alliance had been made consisting of England, the Netherlands and Sweden, that would help Spain stop the French. The primary objective of the Dutch diplomats was to prevent France from having a common border with the Netherlands. For that, the remaining Spanish Netherlands absolutely had to remain as a buffer. The French army was excellent, but Louis XIV, advised by his marshals, knew it was not ready to face such a coalition yet. During the negotiations leading to the signature of the treaty, the ability of Koenraad van Beuningen, ambassador extraordinary of the Netherlands, had upset the proud King of France; rumour had it that van Beuningen had said that he did not care about what Louis XIV wanted to do and only considered what he could actually do. At that point, the Sun King knew he should settle for a peaceful solution and reluctantly signed the treaty. He handed Franche-Comté back to Spain, but kept part of Spanish Flanders including 12 fortresses including Lille, Tournai, Oudenarde, Ath and Charleroi. Nevertheless, Louis XIV and much of France felt they had been robbed of the fruits of the 1667–1668 campaigns.

As for the Dutch, they were quite pleased to see the Sun King stopped in his tracks. There were even popular jokes that Ambassador van Beuningen had stopped the sun's progress when he had appeared in front of the King of France …! This, and the publication of a flurry of mocking cartoons – the Netherlands had a free press – really insulted the Sun King; he of course controlled the French press that praised him as a God on Olympus. From then on, the Sun King was determined to have a future revenge match, so French relations with the Netherlands cooled significantly.

Perhaps the Dutch should not have been so arrogant. The *Blitzkrieg* had, after all, given the southern half of prosperous Flanders to France in record time and this was an amazing gain in itself, the likes of which had not been seen in a very long time. The French army was still formidable and certainly showed no sign of becoming decrepit. The Dutch army was more than seven times smaller, somewhat antiquated and certainly no match against the Sun King's troops. Evidence that Louis could be nasty to deal with came in 1670 regarding the status of the Duchy of Lorraine. It had long been a basically francophone territory going as far back as the ninth century AD, becoming a somewhat semi-independent state within the Holy Roman Empire. Lorraine was occupied by the French army until 1661 when it was given back to Duke Charles IV on the promise that it would revert to France when Charles passed away. But Charles later tried to annul this. The Sun King was angered at this shift and charged Minister of War Louvois to go with a French army corps to Nancy, the Duchy's capital. It was occupied without resistance as were other places by another corps led by Marshal Créquy. The Duke fled to Vienna and Louvois gained much experience that would serve him and the French army greatly in the future, notably in planning the invasion of the Netherlands.[1]

Meanwhile, few in Amsterdam seem to have fully realised the impact that the rapidly growing French navy could have on their own naval trade and power. The Netherlands' naval predominance, which created great wealth and the most powerful battle fleets in Europe, came about through many factors. Perhaps one of the most important was the hitherto unknown way to cut timber with multiple saws to make many planks at the same time in semi-mechanical fashion, using power generated by a windmill. This invention occurred in the Netherlands during the early 1600s, in a country that already had thousands of windmills mainly used to manage the flow of water. The entrepreneurial Dutch, a trading and seafaring people, soon saw the advantages of high volume plank production. Many more windmills with saws sprang up – there may have been up to 30,000 of all types by 1650 – and their products went into new shipyards that could build a modest-sized ship in as little as three weeks. This compared with at least three months in France or England.[2]

As early as 1659, Jean-Baptiste Colbert had written that the most urgent task at hand was to "re-establish the kingdom's glory and honour at sea by putting to sea a considerable number of warships". This fitted exactly the ambitions of Louis XIV and, from 1661, he tasked Colbert to create a powerful French navy as well as to regenerate the merchant navy. It was accomplished over the next decade by creating or enlarging naval bases and shipyards at Le Havre, Brest, Rochefort, Toulon and Marseille. The naval construction programme called for some 110 ships-of-the-line, 60 frigates and smaller vessels for the sailing navy as well as 30 galleys to patrol the Mediterranean. Expertise was sought in and out of France, academies and scientific services such as the hydrographic service were created. As the years passed, French squadrons increasingly appeared off European shores and on all great routes to America and Asia.

For the Netherlands, who had been allies of France in 1667, this was not very good news when added to the then rather hostile attitude of King Charles II of England, who was looking for a way to avenge the humiliation of the Dutch raid on the Medway and secure a good share of global trade. This feeling was noted by the Sun King. Colbert de Croisy, one of the best French diplomats, was sent to England as ambassador to the Court of St James to convince Charles II that Louis XIV felt the same way as he did regarding the Dutch and definitely planned to do something about it. Thus, a secret alliance

---

1 E. de Castelverd, *Mémorial Militaire des Français* (Paris: Dumaine, 1846), pp.208–209; Lucien Bély, Jean Bérenger and André Corvisier, *Guerre et paix dans l'Europe du XVIIe siècle* (Paris: SEDES, 1991), pp.345–346; Jean-Philippe Cénat, *Louvois, le double de Louis XIV* (Paris: Tallandier, 2015), p.54.

2 Data kindly provided by Het Jonge Schaap Sawmill at Zaadam, Netherlands.

was struck between him and the Sun King in the Treaty of Dover, signed on the 22 May 1670. Both wished to humble Holland and take its predominant place.[3]

## The Strength of the Army

At the end of the War of Devolution in 1668, the French regular army had some 131,265 men. This went up in the following years, but not hugely if one relies on published sources. The March 1672 *Mercure Galant* mentioned that it mustered 176,687. Quincy's *Histoire Militaire* later showed that these men were divided as follows:

    Gardes du Corps at four companies: 1,034
    Gendarmes du roi at one company: 200
    Chevaux-Légers du roi at one company: 200
    King's Musketeers at two companies: 454
    Gardes-Françaises Regiment at 30 companies: 3,000
    Gardes-Suisses Regiment at 10 companies: 2,000
    52 cavalry regiments at six companies each: 6,848
    22 cavalry regiments at three companies each: 3,564
    6 cavalry regiments at three companies each: 3,196
    120 companies of recruits for cavalry regiments: 6,000
    46 regiments of French infantry: 83,157
    13 regiments of Foreign infantry: 26.256
    2 regiments of dragoons at six companies: 985
    50 independent companies both French and foreign: 10,000
    300 companies of recruits for infantry regiments: 15,000

Voltaire later rounded out the figure at about 180,000 men. However, the real number was higher. As will be seen in volume 4, there were also many more small regular local units in towns throughout France that usually acted as garrisons.

According to the Sun King's notes kept in his office's desk drawers, a part of the regular army was specifically identified for "the Holland campaign" that could take the field came to about 8,000 men from the royal guard, 56,000 French infantry listed as "exclusive of [units in] garrisons", 30,000 foreign infantry and 25,000 cavalry for a total of about 120,000 men when gunners and staff were added. There were also 97 pieces of ordnance, 72,000 cannonballs, 600 mortar bombs, 150,000 hand grenades and three pontoon bridge units, one having 100 copper boats and the two others with 200 wooden boats. This looked largely sufficient to invade the Netherlands, and it was clear that the King had opted for the doctrine of overwhelming force.[4]

---

3 René Jouan, *Histoire de la marine française* (Paris: Payot, 1950), p.26. For more details, see: *Lettres, instructions et mémoires de Colbert*, Pierre Clément, ed. (Paris: Imprimerie Impériale, 1869), vol. 3.
4 Charles Sevin, Marquis de Quincy, *Histoire Militaire du règne de Louis le Grand, roi de France* (Paris, 1726), vol. 1, pp.311–312; Voltaire (François-Marie Arouet), *Le Siècle de Louis XIV*, (Berlin, 1751) from the (Paris: Gallimard, 2015) edition p.506; Bibliothèque du Ministère des

# THE ARMIES AND WARS OF THE SUN KING 1643–1715 VOLUME 2

Regimental infantry officers, *c.* 1665-1672. At left, a colour bearer; at centre a company or field officer; at right, an officer of pikemen. All three are armed with swords and two have spontoons. The bottom of gorgets are also seen below the cravats. The officer of pikemen wears a cuirass. Note that the colour's pike was hand held at that time and did not rest on the ground. All wear the "justeaucorps" style coat with long skirts that quickly became prevalent in all western countries. A company of pikemen wearing helmets and cuirasses is shown in the background. Engraving in Manesson Mallet, *Les Travaux de Mars*, 1672. (Anne S.K. Brown Military Collection, Brown University Library, Providence, RI, USA. Author's photo)

On 27 January 1672, the secret alliance between Britain and France was renewed. Both Charles II and the Sun King were now ready and eager to attack the Dutch and 6,000 British troops would join the French army of which some 90,000 men were gathering between Sédan and Charleroi. For an invasion by land, it was very important that the small German states bordering the eastern Netherlands be cooperative so that French troops could march through them without any problems. Louis XIV made great promises in gold and added territories so that the Prince of the Palatinate, the Duke of Neubourg and the bishops of Cologne and of Münster were won over and contributed some 20,000 troops; they would be led by Lieutenant General de Luxembourg sent by Louis XIV, since the bishops wanted an experienced army commander. They were especially bitter at the Dutch who had occupied some of their fiefdoms. Now they had a powerful ally in France's Louis XIV whose troops were welcomed in Huy, Liège, Dinant and Bonn as well as other smaller towns. The French contingents were thus within easy striking distance of Maastricht, the Netherlands' sentinel of its southeastern frontier. Most of all, the French troops would not have to go through Spanish Flanders nor the somewhat hostile German states aligned with Vienna's Holy Roman Emperor.

Besides England, Sweden was the more distant and somewhat lukewarm ally of the Sun King with whom it shared a dislike for the Dutch. The Swedes had signed a treaty in April by which they would enter a conflict only if and when Brandenburg-Prussia supported the Netherlands and spilled the fighting into Germany. By then, the British fleet was on a war footing and French army corps were moving towards eastern Flanders. Dutch diplomatic overtures were spurned by Louis XIV. In case of war, they were confident that their fleet could hold its own, but they now realised that their army had not campaigned for 24 years, was outclassed and only had about 24,000 men. The Dutch government thus made frantic diplomatic appeals to other nations to help contain the

---

Armées (henceforth cited as: BMA), Ms A1b, 1626, 'Tiroirs de Louis XIV'; Camille Rousset, *Histoire de Louvois et de son administration politique et militaire jusqu'à la paix de Nimègue* (Paris: Didier, 1864), Vol. 1, pp.346–347. Victor Belhomme's *Histoire de l'infanterie en France* (Paris, 1892), Vol. 2 has 138,620 infantrymen in 1672.

French. Should the French win, it argued, German principalities and Spanish Flanders would likely be invaded too. This possibility spurred the Elector of Brandenburg-Prussia, Frederick-William, to vow 20,000 troops and Spain sent 6,000 soldiers to Ostend, while other states allowed volunteers to join the Dutch. The Netherlands were badly deficient insofar as their army was concerned, but their finances were in a good state. Therefore, they were prepared to subsidise troops from allied nations as well as to raise 6,000 Protestant mercenaries in Switzerland and 20,000 in Germany. The Dutch Republic could now clearly see the war clouds. The Dutch fleet mobilised 72 ships of the line under the command of Admiral Michiel de Ruyter. Many Dutchmen saw hope in the 22-year-old William, Prince of Orange, descendant of the leaders that had driven the Spanish out of the Netherlands and proclaimed the nation's independence. Although he had never drawn his sword in battle, on 25 February 1672 he was elected captain-general of the army.[5]

But it was too late and such land forces would still never be enough to repel a French attack even if they could arrive in record time. In mid March, the Dutch learned of the secret alliance between France and Britain. By then they also were warned by their informants that French troops estimated at 100,000 infantry and 30,000 cavalry were marching towards the Netherlands. And it was true. As Jean Racine, Louis XIV's historiographer, put it, "The King, tired of suffering these insolences [from the Netherlands] resolved to prevent them. He declared war on the Dutch in early spring [on 6 April 1672] and immediately marched against them."[6]

Infantry musketeer, *c.* 1665-1672. In Maneson Mallet's *Les travaux de Mars* 1672, Paris edition. (Anne S.K. Brown Military Collection, Brown University Library, Providence, RI, USA. Author's photo)

## Command Crisis in France

All this diplomatic and military activity kept the French general staff busy. The King appointed Marshal Turenne as chief of planning and operations for the impending invasion, which made him a de facto senior commander of

---

5   M. de La Neuville, *Histoire de Hollande* (Paris: Libraires associés, 1703), Vol. IV, pp.7–12; M. de Larrey, *Histoire de France sous le règne de Louis XIV* (Rotterdam: M. Bohm, 1718), Vol. 4, p.63–65; Bély, Bérenger and Corvisier, *Guerre et paix dans l'Europe du XVIIe siècle*, p.347.

6   Jean Racine, *Précis historique des campagnes de Louis XIV depuis 1672 jusqu'à 1678* in the *Bibliothèque de souvenirs & récits militaires*, Paul Gaulot, ed., (Paris: Henri Gautier, *c.* 1890–1900), No. 57, p.133. Racine is most remembered as the playwright of timeless classics such as *Britannicus* and *Phaedra*.

Infantry ensign, c. 1670. Print after Louis François du Bouchet. (Courtesy Rijksmuseum, Amsterdam. RP-P-2007-174)

the army. He officially was in terms of protocol seniority of command, which was then as follows: the King, the King's brother, the Prince de Condé and the Vicomte de Turenne, who was a marshal of France. In the structure of the time, the marshals were all equal and the King the supreme commander. As such he had appointed his best marshal, Turenne, to plan the invasion operations and his next best field commander, Condé, to lead part of the invasion army. Condé, being a prince of the blood and not a marshal, was acceptable to the marshals, but Turenne, who was a marshal and their theoretical equal, had no rights to give them orders as if they were subalterns. Most marshals grudgingly realised that this was the King's will as commander-in-chief and complied but some did not. Indeed, three of them flatly refused to acknowledge Turenne.

In a telling letter of 22 April 1672, Louvois wrote to Marshal Créquy about the King's reaction on learning that Marshal Bellefond's disobedience to serve under Turenne in the upcoming campaign: "… His Majesty … wished to be obeyed … and would not admit any excuse … and would not even agree to a request of being dispensed from service." The Sun King personally met Marshal Bellefond, reminded him of all the royal favours he had been granted, and told him that if he created "any difficulty", he would never wish to see him again. Bellefond stuck to his rather outdated code of honour, which earned him exile to his estate in Tours with instructions to remain there, the cancellation of all his duties and being forbidden to carry out any military functions as a marshal "until called upon" by the King. This was very unlikely. Perhaps out of solidarity marshals Créquy and Humières followed suit, but while making amends for their situation. The King was uncompromising, but gave them a chance for eventual redemption: both marshals were told to rally Turenne's army and serve with the rank of lieutenant general under the command of … Marshal Turenne. They did. Bellefond eventually also rallied and was forgiven by the King who sent him to serve under Créquy.

In all this, the King showed great leadership. He was as firm as a rock with regard to his authority, yet would forgive everything once that was understood. There were some good and there were some less talented marshals, but all who had risen to that rank were fine officers and the Sun King needed them to lead his expanded army. This incident of course made the gossip mill really turn. Even the Dutch soon heard about it and later reported that "the French marshals, who had refused to obey Turenne, had been disgraced by the King because of that, went to the army to see him; the King forgave them so long as they would obey the orders of his general." In fact, the King had settled remarkably quickly a command crisis that could have been extremely

# THE NETHERLANDS

Soldiers in camp playing cards, 1667. Detail of a print of the siege of Douai after van der Meulen. (Courtesy Library and Archives Canada, Ottawa. NL15529)

damaging to senior military authority, army cohesion and general staff planning. In former days, each marshal usually led a relatively modest-sized army independently whereas now, with a force of 130,000 men moving on the same front and target, several marshals would be in the same large force and the chain of command had to be clear and respected. Thanks notably to the seniority that L'Ordre du tableau eventually imposed (see Volume 1, chapter 6), such dissension was not seen again during the reign.[7]

---

7   *Mercure Hollandois*, 1672, p.524.

# 2

# 1672: Invading the Netherlands

Marshal Turenne came up with a shrewd strategic plan for the invasion. The element of surprise certainly could not be used when such a huge army was on the march as the Marshal well knew. Therefore, where it would actually strike remained the one great advantage of the attacking force. There were two main ways to invade the Netherlands: by the Meuse or Rhine rivers. If one chose the Meuse, the invasion force would have to overcome Maastricht, the fortifications of which were considered very strong. That would surely mean a fairly long siege, which would give time for the Dutch to mobilise their forces and those of their allies to arrive on the scene.

The Rhine presented fewer challenges insofar as defensive works, but it was further away, especially considering the size of the French army that would have to be supplied on the way, and crossing the Rhine also could be difficult. On the other hand, the fortresses guarding the eastern Dutch border on the Rhine were less formidable. That was Turenne's daring strategic choice. If it succeeded, he would take control of the Rhine and the Dutch would be outflanked right in the heart of their country, which would be cut in half. Louis XIV approved.[1]

## *Blitzkrieg* on the Dutch

In late May, the French army divided into four corps to undertake simultaneously four sieges at the fortresses at Wesel led by Prince Condé, at Rheinberg by the King, at Orsoy by the Duc d'Orléans and at Burick by Turenne, these last two being secondary citadels. All four fortresses had surrendered by early May. From Wesel, situated at the junction of the Lippe and Rhine rivers, the French army then marched west along the south shore of the Rhine that would have to be crossed; it provided a natural defence for the Dutch defenders who were nevertheless being outflanked as they tried to gather an army partly made up of militiamen in the area of Arnhem and

---

1   Andrew Ramzay, *Histoire du Vicomte de Turenne, Maréchal général des armées du Roi* (Paris: Jombert, 1773), Vol. 2, pp.173–184.

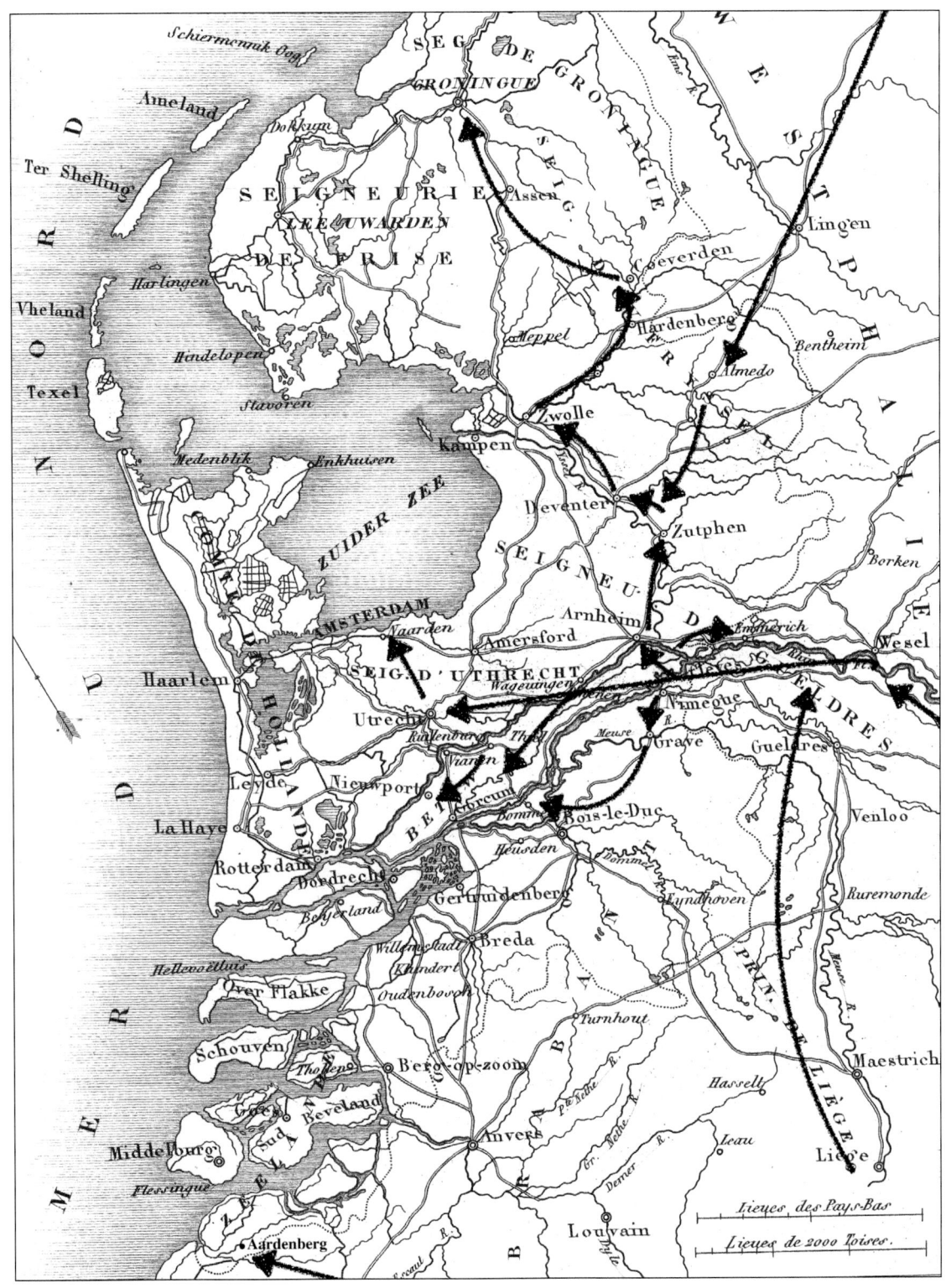

Map of the Netherlands invaded, summer of 1672. The black arrows are overlaid indicating the invasion routes. Print after Hugo's *France Militaire*. (Author's photo)

# THE ARMIES AND WARS OF THE SUN KING 1643–1715 VOLUME 2

Marshal Henri de la Tour D'Auvergne, Vicomte de Turenne, *c.* 1674. This unsigned Dutch print shows the great French commander with a rather though air that may be more realistic than the formal court portraits. (Courtesy Anne S.K. Brown Military Collection, Brown University Library, Providence, RI, USA)

further north along the Yser River. Condé's corps of about 15,000 men was in the van of the French army and reached a small village named Tolhuis where he learned that the weather had been very dry so that the level of the Rhine was lower than usual. Some Dutch troops could be seen on the Rhine's north shore. Soon, a place was found where French cavalry could cross by swimming only "two hundred steps".

By 12 June, the Sun King was on the spot watching about 2,000 cavalry led by the Cuirassiers du Roi attempt the crossing. Dutch troops on the north shore fired at them and some French troopers that were hit then drowned, but most crossed and were then charged by Dutch cavalry. The French cavalry

The surrender of Rheinberg to the French army, 6 June 1672. Print after van der Meulen. (Courtesy Rijkmuseum, Amsterdam, RP-P-OB-82.172)

beat them off, regrouped and countercharged; the Dutch troopers retreated and the French gained a foothold. Soon thousands of French troops were crossing, some in boats, including the King, and eventually many others by a pontoon bridge; the considerably outnumbered Dutch withdrew. There were few casualties, but the Duc de Longueville was killed and Prince Condé wounded, but not seriously: he broke his wrist parrying a Dutch cavalryman, the only wound he ever suffered in all his campaigns.[2]

The crossing of the Rhine was heralded in French propaganda as a next-to-miraculous and glorious victory by the Sun King. In his letter to the King introducing his *L'Art de la Guerre*, Louis de Gaya echoed the official praise in stating that:[3]

> Antiquity can no longer praise the Alexanders and the Cesars; France has placed a Hero at their head, under which they could only serve as Aides de Camp. The passage of the Rhine will no less surprise all for centuries to come as will the conquest of Holland within a month … [and it goes on and on, adding that]… it was not hazard that rendered Your Majesty victorious …

---

2   Voltaire, *Le Siècle de Louis XIV*, pp.166–167.
3   Louis de Gaya, *L'Art de la Guerre* (Paris, 1679), 'Au Roy' n.p.

# THE ARMIES AND WARS OF THE SUN KING 1643–1715 VOLUME 2

The Sun King orders his cavalry to cross the Rhine on 12 June 1672. Detail of a painting by Adam Frans van der Meulen. (Courtesy Rijksmuseum, Amsterdam)

Facing page: Plan of the city of Amsterdam approved in 1664. The extension and urban renewal of the city (upper left) would have been complete by 1672 when French armies invaded the Netherlands. The walls protecting the city were not overwhelmingly elaborate, but the high water level was fully exploited: deep outer ditches full of water made assault very difficult. This, together with the partially flooded countryside, discouraged a French approach to the Netherlands' capital. (Amsterdam Museum, Amsterdam. Author's photo)

Crossing the Rhine certainly had a symbolic significance, but the Dutch troops were not yet beaten. Their commander in that sector was 22-year-old William, Prince of Orange, descendant of the leaders that had driven the Spanish out of the Netherlands and proclaimed the nation's independence. He was courageous, but he knew his troops could not resist the French army that was crossing the Rhine and marching north. Not only were the French numerous, but they were better trained and led compared to the Dutch forces.

The Rhine crossing meant that the French army would soon control the centre of the country from east to west. The nation's capital, Amsterdam, was threatened. The Dutch line of defence of the Rhine was pierced and tens of thousands of French soldiers were pouring in. The eastern sector of the Rhine defence line with that of the lower Yssel River should have been evacuated by the Dutch, but it was not and thus some 13,000 Netherlands troops were trapped – a huge additional setback – it was nearly half of the regular army. Soon the French troops overcame Arnhem on 16 June, besieged and took Doesburg on 17–21 June, Zutphen on 17–25 June and the very strong fort of Schenkenschans on 18–21 June. Nothing seemed to stop the French and they were now marching north.

By 30 June, the French army had captured Utrecht and was getting closer to Amsterdam, marching north towards Naarden, which was only 24km east of Amsterdam. It fell a few days later. Like Amsterdam, Naarden faced

# 1672: INVADING THE NETHERLANDS

# THE ARMIES AND WARS OF THE SUN KING 1643–1715 VOLUME 2

William of Orange, 1670s. This young general was elected *Stadholder* of the Netherlands in July 1672. He was only 22 and yet proved equal to lead his invaded country out of a desperate time. Also crowned king of Great Britain as William III in 1688, from 1672 right up to his death in 1702 he proved to be Louis XIV's most effective opponent. Portrait by Caspar Netscher. (Courtesy Rijksmuseum, Amsterdam. SK-A-3331)

Dikes breached at Coevorden, early 1673. A rather dramatic portrayal of the effects of flooding the Netherlands. Print attributed to Romeyn de Hooghe. (Courtesy Rijksmuseum, Amsterdam. RP-P-OB-82.379)

the huge Zuider Zee bay. Other French troops led by Marshal Turenne also marched west along the Rhine, some turning south and besieging Nijmegen on 3–9 July, taking Grave on 3 July, then the Crevecoeur fort and Bois-le-Duc besieged and captured on 16–19 July and Bommel on 20–22 July. This eliminated any substantial threat to the French army's southern flank.

Young William of Orange, a stern and pragmatic officer in frankly desperate times for the Netherlands, who was becoming the champion and only hope of many Dutchmen, correctly chose to withdraw towards Amsterdam so as to save his troops before they too were surrounded and overwhelmed by the French. On 22 June, he resolved to have the dams that retained the sea water opened to flood the countryside behind his soldiers. For a Netherlander, it must have been a terrible, soul-wrenching decision, but it was the right one in military, tactical, and national survival terms. The Dutch people understood it was the last card they could play.[4]

## Political Revolution in Amsterdam

By late June, the military situation had truly become nearly catastrophic for the Dutch. The only positive event, if it can be called that, was the inexorably rising water that was slowly and surely surrounding and sealing off Amsterdam and The Hague from the French armies. The Dutch government now made overtures to negotiate a peace settlement. At that point, disregarding whatever Charles II felt about this, Louis XIV thought he had the Dutch on their knees begging for his mercy and so made very demanding and humiliating conditions. The King wished to have Maastricht and the towns outside of the Seven Provinces, but Louvois persuaded the King to press also for Upper Brabant, 20 million pounds in war damages and the re-establishment of Catholicism as the official state religion. When the Dutch people heard of these terms dictated by the Sun King, many were so outraged as to revolt against their own government. In an outstanding reversal of attitude, the Dutch now became committed to fight the French to the bitter end, no matter what the cost to themselves and their nation. Public anger in Amsterdam became rife and was unfortunately first aimed at the politically very powerful de Witt brothers, Jan in particular. He was the Republic's leader as Grand Pensionary and Regent since 1653 and now blamed for everything that went wrong in the country. Even before the invasion, de Witt was in a very difficult situation steering between England's commercial ambitions and France's territorial appetite. Now, part of the country had fallen without much of a fight to Louis XIV's troops who had achieved another *Blitzkrieg*, as in 1667.

Already, on 21 June, there had been a foiled assassination attempt on Jan de Witt. His Regent powers melted thereafter. His brother Cornelis, a distinguished naval officer who had fought with Admiral Trump against the French and the British, was arrested on trumped-up charges by the Orange

---

4 Quincy, *Histoire Militaire*, Vol. 1, pp.314–339; W.J. Knoop, *La République des Provinces-Unies en 1672 et 1673 – étude militaire*. Translated by P.G. Booms (Bois-le-Duc: Muller, 1854), pp.36–86;

Dutch troops participating in the murders of brothers Johan and Cornelis de Witt at Dortrecht on 20 August 1672. Cornelis de Witt is shown being murdered in this detail of an anonymous 1672 print after Romeyn de Hooghe, which depicts Dutch soldiers armed and dressed much like their French enemies. (Courtesy Rijksmuseum, Amsterdam. RP-P-OB-55.172)

party and roughly treated in prison by the most extreme avocates of appointing a member of the House of Orange. On 4 July, young William of Orange was proclaimed as *Stadholder*, to be the nation's leader in truly trying times. Jan de Witt finally resigned his office on 4 August, but bitter feelings remained. On 20 August when he visited his brother in prison, a large angry crowd gathered there and, at first calmed by the militiamen on guard, its anger erupted again when most militiamen were called away on a false report of another riot. The mob, with some remaining militiamen, broke into the jail and killed both de Witt brothers whose bodies were later hung up, desecrated and cut up by a frenzied and drunken crowd in a gruesome night spectacle.[5]

---

5   Castelverd, *Mémorial Militaire des Français*, p.210; Anthony Bailey, 'The World of Jan de Witt', *Horizon* (Winter 1975), Vol. XVII, No. 1, pp.13–14.

# Aardenburg

Before and during this political revolution in Amsterdam, French columns were sweeping what remaining Dutch defenders there remained north and south of the Rhine that tried to stop them; it was an ever-victorious campaign until late June, when a French corps of 8,000 men reached the small fortified town of Aardenburg situated near the border of Flanders in the southwestern Netherlands, south of Walcheren Island and Flushing. General Claude de Dreux, Comte de Nancré, French governor of Ath, was instructed bring up to the Netherlands part of the troops in Flanders as reinforcements to the Comte de Chamilly's force so he could march into Dutch Brabant. However, as he was about to depart from Ath, de Nancré received intelligence that Aardenburg had only 70 Dutch regular soldiers and some town militiamen for a garrison that was even devoid of a commander since there was no governor present. Full of confidence at such an easy prize, de Nancré marched there with his corps, led by equally optimistic officers, without even advising his superiors. On 26 June, the town was in sight and it refused to surrender. Young Ensign Elias Beekman was the commander of, in fact, only 40 soldiers and only about 50 inhabitants still in the town, but all were resolute. The women even put on men's hats and clothes to look like soldiers. The French attacked, but were repulsed and about 450 Dutch troops meanwhile reached the town as reinforcements. De Nancré had obviously neglected to surround the place properly. The French made another attack at night, just as uncoordinated and ill-organised as before, and were again repulsed with heavy losses. During the assault, French troops were heard shouting *Tue! Tue! Tous à mort! Point de quarter!* (Kill! Kill! All must die! No quarter!), but they were mowed down and beaten back by the defenders. After suffering some 50 officers and 400 soldiers killed or wounded plus about 575 more officers and men taken prisoner, de Nancré and his force withdrew.[6]

Although this amazing action has since been unheralded in most French histories, it had a tremendous morale-boosting effect on the Dutch. For the first time since Louis XIV had taken power 11 years before, a sizeable French corps had been beaten, and by a tiny garrison in a paltry fortress that should have been easily taken, especially as the French had artillery that they could have used. The message that went out everywhere was that, contrary to popular European belief up until then, the French army could be beaten.

When Louvois learned of this most embarrassing defeat, he was very upset and on 15 July, wrote to de Nancré that when a commander who had received instructions to make an attack and had failed, he could be pitied but not blamed. When a commander acted without approved orders and failed, his superiors had every reason to be extremely upset at a commander "who commits troops in such a manner". Needless to say, de Nancré was relieved from command and told to stay in Ath. A ransom was paid to release the

---

6 Harold van Damme, *Franse aanval op de stad Aardenburg d.d. 26 en 27 juni 1672.* (1790_0_nl_berenning_aardenburg.pdf). According to the 1672 *Mercure Hollandois*, pp.239–240, some 27 officers from the Souche, Châteauneuf, Carignan regiments and unspecified units were taken prisoner along with 350 soldiers, 180 wounded officers and men also brought in town and an estimated were 220 killed.

The French attack on Aardenberg, June 1672. A large French force failed to take the town, which was defended by only 40 Dutch soldiers and a few hundred militiamen. It was one of the few successes in an otherwise very difficult year for the Netherlands. Detail from an unsigned contemporary print. (Rijksmuseum, Amsterdam. RP-P-OB-77.104)

captured French officers who had behaved bravely while Louvois insisted the others were assured they would "never re-enter the [army's] service again after the cowardly action they made".[7]

The large fortress of Maastricht remained Dutch although blockaded by another French corps, which was sufficient to neutralise it as there was no plan nor urgent need to actually capture it. Marshals Turenne and Condé felt that the defences of many captured Dutch towns should be destroyed and that

7 Rousset, *Histoire de Louvois*, Vol. 1, pp.372–373; Damme, *Franse aanval op de stad Aardenburg d.d. 26 en 27 juni 1672*. De Nancré was kept at Ath for the rest of the war managing minor operations, proving his 'capacity, courage and talent' according to an admiring biographer who blames the failure at Aardenburg on preposterous factors such as having no scouts to guide his force, as per: J.B.P. de Courcelles, *Dictionnaire historique et biographique des généraux français* (Paris: Author and Bertrand, 1820–1823), Vol. 5 pp.303–304.

# 1672: INVADING THE NETHERLANDS

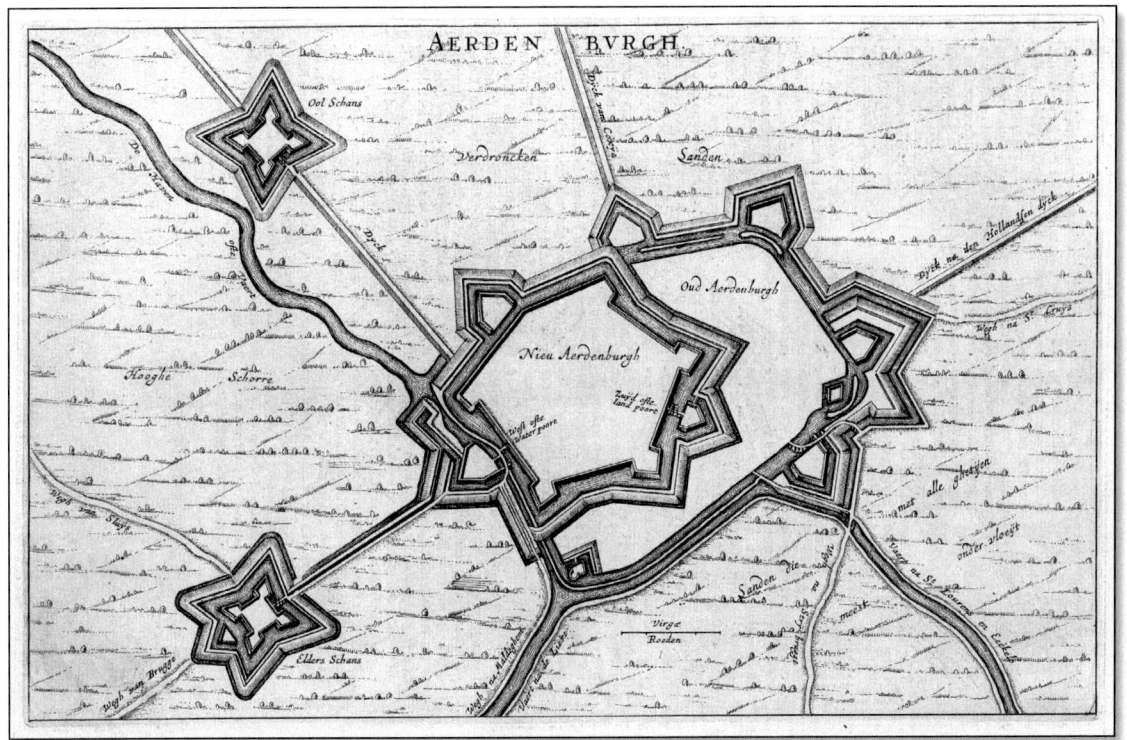

Plan of the small fortress of Aardenburg in 1652. This town has two curtain walls built in about 1650, the smaller enclosure being "new Aerdenburgh [old spelling]" which was an expansion of "old" Aardenburg. This was later consolidated into a single curtain wall with seven bastions surrounded by a moat as per a *c.* 1702 plan. (Courtesy Rijksmuseum, Amsterdam, RP-P-AO-16-9A-1)

the French army in the field should be as large and strong as possible and concentrate on taking Amsterdam and other large centres. Louis XIV and Louvois wished instead to garrison everything they captured, which resulted in a dispersal of forces that actually weakened the army.

## The Bishop's Invasion

The Sun King had secured the assistance of the Bishops of Münster and of Cologne for his invasion of the Netherlands. Their troops were estimated at about 20,000 men to which a French army corps led by Marshal Luxembourg would be joined. The Bishop of Münster was the military leader of this bishops' contingent and an aggressive leader who had no affection for the Dutch (see volume 1). Now, he had his chance to even the score. In late May he set out with his army, and entered the Netherlands' border province of Over-Yssel at its eastern frontier, taking the small Dutch towns of Lingen, Almedo and others in the vicinity. Whatever resistance there was in this basically undefended area was very weak, especially as part of the border population wished a union with Münster. The Bishop's objective was to link up with Luxembourg's corps, marching north from Arnhem. The link was made somewhere in the area between Zutphen and Deventer. This was accomplished and Zutphen quickly taken, but the area further north now had more Dutch defenders.

Dutch Major General Hans Willem, Baron van Aylva was on the spot. Seeing the invasion as it developed, he set a tactical defence line from the west bank of the upper Yssel roughly between Deventer and the Zuider Zee to the north of Zwolle and Kampen. He managed to raise Dutch forces in the area from about 1,300 men to up to 8,000 regulars by withdrawing what troops there were in Overyssel before they were overwhelmed and rallying all other more or less marooned soldiers. Another 5,000 peasants volunteered as embodied militiamen. Such forces would not stop the Bishop's army, but could be relatively effective behind the field fortifications of the Ysser line. For its part, the combined French and Bishop's army arrived outside the walls of Deventer on 16 June; the place put up a fight against overwhelming odds until it capitulated on 22 June. However, Marshal Luxembourg was called back to attack Woerden west of Utrecht, leaving command and some French troops to the Bishop of Münster, about 3,000 of which were said to wear blue coats. The Bishop's plan was simply to conquer and occupy the northern Netherlands. He led his army north keeping it east of the Ysser, occupied Zwolle then Hardenberg and, on 29 June, laid siege to the fortress of Coevorden that finally surrendered after a spirited defence on 11 July. The Bishop was nearing the prize that would win the whole area, the great fortress of Groningen near the North Sea.

Dutch General Aylva also went north, but further east. He established another defence line that went from the Zuider Zee north of the Linde River and several other rivers going east reaching Groningen. The dikes were opened to hamper French movements. Having been reinforced by several regiments from Cologne, the Bishop of Münster left Coevorden leading about 20,000 men, which included some French troops, kept to high ground and came within sight of Groningen on 19 July. He also had a train of siege artillery. Peasants living in the suburbs outside Groningen's walls burned down their lodgings and took refuge inside while Dutch cavalry went out and skirmished with Münster's advance guard.

Groningen was the most important fortress in the northern Netherlands. It was the sentinel with Germany, the nearest other fortress city being the German seaport of Emden. Groningen's Dutch garrison consisted of 2,200 soldiers with 22 companies of militia (about 2,500 men). Further reinforcements were later received, notably 14 companies (about 1,400 men) of Colonel Jorman's Regiment carrying "a white [colour] and the others three [colours], all bearing very fine mottos." The garrison was led by Governor Carl von Rabenhaupt with the Duke of Holstein as cavalry leader. The ramparts were in good repair as was the town's artillery and the town was surrounded by water due to the opening of the dikes. There were nevertheless dry mounds around and Münster's siege artillery batteries were built for bombardments that, it was hoped, would pound the fortress into submission. The bombardiers indeed shot a multitude of bombs into the fortress during the following weeks. Sappers were also building passageways above the water level so that assaults could be attempted. When assault or prodding attacks were made, the defenders always made a vigorous defence and all attempts failed. The garrison was well supplied by boats, while the line of communications for Münster's troops was very long; the Bishop could not obtain enough supplies locally and the Elector of Brandenburg had decreed that none would be sent to Münster's troops from nearby Emden. So Münster's army's rations had to be reduced. After a while some

# 1672: INVADING THE NETHERLANDS

Lieutenant General Carl von Rabenhaupt, *c.* 1670. He successfully repelled the Münster and French troops at Groningen and recaptured Coevorden in late December, thus compelling the Bishop of Münster's evacuation of the northern Netherlands. (Courtesy Rijksmuseum, Amsterdam, SK-A-1422).

Major General Hans Willem van Aylva, *c.* 1672. Nicknamed "the Formidable General", his organisation of the defences in the northern Netherlands was largely responsible for a significant part of the country not being overrun during the summer of 1672. (Courtesy Rijksmuseum, Amsterdam, SK-A-1)

of the artillery wore down, notably the mortars, while some French heavy 36-pounder siege cannons were captured during a daring battery raid sortie by Groningen's defenders. Finally, on 18 August, the Bishop raised camp and gradually evacuated most of the northern Netherlands except for Coevorden, that became his main base in Over-Yssel. The siege had been costly and while the Dutch obviously inflated numbers, there can be little doubt Münster's losses were high. The garrison suffered about 100 casualties.[8]

## The *Blitzkrieg* Ends

For Louis XIV, May and June had been truly extraordinary. His French army had, thanks to its large numbers, training, technical superiority and fine generals, achieved the nearly unthinkable: conquer much of the Netherlands in barely a month. The provinces of Gelderland, Utrecht, Over-Yssel and part of the province of Amsterdam were now occupied by the French army. Everyone was stunned at the news. The Netherlands were a small country on a map, but one of the world powers thanks to its redoubtable navy and riches from world trade. But militarily, they had put their faith in fortresses and neglected their small army. French writers exalted Louis as the true sun whose powerful rays had terrorised Dutchmen and ruined their nation. Militarily, the Sun King likely thought that the campaign was over and the Dutch utterly beaten. On 16 July, he left the command of the French army in the Netherlands to Marshal Turenne and went back to France to be celebrated as the reincarnation of Alexander and Cesar combined.

In the Netherlands, the war was actually still on and it took on a "bogged down" aspect. The opening of the dikes to flood the land had considerably changed the tactical situation. By mid July, many a soldier must have lost his shoes stepping in a watery ooze of mud if he ventured too far. Both the French and the Dutch forces were forced to a standstill, which really favoured the defenders of the unoccupied Netherlands. In spite of all the French propaganda, major Dutch cities such as Rotterdam, The Hague and the capital, Amsterdam, were under the tricolour standard of the Netherlands. Towns were generally sited on slightly higher ground so they could be surrounded by water, but still be relatively dry within. At Amsterdam, the bridges over the moat were destroyed so that the city became something of an island, which it already was in some ways. The other Dutch cities followed suit and, in effect, it became all but impossible for the French army to conduct siege operations or even try surprise assaults in such conditions. William of Orange and his officers made the most out of the flooding, which gave him and his general staff time to regroup and raise a new Dutch army. For the short term, he posted his available troops at the water's edge as a defence line. The population of the cities did not succumb to starvation. Ironically, with the countryside largely flooded, both

---

8   *Mercure Hollandois,* 1672, pp.321–350. This account put the Münster and French troops at 14,000 when they left, some 4,000 had died, 426 wounded, 600 deserted into the fortress and some 5,000 had 'retired elsewhere'. The French soldiers in blue coats were said to be a 'gift by the King of France to the Bishop of Cologne'.

the French and the Dutch had difficulties finding drinking water. Food stocks were sufficient as well as arms and equipment for the rising number of Dutch defenders, as volunteers came forward.

Furthermore, the North Sea coastal ports were active and the Netherlands controlled the all-important Zuider Zee by which ships came in and out constantly, thanks to the protection of the redoubtable Dutch warships. In the original vision of the invasion, both Louis XIV and Charles II were optimistic that the French and British navies could neutralise and even defeat the powerful Dutch fleet, and blockade the Dutch harbours thus strangling supply routes to cities. To prevent this, Admiral de Ruyter attacked by leading his 75 ships onto the anchored 93 ships of the combined Anglo-French fleet at Solebay (Suffolk, UK) on 7 June 1672. The hard-fought battle was indecisive and both sides claimed victory, but it was really a draw in terms of fleet destruction. In terms of strategic objectives, however, the Dutch had the advantage. The British and French navies gave up the idea of a blockade against such a powerful opponent; the Dutch kept control of access of their coast and this had a considerable impact on the land war. Overseas trade was not affected as shown by the arrival, in August, of the "India Fleet" filled with valuable exotic goods from the Orient for the European markets. The interior economy was certainly very affected by the invasion, but, unlike France, much of the nation's economy rested on international trade, commerce and banking. Thus, there would be funds for military expenditure. Most of all, the heartened Dutch population became even more resolute.[9]

Nevertheless, the King of France may have gone back satisfied at his conquest, but a lot of his troops stayed in the Netherlands, especially in the Rhine area south of Amsterdam. In the early autumn, Marshal Turenne moved eastward towards Cologne and Bonn in Germany to counter the vanguard of Brandenburg and Imperial troops that were slowly coming towards the Netherlands. After a few skirmishes, it was clear to Turenne that they would not advance further and that their main army was not likely to be on the spot as a real threat for months, especially as the colder season was coming; a French army corps was left in the area to watch them.

In the Netherlands, the French army's command centre was in Utrecht with Marshal Luxembourg as area commander. The war of great and swift strategic advances was basically over and, with a lot of the countryside underwater, movements were limited for both the French and the Dutch troops. All the same, instead of just watching the French, William of Orange opted to attack them at Woerden, which had been occupied by the French since July. It was situated only 16km west of Utrecht. Its garrison was about 2,000 men led by

Regimental colour of the Navarre Regiment, early eighteenth century. Medium brown field, white cross with gold crowns and lilies, red shied with gold chains of Navarre's coat of arms, gold and silver knighthood order's collars. (Private collection. Autho's photo)

---

9   *Mercure Hollandois,* 1672, pp.389–393. The goods on board are listed and were said to be worth 150 tons in gold.

the Comte de La Mark. In early October, William made a false attack on Naarden that alarmed Marshal Luxembourg enough for him to leave Utrecht and go there with most of his troops. Since his ruse worked, William, leading about 8,000 men, approached Woerden on 10 October and a corps of 1,500 infantrymen attacked, but the French garrison stopped it and boldly counterattacked. Marshal Luxembourg soon learned of William's attack and leading a vanguard of 3,000 French troops quickly arrived next day, attacked and outflanked a corps of Dutch troops on 12 October; another Dutch corps came to the rescue. In the ensuing fierce five-hour struggle, the Navarre Regiment especially distinguished itself, crossing flooded land and taking five Dutch field defence trenches, a windmill and two small forts, Luxembourg later reported. The Dutch finally retreated. About 1,000 men on each side were killed or wounded. It was clear that the Dutch troops were regaining confidence and would henceforth put up a fight. But they were facing the best infantry in Europe and it was not about to give up.[10]

Marshal François-Henri de Montmorency, Duc de Luxembourg c. 1674. This not overly flattering Dutch print mentions he was governor of Utrecht while in the Netherlands. The background shows French troops slaughtering Dutch men and women, something this rough and ready soldier probably tolerated having been raised in a robust family context; six months before his birth, his father was publicly executed for repeatedly disobeying Louis XIII's duelling ban. The Duc was born humpback, which did not deter him from rising to be one of France's top soldiers. Print after Abraham de Wicquefort's *Journael* (1674). (Courtesy Peace Palace Library, The Hague)

## A "Rape and Pillage" Reputation

The Sun King thus had found in William of Orange a very determined and ambitious opponent with tremendous energy, tact and shrewdness. He undertook a crusade-like struggle to convince rulers of Europe that the King of France vied to have them all eat out of his hands and be subject to his ferule. The summer *Blitzkrieg* of 1672 endured by the Netherlands was a supreme example of the evil that could fall on their own kingdoms if they did not unite to counter Louis XIV's ambitions. And evil there was. The French army had not always been a model of discipline once it took a town. In Naarden, the old "rape and pillage" practices of the Thirty Years' War were tolerated again as were murders of hapless townsfolk. Unlike Marshal Turenne, who did not approve of such behaviour, Marshal Luxembourg had a cruel tinge and turned a blind eye. As late as November 1672, he was writing to Louvois about his troops shooting "many peasants and women" as well as burning 150 houses in one place; destroying the castle and village of Liesseld and shooting many peasants, since some had shot at French troops a few days earlier; burning the village of Overmeer making sure no one escaped, including its "peasants, women and small children"; and not failing to mention the destruction of Waerder, and later, at the end of December, of Zwammerdam and Bodegraven, including the elimination of all

---

10   Knoop, *La République des Provinces-Unies*, pp.90–95; Demiau, *Historique du 5e régiment d'infanterie de Ligne* (Caen: Brulfert, 1890) pp.50–52. Navarre lost about 350 officers and men at Woerden.

their inhabitants and livestock. Amongst the French troops present were officers and men of the otherwise elite La Reine Regiment.[11]

As seen in prints reproduced in this volume, this suffering inspired many engravings depicting all these cruelties as to what to expect if French soldiers came. It made great propaganda and since the Netherlands had a free press with an excellent distribution network, these scenes of utter horror were soon seen all over Europe. Whatever intellectual and moral reasons there might have been to make arrangements with Louis XIV's France, they were totally swept away by the cruel actions of French troops, from common soldier up to marshal. Many decades later, Voltaire wrote, regarding these massacres, that it was "surprising that the French soldier is so barbaric, being led by so many officers that have the just reputation of being humane and courageous", which contradicts Dutch accounts of officers participating in rapes, pillage and killings. He further correctly noted that these outrages on defenceless people left such a profound impression that Dutch schoolbooks half a century later recounted the fate of these villages to new generations that would grow up hating the French. He did not elaborate as to why the King tolerated such conduct in the first place.[12]

What the King seems to have perfectly understood is that the outlay of luxury and grandeur had a tremendous effect on peoples minds in that they became admiring, and enviously recognised superior qualities in those who wielded such wealth and thus power. They might benefit from the prince's benevolence as good subjects. It made excellent propaganda for France regarding the high virtues of its culture, the heights of its civilised ways and the invincibility of its armies. For those who did not see it that way, terror at the hands of crazed soldiers might reduce civilians to obedience.

On the opposite side, William of Orange knew, as his ancestors had realised, decrying the horrors the Spanish inflicted on the Netherlands during their war of independence, that he was being handed an immensely effective propaganda tool that was not only concerned with the Netherlands, but went to the very heart of human morality. How could civilised soldiers behave against their fellow defenceless men, women and children in such a way? What awaited anyone or any country that French soldiers would occupy? Both Louis and William of course knew that war and cruelty went together and that terror could be an efficient way to subdue populations, but William had the advantage; Dutch publications were distributed everywhere so that common people in other countries soon became aware that something awful was going on in the Netherlands. Like their rulers they were disgusted by such actions, and fearful if not quite terrified that they might be next. Thus then, and for the rest of Louis XIV's reign, William of Orange and his successors could and did mount remarkable coalitions to fight the Sun King's armies.[13]

---

11  Knoop, *La République des Provinces-Unies*, pp.30, 52, 153; the outrages by French officers and soldiers at Bodegraven and other places, too awful to relate here, were published in the *Mercure Hollandois* 1672, pp.585–586; Louis Susane, *Histoire de l'infanterie française* (Paris: J. Dumaine, 1876), Vol. 4, p.24.
12  Voltaire, *Le siècle de Louis XIV*, p.178; Rousset, *Histoire de Louvois*, Vol. 1, pp.431–450 shows that Louvois received reports and was ambivalent regarding these deplorable events.
13  Olaf van Nimwegen, *The Dutch Army and the Military Revolutions 1588-1688* (Woodbridge, UK: Boydell, 2006), p.459.

French officers looking at a Dutchman vomiting the many towns and fort captured by the French army during its *Blitzkrieg*-like invasion during the summer of 1672. This detail from a satirical French print after Le Poffre published in 1673 (or possibly earlier, a relatively scarce view) shows the dress of a presumably senior officer with another holding a partisan, who could also be a general's personal bodyguard. (Courtesy Rijksmuseum, Amsterdam, RP-P-OB-82.392).

## Dutch Resistance

Since the summer, the Dutch had not been inactive and small parties of mobile troops raided French troops. The *Blitzkrieg* period was definitely over and the occupation of the country was increasingly difficult. Thanks to the efforts of William of Orange and his senior officers, the Dutch army was reorganising and gaining strength in the areas it controlled. The French, in the areas they occupied, were reportedly treating inhabitants very badly; in Utrecht they were ransoming the burghers after seizing such items as church tapestries to raise money. In November, the French took the church bells in Woerden and send them to Utrecht to make cannon barrels. Hearing of this, Count van Horne intercepted the French convoy and sent them to Oudewater. Repression followed, but while destroying anything and anyone, the French soldiers burned boats and wood that they would soon need in winter, which was then quite cold in the Netherlands. Ice would cover the canals and vast flooded areas upon which thousands of Dutchmen would skate, not only for pleasure, but to raid French outposts. Thus, the French troops in Holland were increasingly hemmed in and their numbers were diminishing due to withdrawal of some units as well as to increasing sickness due to unfamiliar winter conditions. In late December Marshal Luxembourg, seeing the waters frozen, gathered about 12,000 men to march over the ice and attack The Hague. But then came a warm spell and the French army came back with difficulty by whatever high ground

# 1672: INVADING THE NETHERLANDS

"Warfare and cruelties of the French in the Netherlands, 1672 and 1673". Men and children are killed while women are stripped and raped by troops under the benevolent approval of their officers. Unfortunately, events such as this were genuine. Print after Romyn de Hoogue. (Anne S.K. Brown Military Collection, Brown University Library, Providence, RI, USA. Author's photo)

such as the top of dikes that they could find.[14]

Meanwhile, William of Orange was becoming a hardy and innovative general. He wanted to gain the tactical initiative. For that, he left just enough troops to watch Marshal Luxembourg's army around Utrecht and, in late November and December, marched south-east leading 6,000–8,000 men to the vicinity of Maastricht and Liège, linking with a Spanish force from Flanders, and taking several small forts occupied by the French. By mid December he was threatening the fortress of Charleroi before going east towards Cologne and then west back into Holland. None of the French-held fortresses were attacked. William just wanted to show that the Dutch army was now very mobile and redoubtable. It was also a tremendous morale boost for his army and the nation in general.[15]

Up north, a mixed force consisting of most of the garrison of Groningen with some German troops from Nassau stormed and took Coevorden on 27 December, thus eliminating the Bishop of Münster's troops as viable forces in that area. By then, the *Mercure Hollandois* of December mentioned

---

14 Quincy, *Histoire Militaire*, Vol. 1, pp.339–340; Voltaire, *Le Siècle de Louis XIV*, pp.177–178; Knoop, *La République des Provinces-Unies*, pp.103–105.
15 Knoop, *La République des Provinces-Unies*, pp.96–100.

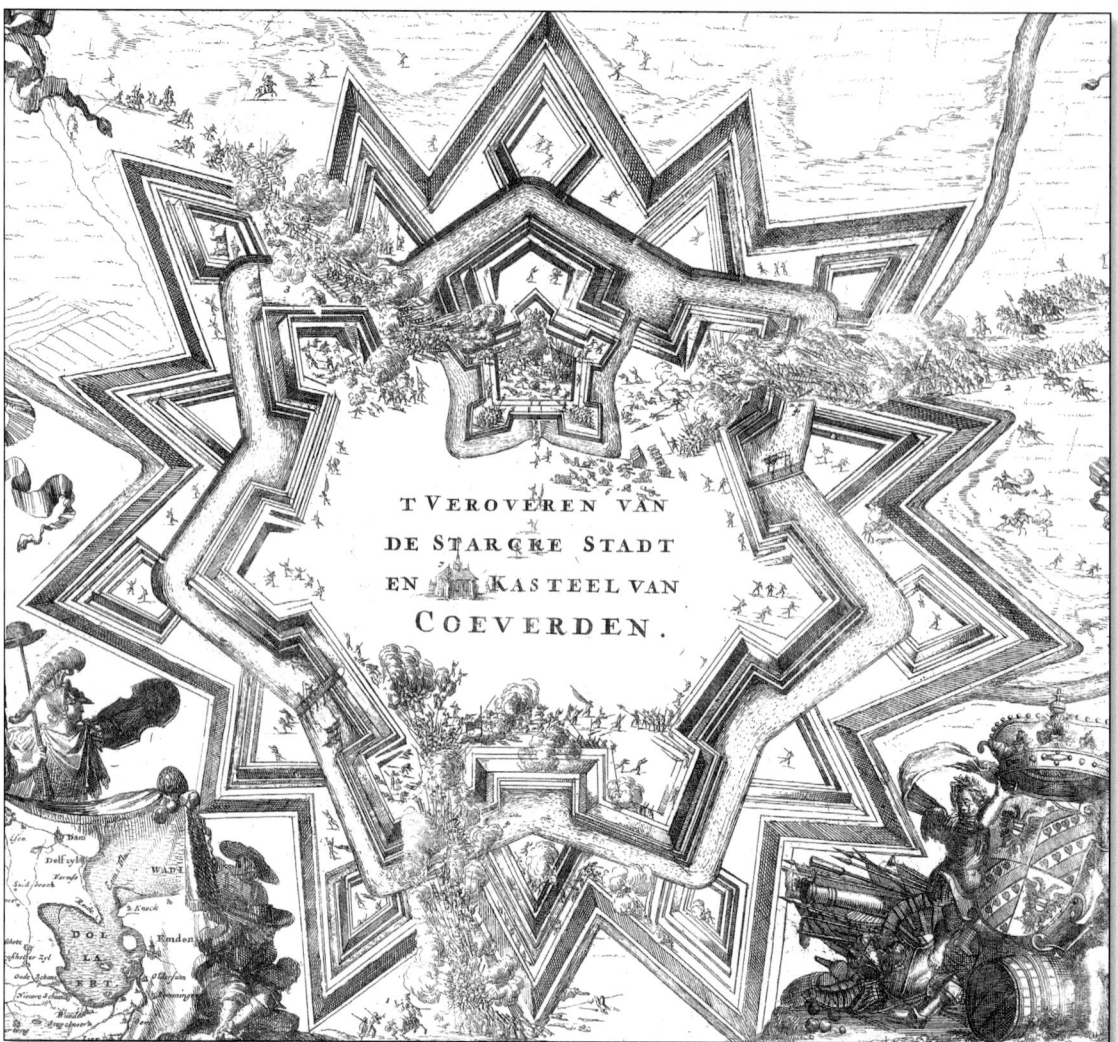

Dutch Assault on the fortress of Coevorden, 30 December 1672. Print after Romeyn de Hooghe. (Courtesy Rijksmuseum, Amsterdam. RP-P-OB-79.270)

that a list had been found in Arnhem compiling the losses of the French and the Bishop's troops at 72,464 dead, wounded, deserted or disappeared. While this total was certainly much exaggerated, it clearly showed that the French army was now on the defensive in the Netherlands. Thus ended, after starting so badly, what Dutchmen came to recall as the *Rampjaar* (The Year of Disasters).[16]

---

16  *Mercure Hollandois* 1672, pp.579, 609–619.

# 3

# 1673–1674 : The War Expands

## 1673 and Maastricht

Spain was not at war with France, but there were fears of invasion in Spanish Flanders and Madrid that the Sun King would nevertheless invade what was left of the Spanish Netherlands. This seemed to become more possible when spies reported that many French troops coming out of winter quarters were assembling near Courtrai, that many tools for siege operations were being stocked at Oudenarde and that great quantities of bread rations were to be made. The Spanish feared that a great French army would besiege Brussels. The spies were right about the French army preparing for a siege, but it would not be that of the capital of Spanish Flanders, but of the Dutch fortress of Maastricht.

This prize had not been included in Turenne's 1672 invasion plan of the Netherlands, but, a year later, the King was still frustrated about it and resolved that it be taken in his presence. Although William of Orange was putting up quite a resistance to the French troops occupying parts of the Netherlands, his army of about 18,000 men was too small to drive out the enemy. Louis XIV meanwhile assembled a French army of some 40,000 that marched towards Maastricht in May. This included about 6,000 allied English troops led by the Duke of Monmouth sent by King Charles II. On 6 June the surrounded fortress city was invested and the lines of circumvolution were completed by the night of 14 June, and trenches were begun approaching the city's walls from the night of 17 to 18 June. General Vauban was in charge of siege operations. The Dutch garrison consisted of about 5,000 men led by Major General Jacques de Fariaux and it could not expect any relief from William of Orange nor from Austrian or German forces – indeed, fearing devastation of his possessions in nearby Westphalia, the Elector of Brandenburg had signed a peace treaty with France in April. Another factor favouring the French army was the very presence of the King, which required the application of the principle of overwhelming force. His victory had to be guaranteed.

Meanwhile, the French trenches nearing the wall were unlike anything else previously seen. Previously dug as narrow and cramped affairs, Vauban had designed them to be wide with stations for arms, supplies and extra

Captain John Churchill (later Duke of Marborough) at the siege of Maastricht, 24 June 1673. The city was besieged by a French army of some 40,000 led by Louis XIV and General Vauban for siege operations. An English contingent under the Duke of Monmouth was attached to the French army. On 24 June, an assault was made on the Dutch fortifications where Captain John Churchill distinguished himself by planting a standard on the outwork, but the attack failed. Vauban's siege operations nevertheless ensured success and Maastricht capitulated on 30 June (Private collection. Author's photo)

troops; they also had parallel trenches to link the trenches going towards the city. It was said that Vauban had borrowed these ideas from the Ottoman Turks as related by one of his engineers, the Chevalier Paul, who had been with the besieged Venetian and French garrison of Candia four years earlier. The Dutch defenders in Maastricht, while amazed and even admiring these trenches, nevertheless put up a stout resistance from within their fortifications, which included several horn works, that were so pounded by French siege guns that much of the fortress' artillery was reduced to silence after four days. The defence works were not destroyed, however, and the Dutch garrison was protected by a good curtain wall, many revetted half-moons and an excellent covered way. General de Fariaux proved to be a fine commander determined to put up an outstanding defence no matter the odds against his troops, and so did his soldiers. A first assault on the city's Tongres gate was attempted on the night of 24 and into 25 June by six battalions, half of guards and the others of Picardie and Royal, with eight squadrons of guards cavalry, but the French forces were fiercely counter-attacked by several Dutch sorties before they finally reached the covered way and the ditch. The casualties were high on both sides and the assault force was reinforced by the Gardes du Corps, the King's Musketeers on foot under Captain d'Artagnan and the

# 1673–1674 : THE WAR EXPANDS

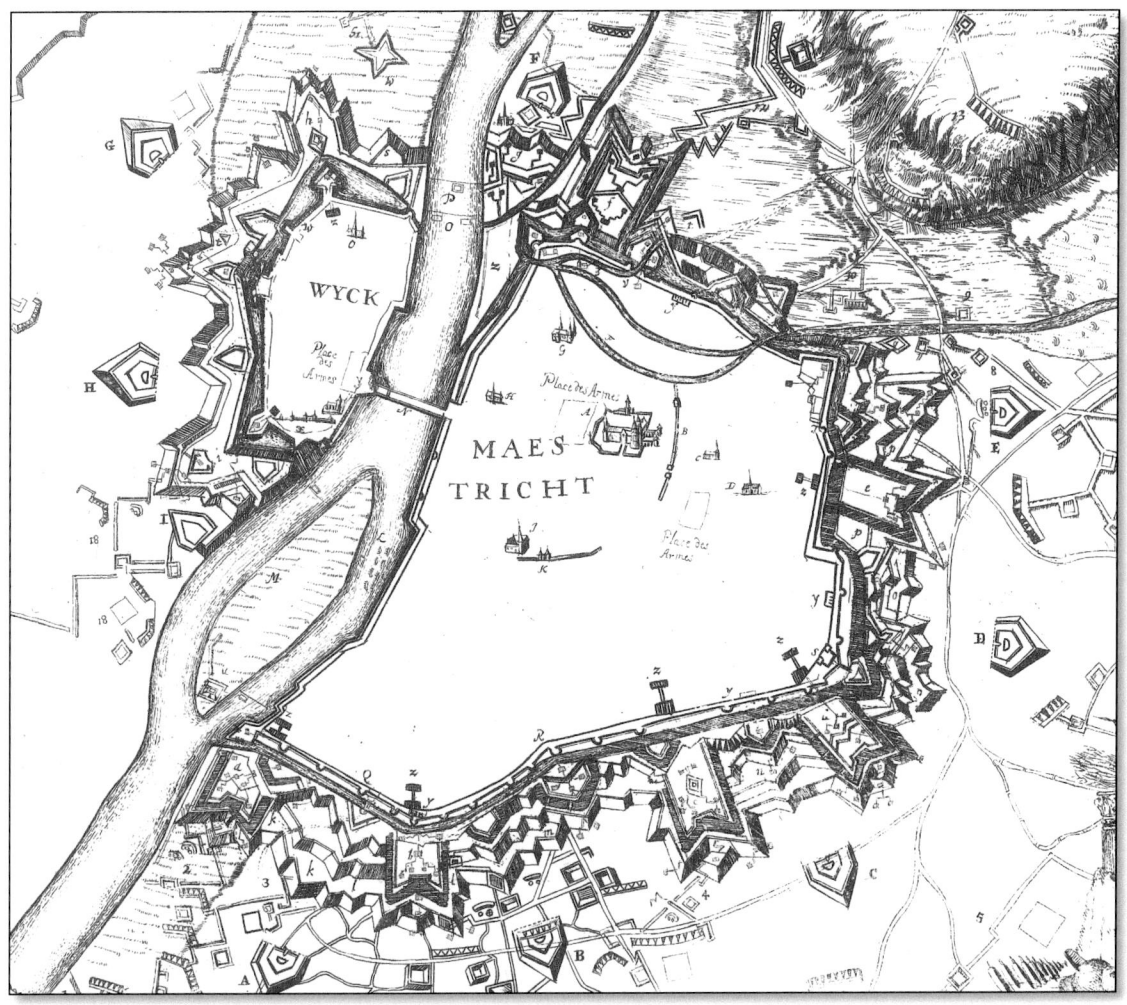

Plan of the siege of the Fortress of Maastricht, June 1673. Detail after an anonymous plan.
(Courtesy Rijksmuseum, Amsterdam. RP-P-1896-A-19328)

English troops led by Monmouth. Led by d'Artagnan, the first assault party took the half-moon after half an hour of fighting. However, Fariaux, who had assembled his best Dutch defenders on the spot, ordered a mine exploded, and attacked and drove out the French in a ferocious struggle where the famous d'Artagnan was killed in action.

Seeing all this, the King called for more troops to recapture the half-moon and Monmouth led his English soldiers into another assault. This included young Captain John Churchill who had already been noticed by Turenne as an uncommonly bright, cool and efficient officer – such was the future Duke of Marlborough. He was the first to plant a colour on the walls of Maastricht amidst two more mines exploding and furious hand-to-hand fighting by heroic men on both sides. British military histories usually mention at length Churchill and his British comrades at Maastricht, Fortescue pompously even adding that "the most brilliant little action of the war was the work of the red-coats." It gives the impression the French were hardly involved …! Yet one also reads of the Sun King's dismounted Gardes du Corps armed with partisans for the attack who "did marvels on this occasion", according to Quincy. And none of this outstanding bravery could have occurred without the extraordinary valour of the Dutch defenders. Ultimately, the half-moon was taken. Although Quincy of course mentions "very few losses" in this action while mentioning the Dutch had some 1,200 men missing; it was certainly a statement for propaganda. Maastricht finally capitulated on 2 July and the garrison paraded out of the city in view of the King. He finally had Maastricht, but the cost was certainly higher than foreseen, although unknown in detail. The dead and wounded Dutch have been estimated at 1,200 to 1,700 men, the French army's from at least 2,300 to over 9,000 men.[1]

The tactical value of Maastricht was basically its importance as a strong sentry forbidding eastern access into the Netherlands. However, the French were already occupying part of the Netherlands and the Dutch were too weak to drive them out. The French methods of occupation were certainly not benevolent. Forced taxes and loans were levied to pay for the garrison; if the leading inhabitants expressed reluctance at this, French troops might take them away as had been done for 24 of them in Utrecht. For all that, the theatre of war was actually moving east into Germany. A French corps had thus taken Trier on the Rhine while William had retaken Naarden in September, securing Amsterdam further. The French also knew that an Imperial army led by Marshal Montecuccoli was approaching Westphalia hoping that Dutch troops could join him to attack Bonn, the residence of the Bishop of Cologne allied to France. Its fall would cut off communications with neutral but French-leaning Bavaria, and the French army in the Netherlands. Spain had declared war on France by joining the League of The Hague, consisting of the Netherlands, the Holy German Empire and the Duke of Lorraine, on 30 August 1673. Part of the Spanish army in Flanders joined William's field force; thus, about 12,000 men set out towards Bonn in mid October.

Faced with this, Louis XIV and Louvois had little choice but to decide on the evacuation of some 18,000 troops at Utrecht and its vicinity so that marshals Turenne and Luxembourg could try to prevent the allies from reaching Bonn. Marshal Bellefond was meanwhile concentrating 26,000 men at Zutphen, Arnhem, Nijmegen and Grave that could either reoccupy the Netherlands or go south towards France along the Meuse. Marshal Luxembourg tried and failed to intercept William's Dutch–Spanish force and it marched

Dutch medal commemorating the conquest of Naarden and the expulsion of the French from Utrecht, 1673. (Courtesy Rijksmuseum, Amsterdam. NG-VG-1-1143)

---

1   Quincy, *Histoire Militaire*, Vol. 1, pp.350–353; Rousset, *Histoire de Louvois*, Vol. 1, pp.458–464; Nimwegen, *The Dutch Army*, pp.459–461; James Grant, *British Battles on Land and Sea* (London: Cassell, 1888), Vol. 1, p.346; John W. Fortescue, *A History of the British Army* (London: Macmillan, 1899), Vol. 1, p.296.

## 1673–1674 : THE WAR EXPANDS

The siege and recapture of Naarden by Prince William of Orange and his troops, 12 September 1673. This was the prince's first substantial military success against the French. Detail of a print after Romeyn de Hooghe. (Courtesy Rijksmuseum, Amsterdam, RP-P-OB-79.2780)

The junction of the armies of General Montecuculi and Prince William of Orange, 4 November 1673. A powerful imperial Austro-Geman force with troops from Spanish Flanders joined the Dutch army in the area of Rhinbach. It was a major turning point of the war. Austrian General Montecuculi is shown wearing a blue coat and Prince William of Orange has a red coat. Other officers include the Prince of Courlant and Spanish marquis of Spaanse and of Grana. This led to the surrender of Bonn on 18 December. Detail of a print attributed to Romeyn de Hooghe. (Courtesy Rijksmuseum, Amsterdam. RP-P-OB-79.420)

into Cologne's territory, plundering it terribly in late October. Dutch soldiers in particular sought revenge for the ruin and massacres that had occurred in their country. At the small town of Rheinbach, they even massacred many of its armed militiamen, an event not glorified in Dutch propaganda prints. Further east, Turenne wished to prevent Marshall Montecuccoli besieging Bonn and make the conjunction with William's troops, but he realised that the Austrian marshal was a good tactician with superior forces so, after a few skirmishes, wisely withdrew eastward. William marched on and, by 6 November, was in sight of Bonn, to join Montecuccoli's army which was already there. The siege went swiftly and Bonn's 1,200 French and Cologne defenders capitulated six days later. Not wishing to face around 28,000 allied troops, Marshal Luxembourg retreated to Charleroi while Turenne went further east towards Alsace. The following months saw reversals of alliances. England withdrew from its alliance with France in February 1674, the allied bishops followed suit to escape occupation by the allies in April and May. It was now obvious the remaining French-occupied Netherlands had to be evacuated and, by the end of May, only Grave and Maastricht remained garrisoned by about 9,000 French troops.[2]

---

2  Quincy, *Histoire Militaire*, Vol. 1, pp.363–364; Nimwegen, *The Dutch Army*, pp.465–468; Charles-Auguste, Marquis de La Fare, *La dernière campagne de Turenne* in the *Bibliothèque de souvenirs & récits militaires*, Paul Gaulot (ed.) (Paris: Henri Gautier, *c*. 1890–1900), No. 68, pp.67–69. La Fare blamed Louvois (whose jealousy made him dislike Turenne) for not providing reinforcements thus dooming Bonn and forcing Turenne's withdrawal, a valid argument.

# 1673–1674 : THE WAR EXPANDS

# 1674 Franche-Comté, Rhineland and Senef

The fighting in the Netherlands was over and nearly all the French army had left. The terrible way it had been occupied had raised wide reprobations in neighbouring countries and many people in France were also undoubtedly troubled by such actions, even in an age when violent persecutions were frequent, not only in their country, but in much of Europe. Conversely, all in Europe were amazed and admired the feats of the French army who had captured many cities so quickly in the 1672 *Blitzkrieg*, followed by the surrender of the great fortress of Maastricht in 1673. It was obvious that the French army was not only the most numerous, but still the best in Europe. It was now regrouping in southern Flanders where the land was dry and not below sea level.

The Sun King was in no way discouraged and instead saw Spain's entry into the war as an opportunity. Attacking Spanish Flanders was an option, but Spanish Franche-Comté – which had been taken and given back in 1668 – was again ripe to pick. In February 1674, a French corps under Lieutenant General the Duc de Navailles entered Franche-Comté, taking several small towns and, on the 28th, started the siege of the fortress of Gray. It was stormed by the Lyonnois (modern spelling: Lyonnais) Regiment and capitulated after a five-hour battle, followed by the capture several other small towns. Navailles then marched to Besançon and laid siege to it from 25 April. The King joined him on 2 May. Siege operations were supervised by Vauban. The town of Besançon itself capitulated on 14 May while its citadel, situated on a cliff, continued to resist bravely until its garrison surrendered and was granted the honours of war. The last fortress, Dole, was besieged from 27 May until its capitulation on 6 June. Salins and a few smaller places

Regimental colours of the Toulouse and Agénois regiments, early eighteenth century. Toulouse, 1 and 4, brown with green bar, 2 and 3 green with brown bar, grey anchors with blue bars with yellow lilies at ends of white cross. Agénois, buff and purple quarters. (Anne S.K. Brown Military Collection, Brown University Library, Providence, RI, USA. Author's photo)

The Sun King with General Vauban leading the French army's invasion of Franche-Comté, culminating in the siege and capture of Besançon in May 1674. Staff officers are at left and, at right, the French army is seen with the city of Besançon in the distance. Its fortifications were later greatly improved by Vauban. From a large brass plaque by Martin van der Bogaert, called "Desjardins in France". (Musée du Louvre, Paris. Author's photo)

were taken later. Franche-Comté had been conquered in six weeks from the time the Sun King arrived there – it was *Blitzkrieg* again for the French army.[3]

Previously, Louis XIV had sent troops to occupy certain territorial enclaves in France and western Germany belonging to various princes. He was reactivating his policy of reunion. Thus, the town and area of Orange in southern France that belonged to the Prince of Orange with the Spanish Charolais County were annexed as was Cleves and several small Imperial towns in Alsace. For the opponents of France, all this meant that Louis XIV was once again in a mood to invade his neighbours thanks to his powerful army. Thus, the Holy German Imperial assembly in Regensburg declared *Reichskrieg* (Imperial war) to France on 31 March followed by the Elector of Brandenburg who re-entered the war on 1 July.

From various intelligence reports received during the early spring, the allies considered that about 65,000 men of the French army would be deployed in Flanders, the Rhineland, Franche-Comté and Roussillon and this was proving correct already in the case of Franche-Comté. In theory, the allies could mobilise about 130,000 men to counter the French on the three other fronts. There were large concentrations of French troops under the Prince of Condé south of Spanish Flanders so the allies could safely conclude that this would be the most threatened area. There, its governor, the Conde de Monterrey, estimated that he would need about 60,000 men, half in garrisons

---

3   Quincy, *Histoire Militaire*, Vol. 1, pp.374–379

and half in the field, but was short of 20,000 men to have a viable field army, which then only stood at 10,000. As spring slid into summer, the promised German Imperial contingents were only slowly arriving in Flanders and the Rhineland, and in lesser numbers. The main corps under General Raduit de Souches would reach 30,000 men only in late July. Allied leadership was also hampered by having three commanders: William of Orange, Monterey and Souches, all of whom had different priorities; Souches was not even sure if he should cross the Meuse at Namur to reinforce Spanish Flanders. He finally did cross in July, boosting the allied army to about 70,000 men.[4]

In the field elsewhere, the situation of the French armies was not as secure. Marshal Turenne, now French commander in the Rhineland, wanted to move on Germany from Alsace. He felt that front was the most important for the 1674 campaigns, but had been overruled. His army was therefore weak at only about 10,000 men and while calling for reinforcements, he was in a defensive posture when two allied armies approached. Turenne knew he had to seize the opportunity and attack one before both armies united. He crossed the Rhine with 9,000 men and met the small army of 7,500, led by Imperial general Aeneas de Caprara, at the village of Sinsheim on 16 June 1674. Both armies consisted mostly of cavalry although some of Turenne's consisted of dragoons that could also fight on foot. Caprara deployed his 1,500 infantry outside Sinsheim, which were overwhelmed by about 4,000 of Turenne's infantrymen and dragoons on foot, and fierce fighting went on in and around the village, which was utterly destroyed in the battle. The Imperial troops withdrew after a failed counter-attack, and so did Turenne soon thereafter, as Sinsheim itself had no tactical value. Both sides had high casualties, about 1,500 for the French and 2,000 for the Imperials. Louis XIV congratulated Turenne and it was indeed a brilliant and daring move, but it only delayed the union of the two armies, which later occurred at Heidelberg.[5]

Turenne turned west, then north, and skirted Heidelberg. This was his rather infamous march through the Palatinate in which the French army devastated any hamlet it came upon and just about everything else it could reach. It seemingly originated in instructions by Louvois in June to the intendant of Alsace to have orders issued regarding contributions of inhabitants in parts of the Palatinate, which was in the Holy Roman Empire with its elector who protested while his subjects were in no mood to submit to the French. Louvois was clear: no contributions in food, forage or money meant burning down lodgings and seizing whatever was needed. Especially by the standards of the early twenty-first century, this was cruel and illegal, but in the seventeenth century there was no international law and such practices were tolerated and even encouraged by hard-hearted leaders such as Louvois.

---

4   Nimwegen, *The Dutch Army*, pp.471–474.
5   Quincy, *Histoire Militaire*, Vol. 1, pp.381–388; Ramzay, *Histoire du Vicomte de Turenne*, Vol. 2, pp.248–253; John Lynn, *The wars of Louis XIV 1667–1914* (London: Longman, 1996), p.109; Henri Choppin, *Histoire générale des dragons* (Paris, 1879), pp.118. Ramzay lists Turenne's infantry at Sinsheim as a battalion each of Picardie, la Ferté, du Plessis and Douglas for 2,000 men with detachments of Champagne, Turenne, Languedoc, Bourgogne, Hamilton and Monmouth for 1,500 men.

An infantry officer taking a pinch of snuff, c. 1673–1675. He wears a brown "winter coat" with red cuffs, silver buttons and buttonholes, buff breeches, red stockings, white cravat with red bows, black shoes with red hells (said to be reserved to noblemen), grey hat with red plumes, white sash with red lines, buff bandolier. (Anne S.K. Brown Military Collection, Brown University Library, Providence, RI, USA. Author's photo)

Marshal Turenne was not enthusiastic about this sort of repression, but he was a soldier and had to obey higher authority. So his men started to carry out the instructions where they passed. Soon his soldiers found the horribly mutilated bodies – *d'une assez étrange façon* (in a rather strange way) commented Turenne – of their comrades who were stragglers that had been caught by armed villagers. These were what has since been called guerrillas that were called *schnapans* (or *chenapans*, a word still used in French Canada today to denote a wily wrongdoer). This sort of discovery enraged many soldiers who now happily wielded torches to burn dozens if not hundreds of hamlets that had naturally been abandoned by their inhabitants, and only God could help any *schnapans* or other hapless people they caught. This was not the first nor the last time the Palatinate would be ravaged in wars, but the sacrifice of these unfortunate people would make excellent propaganda against the French for many decades to come.[6]

Turenne's army went towards Luxembourg, made a large loop in the countryside and headed to the outskirts of Strasbourg. It met General Bournonville's Imperial troops at Enzheim on 4 October, an encounter which caused some 3,000 French and 3,500 Imperial casualties, but won by Turenne. Four days later, some 20,000 Brandenburg troops led by the Elector arrived and joined Bournonville's army, raising the allied force to some 50,000 men. Although Turenne had received some reinforcements, he only had 33,000 men. So, to confuse the enemy, he marched west past Sarrebruck then wandered south into Lorraine going by Nancy and Épinal.

The main front was Flanders, where the Prince de Condé commanded a French army of about 45,000 men that had to check an allied army of some 70,000 men. The allies were more or less led by the Prince of Orange because there was no really unified command with a supreme commander. Thus there was much debate about what to do; namely, would the emphasis be given to sieges or to field engagements. This last option was favoured by William of Orange and it was supported by German princes, but to satisfy everyone 12,000 men would besiege the French-held fortress of Grave. If William with his superior army of 60,000 men could beat Condé's field force of only 32,000 (according to La Fare, a Gendarmerie officer who was with

---

6  *Collection des lettres et memories troves dans les porte-feuilles du Maréchal de Turenne*, Comte de Grimoard (ed.) (Paris: Nyon, 1782), Vol. 2, pp.537–538, 560–561; Voltaire, *Le siècle de Louis XIV*, p.186–187; Rousset, *Histoire de Louvois*, Vol. 2, pp.78–84. One does not even wish to guess the atrocity that was 'in a rather strange way' alluded to.

## 1673–1674: THE WAR EXPANDS

The battle of Senef, 11 August 1674. Print after Romeyn de Hooghe. (Courtesy Rijksmuseum, Amsterdam. RP-P-OB-82.424)

Condé's army), he would then lead it to conquer Picardie and Champagne in northern France. But the wily Condé was waiting until William's allied army had passed a narrow valley at Senef, near Mons. On 11 August 1674, he attacked the allied rearguard made up of Spanish and Dutch troops, who panicked until rallied by William, while Condé pressed the attack with his soldiers, sword in hand. In this first stage of the engagement, the allies had up to 6,000 casualties and 4,000 men that surrendered, but German and Austrian troops kept arriving in relief and a ferocious general engagement followed with three attacks and counter-attacks, Condé being in the midst of the fighting with three horses killed under him. The fierce battle lasted until the late evening when, according to La Fare and Voltaire, both sides were exhausted and slowly withdrew from the field, each having about 7,000 casualties with the allies losing 5,000 men captured by the French. La Fare reported 7,000 French casualties including 1,000 officers. Racine and Quincy gave a generally similar account except that Condé's troops had remained on the battlefield and taken the baggage and the allied prisoners, so French histories usually attribute victory to Condé while acknowledging that it was a bloody struggle for all.[7]

---

7 Racine, *Précis historique des campagnes de Louis XIV depuis 1672 jusqu'à 1678*, p.140; Quincy, *Histoire Militaire*, Vol. 1, pp.391–394; Conde de Clonnard, *Historia organica de la infanteria y caballeria española* (Madrid, c. 1853), Vol. 4, pp.439–440; Nimwegen, *The Dutch Army*, pp.471–

William's force certainly could not now invade France so, perhaps to keep up morale and keep command bickering to a minimum, as well as giving the impression he had won at Senef, he laid siege to Oudenarde in mid September. Condé saw in this an opportunity to engage him on ground favourable to the French and, on 22 September, was in the vicinity of the besieged city that was bravely defended by its garrison. William, who was a cool-headed general, did not wish to risk an engagement in these conditions with one of the best field commanders of the seventeenth century and raised the siege. In a sense, William's retreat confirmed that Condé had indeed won at Senef since he could make an enemy superior in strength actually retreat before him. Dutch troops had also laid siege to Grave since late July and, led by its tenacious commander the Marquis de Chamilly, its garrison had repulsed all assaults costing thousands of casualties while suffering much less. By mid October, William arrived there with his army and was joined by German troops on the 24th. Grave was not in a situation where it could be relieved by Condé. The besiegeds' stubborn resistance was meant to occupy as many enemy troops as possible, especially as even more allied reinforcements were expected from Brandenburg. At that point, nearly all the city's cannons had been silenced by bombardments that also left it partly in ruins while the weather was getting colder. At last, on 28 October, Grave capitulated. Some 2,000 of its 4,000 men of the garrison were casualties, but the allies took about 5,000 to 6,000 who were mostly Dutch. The campaign in Flanders was basically over. December was approaching and armies would soon be going into winter quarters.[8]

On the Rhineland front, Marshal Turenne was still keeping his many stronger opponents at bay late in 1674. German and Austrian Imperial troops led by the Frederick William, Elector of Brandenburg and Bournonville had occupied several towns in Alsace and everyone thought that Turenne would be going into winter quarters too. The allied troops were taking theirs in lower Alsace mainly at and around Belfort, Mulhouse and Colmar with some infantry on the east side of the Ill River. La Fare happened to talk to Marshal Turenne who asked him what he thought he would do in the winter. Taken aback, the young officer answered that the rumour in camp was that the royal court was pleased with him and that it thought it was time to put his troops in winter quarters and rest. The old marshal replied that the royal court "is sometimes happy when it should not be, and is not when it should be. As for me, I try to do the best that I imagine can be done; and rely on me: there cannot be a man-at-arms resting in France as long as there is one German beyond the Rhine in Alsace." It was a foreboding of things to come.[9]

---

479 and puts the Senef allied casualties 'at 12,000 men, perhaps even 15,000, of whom 6,000 were Dutch troops. The French had suffered 8,000 to 10,000 dead and wounded', and Condé had taken 'a great many colours and standards' and 'seized most of the Dutch army's baggage wagons'. La Fare, *La dernière campagne de Turenne*, pp.71–76.

8 Voltaire, *Le siècle de Louis XIV*, pp.188–189; Racine, *Précis historique des campagnes de Louis XIV depuis 1672 jusqu'à 1678*, pp.140–141; Quincy, *Histoire Militaire*, Vol. 1, pp.381–389.

9 La Fare, *La dernière campagne de Turenne*, p.78; Quincy, *Histoire Militaire*, Vol. 1, pp.424–425.

After having his cavalry forage in Lorraine, Turenne slowly moved his infantry southwards past Épinal, leaving 12,000 men in that area as a rearguard. By late December, through rain and snow "in one of the worst winters that had been seen", related La Fare, Turenne approached Belfort, one of the allied army's winter quarters towns, which did not expect the French to show up; they thought the French too were in winter quarters. The Elector had quartered about 30,000 men that were spread in the area. In late December 1674, they realised Turenne was arriving at the head of some 20,000 men. It was too late to save 6,000 cavalry and 2,500 infantry that were surprised and shattered at Mulhouse on 29 December. The allies took about 300 casualties, but many dispersed in panic some even crossing the Rhine into Switzerland to get away. The French had about 30 casualties. Turenne marched north and a week later arrived and faced the main body of the Elector's troops.

# 4

# 1675–1678: Movements and Sieges

## 1675: the Rhineland and the Moselle

### Turenne's Outstanding Winter Campaign

On 5 January 1675, the Elector deployed his men between Turckheim and Colmar north of the Logelbach stream, but had difficulties extending their line all the way to Turckheim, which was weakly garrisoned. What happened next was classic Turenne tactics at their finest. He deployed most of his troops in two lines south of the stream, slowly moving west. These troops were worried because they exposed their flank to the enemy and La Fare mentioned it to Turenne. He answered that he was right, but the enemy would not move because it was secure in a strong position and its supplies were in Colmar. Thus, it could be outflanked further west. Indeed, Turenne sent another French corps west to Turckheim that was out of enemy sight thanks to hills south of the two towns and it attacked the Elector's west flank. Turenne then had his line move up and attacked the east end of the enemy position near Colmar. French pressure was less intense on the centre and it allowed the Elector to reinforce his west flank. However, after a bloody fight at a windmill, the French prevailed and the outflanked Imperial troops were compelled to withdraw. Turenne reported 918 casualties including 382 killed. The allies' losses are unknown apart from a vague reference to 200 Austrian casualties. One would expect much more from the Brandenburg and other allied contingents. In barely a week, the Elector had been outmanoeuvred and beaten by Turenne who led a force one-third weaker than his own. And now, the allied troops' position was untenable. They left Alsace altogether and took their winter quarters in Germany.[1]

The allies were surprised and shocked at this turn of events in the Rhineland. They resolved to invade Alsace again and this time, Emperor Leopold I sent the best field officer in the Austrian army to lead their forces,

---

1 La Fare, *La dernière campagne de Turenne*, pp.80–82; A. Billich, *La bataille de Turckheim 5 janvier 1675* (Münster,1958), <http://assifarnoldinfos.canalblog.com/archives/2007/08/19/5932161.html> 382 k 536 w 918 t.

## 1675–1678: MOVEMENTS AND SIEGES

Frederick William, Great Elector of Brandenburg, c. 1674-1675. He was an able tactician, but not as talented as Marshal Turenne. The Print after W. von Camphausen. (Private collection. Author's photo)

Marshall Montecuccoli, to face Turenne. In early May, Montecuccoli crossed into Alsace. Turenne was near Strasbourg, which was still a supposedly neutral republic that promised not to let either belligerent enter it. For months, the wily Montecuccoli tried every trick in the book to lure Turenne further out without success. Their armies were at about equal strength with 25,000 men each. These commanders tried to outfox each other while one would follow the other in the countryside with occasional skirmishes. On 27 July, both armies were manoeuvring close to each other near Salzbach when a stray cannonball hit Marshal Turenne, killing him instantly. The grief was great amongst his troops, but they were ready to put up a fight. Marshall Montecuccoli eventually withdrew, as did the French army. Meanwhile, Montecuccoli might have wished that Turenne's passing would lead to the collapse of French resistance in Alsace.

The French army may have been grieved, but it was still very much in a fighting mood, many common soldiers looking forward to avenge their

# THE ARMIES AND WARS OF THE SUN KING 1643–1715 VOLUME 2

Above: Marshal Turenne hailed by his men, after winning the battle of Mulhouse on 29 December 1674. Unsigned drawing from 1704. (Courtesy Anne S.K. Brown Military Collection, Brown University Library, Providence, RI, USA)

Left: Marshal Turenne killed at the battle of Salzbach, 27 July 1675. He was 63 years old when he perished, one of the seventeenth century's greatest strategists and tacticians. On learning of his death, his opponent, Raimondo Montecuccoli, is said to have responded: "Today died a man that honoured mankind." Print after Maurice Leloir. (Private collection. Author's photo)

## 1675–1678: MOVEMENTS AND SIEGES

revered fallen leader. His army had been partly withdrawn to safety after the Marshal's death, when its rearguard was attacked by Montecuccoli while crossing the Rhine at Altenheim on 31 July. The French rearguard put up a fierce resistance, notably the Champagne Regiment whose officers were nearly all casualties, while generals Vaubrun and De Lorges recrossed the Rhine to reinforce the rearguard. They rallied their troops, quickly built field fortifications garnished with artillery and attacked the allies with great vigour while the French cannons poured a murderous fire in their ranks. Montecuccoli, after losing about 3,000 men as casualties and another 2,500 taken prisoner, some with their colours, and seven cannons, now knew that the French army was a still a very dangerous opponent and withdrew. Marshal Créquy, temporary commander by rank and precedence, was not with the army and was soon sent with a corps to the Moselle instead. Louis XIV and Louvois knew they needed an experienced commander and wisely sent Condé from Flanders to lead in Alsace. Montecuccoli therefore had to face the other most renowned tactician in the French army and indeed, in Europe. So the "cat and mouse" games of manoeuvres continued and, just as before, the allied army was held in check by the French forces in Alsace. Leading some 30,000 men, Montecuccoli hoped to take Haguenau and Saverne and laid siege to both, but met a fierce resistance from within their walls and was not comforted by the possible arrival of Condé's army in his rear that would likely be disastrous for the allies. So he wisely abandoned siege operations and, so as to avoid a nasty surprise such as Turenne had perpetrated on the Elector, finally went back across the Rhine to take his 1676 winter quarters in Germany. In all this, the long-term loser may have been the supposedly independent republic of the city of Strasbourg. In the future, the Sun King would not forget the rather obliging stance it had shown to the allies.[2]

The city of Trier on the Moselle that had been occupied by the French since 1673 meanwhile came under threat from an allied army led by the Duke of Lorraine who invested it in early August. A French corps of 15,000 men led by Marshal Créquy came to the rescue, but was attacked at Consabrick (or Konzer Brücke) near Trier on 11 August and utterly defeated by the allied army. The Vermandois Regiment would not surrender and was practically destroyed while others managed to escape to Metz and Thionville in France. The French losses are uncertain but the lower estimates of about 3,500 to 4,000 casualties

General Raimondo Montecuccoli, c. 1675. He was the best Austrian Imperial general and proved a match for the French in the Netherlands. Print after Wouter Jongman. (Courtesy Rijksmuseum, Amsterdam. RP-P-1908-3882)

---

2   La Fare, *La dernière campagne de Turenne*, pp. 86–87; Quincy, *Histoire Militaire*, Vol. 1, pp.438–450; Racine, *Précis historique des campagnes de Louis XIV depuis 1672 jusqu'à 1678*, pp.141–143; Herbert V. Patera, *Unter Österreiches Fahnen* (Vienna: Styria, 1960), p.23.

The city of Trier. Print after Jan van Call. (Courtesy Rijksmuseum, Amsterdam, RP-P-OB-83.204B)

against about 1,000 for the allies would seem reasonable. A trickle of other survivors including the Marshal found refuge in Trier, the siege of which was resumed by the Duke of Lorraine. By 3 September, constant bombardment had made a large breach in the curtain walls and the allies summoned the French garrison to surrender so as to avoid the useless atrocities of a general assault. Marshal Créquy would have none of that, which went against the opinion of most of his officers. In the following days, powerful mines destroyed more of the walls and spread panic in Trier's garrison; the breach was now wide enough for ranks of 40 men abreast to charge in. On the 5th, led by Captain Boisjourdan of the La Marine Regiment, the officers mutinied followed by the rest of the French troops and made an agreement with the enemy to capitulate if they were free to go back to Metz in France. Marshal Créquy with a few others barricaded themselves in a church, but, finally, once surrounded by allied troops, he surrendered his sword.

The mutiny was not appreciated at all in France. The officers from Trier were arrested and tried in Metz, Captain Boisjourdan was beheaded in public and all others not executed were cashiered from the army. In all this, Créquy proved he was not a great tactician, but also showed that he was never discouraged by defeats and ill fortune, "sublime virtue found in few generals", La Fare later wrote. That was recognised by the Sun King. When the Prince of Condé had to give up command of the Alsace army in December 1675 due to health issues, Créquy replaced him. His luck had not totally run out. His defeat and the fall of Trier left the French province of Champagne liable to be invaded, but the allies did not take advantage of this. Possibly because, assuming that they could have assembled a powerful enough army, they were concerned that might be outflanked by an even larger French force. With Louis XIV as opponent, that was a real possibility. As for Créquy, better battlefield times awaited him.[3]

In Flanders, the year had seen many large-scale troop movements and minor engagements, but no really decisive action occurred there. The French hung on to Maastricht and, when the Bishop of Liège, an independent city,

---

3   Quincy, *Histoire Militaire*, Vol. 1, pp.453–454. Voltaire, *Le siècle de Louis XIV*, p.193; The 71-year-old Duke Charles IV of Lorraine became ill during the siege of Trier and was taken to Coblentz where he passed away on 18 September 1675. Command of his army was assumed by the princes of Lunenburg and of Zell.

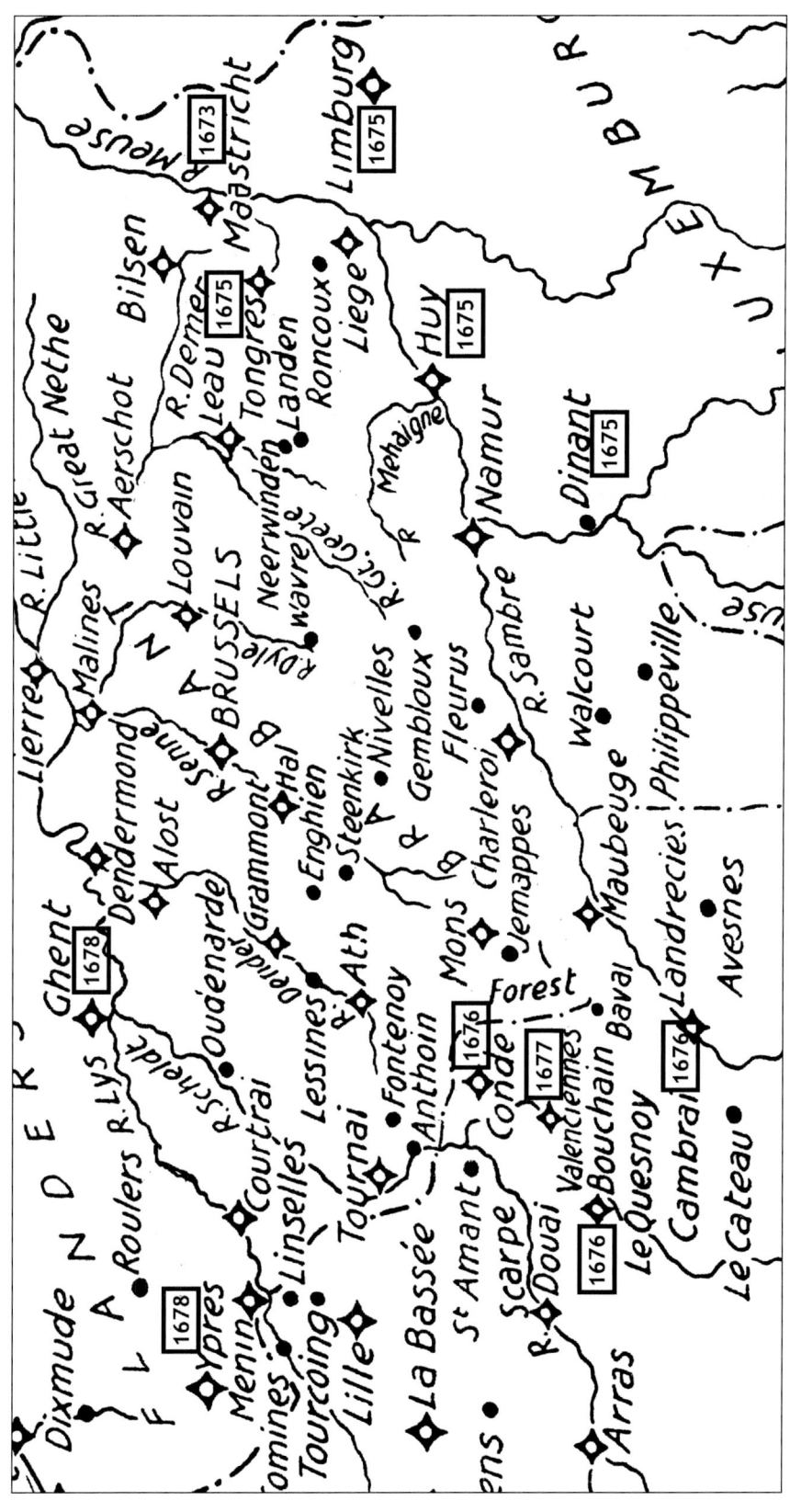

Map of successful sieges by the French army in Flanders, 1673–1678. Besides the many locations shown, Aire (1676) and Saint-Omer (1677), situated west of Ypres and not visible on this map, were also taken. (Private collection. Author's photo with digital additions)

seemed to be leaning towards the allies than France, Louis XIV ordered that it be occupied, which was accordingly done. French troops led by the Comte d'Estrades marched into its citadel on 31 March. In May, the King arrived in Flanders to join some 60,000 men led by Condé. On the 19th the Sun King, accompanied by Vauban for siege operations, was before the walls of Dinant that opened its gates on the 28th. On 1 June the King invested the fortress of Huy that capitulated six days later, then on went on to Limbourg that surrendered on 20 June and, satisfied by his own success, went back to Versailles in July to be glorified yet again. With about 40,000 men, the allies under William of Orange did not risk an engagement with a force a third larger than their own.[4]

Furthermore, the allies could no longer count on the forces of the Elector of Brandenburg. Sweden was France's somewhat lethargic ally and Louis XIV had asked that King Charles XI invade Brandenburg, otherwise the payment of French subsidies might dry up. The message was clear and a Swedish army of about 15,000 men under the elderly and sickly Marshal Carl Gustaf Wrangel entered Brandenburg near Stettin in May 1675; the Elector needed all the men he could muster to repel the invading force. While this must have been satisfying to Louis XIV and his army, it was only for a short period of time. The Swedish army's command was much weaker due to disputes amongst the generals, while Marshal Wrangel was often incapacitated by severe gout, leading an army that was much less effective than it once had been during the Thirty Years' War. The Elector left the Rhineland on 6 June with 15,000 Brandenburg troops to check the Swedes, who had occupied several towns including Spandau near Berlin, the capital. On 21 June, the Elector was at Magdeburg and marching north-east leading about 7,000 men of which 5,000 were mounted. Four days later, the Swedes were forced to withdraw from Spandau and the town of Brandenburg after the capture of Rathenow, to regroup their forces further north. The Elector went after them knowing that he had to intercept them before they fully united. He caught up with the Swedish and attacked at Fehrbellin on 28 June. The Swedes under Wrangel had 11,000 men but managed to deploy only 7,000, who were decisively defeated. This heralded the rise of Brandenburg–Prussia as a major power in Germany. For Louis XIV's army, it lost the hitherto unbeatable Swedish army as an ally that could divert Brandenburg, which had the second largest army in the Holy Roman Empire after Austria.[5]

There can be little doubt that the Elector of Brandenburg's campaign experience against the French was of great benefit to him and his army. Crossing swords with the likes of Marshal Turenne and his troops taught rare lessons to the Elector that served him well against the Swedes. They were something like the Dutch in 1672: their army which had been outstanding in the past, was now somewhat neglected and indifferently led. The speed and efficiency of the Brandenburg army in beating the Swedes at Fehrbellin

---

4 Joseph Halkin, 'Dépêches des officiers au service de la France concernant les opérations militaires des armées de Louis XIVen Belgique pendant les mois de mai, juin et juillet 1675, suivies d'un inventaire des archives du Ministère de la Guerre deFrance concernant la Belgique', *Compte-rendu des séances de la commission royale d'histoire*, VI, 1896, pp.337–414.

5 Robert Frost, *The Northern Wars. War, State and Society in Northeastern Europe* (London: Longman, 2000), p.210.

# 1675–1678: MOVEMENTS AND SIEGES

The army of the Great Elector of Brandenburg and Prussia defeats the Swedish army at Fehrbellin on 18 June 1675. This event heralded the increasing military importance of Prussia in European affairs in the following centuries. (Private collection. Author's photo)

certainly had the mark of the great French marshals that the Elector had observed. Now, the Sun King's Swedish ally was beaten and a new and powerful force was rising in the allied camp.

A much smaller, but still important front, was the border of French Roussillon and Spanish Catalonia, a mountainous but still passable area. General Schomberg led his troops in a two-month foray along the border marked by many small engagements and capture of small towns, but there were no great engagements with the Spanish. They were in a defence mode, part of their troops having been sent to reinforce Sicily. The Spanish Miquelet light troops were noted by the French general staff for their bravery and their tactic of taking cover to fire and retreat when dragoons charged them. There were Miquelets on the French side of the border too and some were mustered. For Schomberg's army, the important engagement was the capture of the Spanish fortress of Bellegarde on 20 July. Ten days later, Schomberg was promoted to marshal of France.[6]

## Tax Revolts in France

During the year, Louis XIV and his government were faced with tax revolts that erupted in many places. On 28 March, crowds in Bordeaux's streets were

---

6  Quincy, *Histoire Militaire*, Vol. 1, pp.455–459; Clonnard, *Historia organica de la infanteria y caballeria española*, Vol. 4, p.441.

shouting *Vive le roi sans gabeles!* (Hail the King without salt taxes) wishing that the hated salt tax should be abolished. Not wishing to deploy troops needed on the eastern border, the Sun King announced an amnesty to the demonstrators and kept the salt tax. As Louvois feared, an amnesty might actually encourage others to come out in protest and, sure enough, it was not the end of it. Soon, crowds were shouting the same slogans in the provinces of Guyenne, Brittany and Franche-Comté as well as in many towns. The tax revolt had spread across the kingdom and there was violence against officials in some places. A group in Brittany even plotted that a Dutch fleet land 6,000 troops there. In the short term, with campaigns getting under way in the east and William of Orange hoping the revolts would be big enough to weaken the French army facing him, the only thing that could be done was to contain the uprisings.

In April, the elderly Marshal d'Albret went into Guyenne with two infantry regiments and two of cavalry. In May a battalion of the La Couronne Regiment and 600 archers of the Maréchaussée armed constabulary were sent to Brittany. After the King came back from Flanders in July, royal guard detachments arrived in Brittany to further disarm suspicious peasants. The real repression occurred during the late autumn. On 17 November, 7,000 troops marched into Bordeaux to disarm its inhabitants including members of its Parliament and proceeded to demolish the city's walls. There were some violent incidents, the worse being Marshal d'Albret assailed and beaten up in his carriage before his guardsmen could intervene. After this, the city had a difficult occupation and some cavalry that should have departed, to be quartered in its winter quarters elsewhere, stayed in the city and was still patrolling the city in January. For Bordeaux's inhabitants, it was close to a reign of terror at the mercy of none too sympathetic troopers and dragoons. Some 1,200 families fled the city, business in which simply collapsed. By then, the provinces were in no state nor humour to resist paying tax when they bought salt. Especially as the despised archers of the salt tax police nicknamed the *Gabelous* were more present than ever. Being caught by them could earn the guilty a seat in a rowing galley of the Mediterranean fleet or deportation to overseas colonies.[7]

## 1676: the *Pré carré*, Flanders, Rhineland, Roussillon

The war was in its fourth year and all sides were feeling the strains of conflict. The allies had yet to find cohesion and a unified military and political command, without which effective strategy is very unlikely. Denmark was mostly an effective ally at sea. Spain had joined the coalition and while it could put up a stubborn defence, its armies were too weak to have an important impact and tilt the balance. Furthermore not all of Germany and other nations rallied to oppose Louis XIV. For France, the happy summer of 1672 Blitzkrieg on the Netherlands had been literally stopped by muddy waters when the desperate Dutch opened the dikes that protected their

---

7   Rousset, *Histoire de Louvois*, Vol. 2, pp.134–137, 197–201. As usual in Ancient Régime judicial administration, troublesome ringleaders were rounded up and condemned to the navy's rowing galley fleets in the Mediterranean.

nation from the North Sea. England might have been a good ally of France, but its domestic response forced King Charles II to seek neutrality in 1674. Some small German states near France were allies and Bavaria remained neutral. Sweden as an ally proved to be a disappointment.

It was basically a draw. In the field, the nature of the fighting was slowly departing from field engagements to an increased preference for sieges. This was partly due to Louis being concerned about an invasion of France. During the Fronde, he had seen Spanish troops in Paris as part of the nobles' army and was determined that this would never happen again, not only for political and military reasons, but also for the economy since revenues would be dramatically lessened. It made much better sense to massively invest in defence by raising the strength of the army to unseen levels and to build and repair fortifications by adopting General Vauban's concept of the *Pré carré* (literally the square field) that he had been mooting for a while (of which more in the next two volumes). Vauban outlined his concept to Louvois in the autumn of 1675 and it was obviously the work of a brilliant mind. Since there were so many opponents against which the army in Flanders in particular had to last a long time, the idea was to concentrate the forces in a series of strong points that would interlink with each other. Lines or circles of defence were already in vogue, but this particular proposal took the square as the model to, in effect, envelop northern France and somewhat beyond in a square field, the *Pré carré*, whose fortresses would be as many strong bases for French field armies as well as a string of redoubtable places that an invading enemy could not ignore; if he did, he might be outflanked.[8]

The King was of course quickly convinced, especially as he increasingly favoured siege warfare and looked to occupy more permanently the places that the French army held. In the seventeenth century up to that time, places were besieged, taken and sometimes evacuated shortly thereafter for lack of troops to garrison them or because they had lost their strategic importance. However, the withdrawal from the Netherlands and the arrival of strong German forces at the Alsatian border put opposing forces close to the French frontier. A large enemy army could dare to advance deeply into France and the most likely place for this to happen was in Flanders. With an interlinked network of fortresses built or upgraded to the very latest fortifications techniques that the genial Vauban had imagined, the obstacles to such an invasion became nearly insurmountable.

Another factor was that a diplomatic start at negotiating a peace settlement had been made, but it was going to be a long process; no one was ready to really bargain anything as yet. French negotiators expected the Spanish to try everything in the book to revert the situation in Flanders to the terms of the previous 1668 treaty. To avoid that, France had to come up with a peace negotiating process that would give it the advantage, but only as long as a few allied fortresses were captured to refine the line of fortifications and have a few bargaining chips.

---

8  Rousset, *Histoire de Louvois*, Vol. 2, pp.202–204 quotes at length Vauban's remarkable correspondence to Louvois of 21 September and 4 October 1675.

Plan of the fortress of Philippsbourg, *c*. 1680. The French 2,800-man garrison sustained a long siege against some 40,000 allied troops in 1676. Granted the honours of war, 1,200 men marched out of the city on 9 September. Print from Georges Fournier's 1688 *Traité des fortifications*. (Author's photo)

French troops movements with heavy artillery in early April had nearly all the Spanish fortresses in southern Flanders such as Ypres, Mons, Namur and even Trier on the Moselle wondering anxiously if they would be besieged. The smaller town of Condé did not really expect it. Nevertheless, on 17 April, the place was invested by Marshal Créquy's army of about 45,000 men and four days later, Louis XIV himself joined his army there. Condé's best defence was the water surrounding its walls. Knowing this, Vauban previously had rafts built as floating redoubts armed with guns on naval carriages to shoot at and bombard the place, the walls of which were badly damaged. On the night of 25 to 26 April, a successful assault was made and the fortress capitulated. On 2 May the French army laid siege to Bouchain, but soon learned that the Prince of Orange was in the area near Mons, so the French army marched to meet him and, on 10 May, both armies came within sight of each other near Valenciennes. However Louis XIV agreed with Louvois and three of his marshals who advised caution, while Marshal de La Feuillade wanted to attack William's apparently weaker force. So the allied troops were only too glad to withdraw and we agree with historian Camille Rousset that the only fairly sure opportunity to crush William and his army was lost and would never again occur. The next day, Bouchain surrendered. The King went back to Versailles and later also Louvois leaving Marshal Schomberg in command; Aire was besieged on 21 July and surrendered 10 days later.

The *Pré-carré* was coming along and the French thought William of Orange had retreated to safety in the Netherlands. He was in fact in fighting mood and his army of about 50,000 men invested Maastricht on 7 July. That great fortress was important, but somewhat less so since the evacuation of the Netherlands, the bulwark of the French defences being now further south. It was nevertheless a very strong place commanded by the Comte de Calvo with a garrison of 4,500 men. Calvo proved more than equal to the challenge and had a spirited garrison that put up a stubborn resistance for months until 9 September, when a disappointed and apprehensive William abandoned siege operations. There was a tremendous sigh of relief in Versailles as witnessed by generous gratifications and promotions to the heroic defenders. This essentially concluded operations on the Flanders front.[9]

---

9 The French garrison of Maastricht consisted mostly of elite units: a battalion of Picardie, three of Piémont, two of Bourbonnais, one of Jonsac, one of Vierzet, two cavalry regiments and one of dragoons as per Quincy, *Histoire Militaire*, Vol. 1, p.482.

On the Rhineland, Charles V, Duke of Lorraine had replaced Marshal Montecuccoli leading the allied army of some 40,000 men, while Marshal Luxembourg was commanding French forces of about the same strength. There were several engagements when both armies were moving in Alsace, Luxembourg wondering what the Duke of Lorraine was up to until he learned that his infantry and artillery had boarded boats in Strasbourg, arriving at Philippsbourg, and beginning siege operations on 10 May 1676. There was a vigorous defence by its 2,800-man French garrison for months and Luxembourg approached the place with his troops hoping to make the enemy give up, but he then saw that the camp of the numerous allies was too well entrenched; his force was not strong enough to risk an assault and withdrew; as he put it, the King could either lose Philippsbourg or his army in Alsace. The town capitulated on 9 September.

In Roussillon, Marshal de Navailles replaced Schomberg and, learning of the depredations caused by Spanish Miquelets, mustered and disciplined a corps of French Miquelets that opposed the enemy's successfully. Navailles initially led an army of about 15,000 men, but this was reduced by 4,000 being sent to Sicily, which was also the case in the Spanish camp. The rest of the year was thus relatively stable, punctuated by small border engagements and raids.

# 1677

The year started with more diplomatic activity in a somewhat deadlocked war. Each nation hoped for a break in its favour, so hostilities went on. Louis XIV had an army of about 300,000 men, the highest it had ever been France's long history; Voltaire even advanced the figure of 450,000 when adding the naval, overseas and other troops not counted as part of the regular army's establishment. So the Sun King certainly felt he stood a chance. His immediate objective was to capture Saint-Omer and Cambrai that had been given back in 1668 and to make new captures, especially Valenciennes, that would fit in nicely as a French fortress in Vauban's defence network.[10]

The King was quite anxious that the campaign should get going early and, on 1 March, Valenciennes was invested and Vauban had parallel trenches dug. The King was present with 35,000 men led by Marshal Luxembourg. At dawn on the 17th, an assault column consisting of the guard's Grenadiers à cheval and the King's Musketeers broke into the city; the King was looking from a distance and seeing his guardsmen disappear amidst the haze and smoke, thought they would all be lost. Luxembourg was looking too and his experienced soldier's eyes understood what was happening: the guardsmen were fighting like devils to take Valenciennes almost by themselves. He immediately rushed in with other troops to demolish the gates and support the brave guardsmen. It was a brilliant assault and the city capitulated. Cambrai was next besieged by Luxembourg from 22 March and capitulated on 5 April.

---

10   Voltaire, *Le Siècle de Louis XIV*, p.506. Voltaire's figure is certainly exaggerated, but indeed reveals that France had several smaller establishments of regular troops.

Attack by the King's Musketeers at Valenciennes, 16 March 1677. In a daring action, they managed to take a gate and penetrate into the city. Print after J. Alaux. (Courtesy Yale University Art Gallery, New London, CT, USA)

Caught somewhat by surprise by the early campaign season that gave the initiative to the French, William of Orange hurriedly gathered a force of about 30,000 men hoping to stop the French and prevent the loss of Saint-Omer. Marshal Luxembourg marched north from Cambrai to meet William's army. On 11 April both armies met at a small river named Peene Becque, which is why the battle of Cassel is sometimes called battle of Peene, near the town of Cassel, about 15km east of Saint-Omer. The battle was basically a succession of French and Dutch charges and counter charges at the small river. It was a hard and bloody fight, and by evening William's flanks were threatened and he withdrew. The French had about 4,000 casualties and William's army double that figure. The immediate result was that Saint-Omer surrendered on 19 April. The main front then moved to the Rhineland so the French forces in Flanders under Luxembourg were weaker, but sufficient to keep mostly at bay about 60,000 men under William and the Duke of Villahermosa. William besieged Charleroi from 6 August, but Luxembourg, with over 40,000 men, came nearby while a smaller corps led by Marshal d'Humières blocked other allied troops and supplies reaching William from Brussels. Yet another French corps under Marshal Créquy prevented allied reinforcements from crossing the Meuse. William had to raise the siege of Charleroi on 14 August not wishing to expose his army to risk another battle

although Villahermosa did, so there were command dissension as well. In December, the French army captured Saint-Ghislain in Spanish Flanders. On the whole, it was not a good year for the allies on that front.

The Rhineland front was marked by constant troop movements between the French and the allied armies that were occasionally punctuated by small engagements, but there were no decisive battles. Marshal Créquy led an army of 32 infantry battalions and 110 cavalry squadron to match the Duke of Lorraine's at about the same strength. In June, Créquy notably marched on Nancy in Lorraine and the Duke evacuated, never to return again to his fiefdom. The allies took their winter quarters in early October and Marshal Créquy then saw his chance; he made the Duke withdraw at a small battle on 7 October at Kokersberg, and invested Fribourg in Germany

Map of Marshal Navaille's foray into Spain, in the summer of 1677. After taking Figueres, he withdrew when a strong Spanish army pursued him. Unexpectedly, Navaille turned back and attacked the Spanish on 4 July at the village of Espouilles/Espolla. The charge of the Furstenberg Regiment, wielding swords, was notable. The black arrows indicate the French troops' movements. Print after Hugo's *France Militaire*. (Author's photo)

*L'Espagnol sans Gand*, 1678. Satirical print showing a smiling French officer with a glove on the end of his sword, which is a play on words with regards to the loss of Ghent – *Gand* in French which is also *gant*, a glove – by the Spanish to the French army. The Spaniard at the centre is helped out by a somewhat distraught Walloon. The costume details of the French officer are remarkable. Anonymous print. (Courtesy Rijksmuseum, Amsterdam, RP-P-1989-194)

on 9 October. It capitulated on the 16th when it obtained the honours of war and its 1,600 men garrison paraded out the next day with drums beating and colours. Thus ended Créquy's long campaign in a manner worthy of Marshal Turenne, in Quincy's opinion.[11]

On the Pyrenees and Roussillon front, the Spanish court made it its priority and put in command of the reinforced Spanish troops, now numbering some 12,000 men, the Conde de Monterey, an experienced soldier who had been governor of Spanish Flanders. Marshal de Navailles in Roussillon led a modest French force of 8,000 men. Nevertheless, in June, he entered Catalonia and occupied Figueres, but his force was too weak and he withdrew, now pursued by a strong Spanish force led by the Conde de Monterey. Contrary to Spanish expectations, the wily Navailles turned his force around, regrouped, and marched south towards Monterey's troops. Both armies met at Espouilles (Espolla, Catalonia) on 4 July. The Spanish were obviously surprised. The soldiers of the Furstenberg Regiment fired a volley on the lead Spanish troops, dropped their muskets, drew swords and charged two battalions of Spaniards trying to entrench at the foot of the mountains; the startled Spanish soldiers were "cut to pieces" while Furstenberg's had 191 casualties. A French cavalry charge on the left flank decided the issue; the Spanish broke and ran, losing some 4,000 men compared to about 1,000 of Navaille's troops. Both armies withdrew and thus ended the campaign. Again, it was not a year to celebrate in the allied camp.[12]

## 1678

The marriage of William of Orange to Princess Mary, daughter of Charles II of England, in late 1678, had a profound effect on France's geopolitical situation. It resulted in a treaty of alliance between the Netherlands and Great Britain signed in January 1679 followed by the London Parliament approving funds to put the armed forces in a war footing. Consequently, regiments of Britons still in the French service were recalled. The allies were encouraged by this turn of events. The French army was nevertheless very strong and the loss of a few foreign regiments had no impact on it. It

---

11 Quincy, *Histoire Militaire*, Vol. 1, p.561.
12 Susane, *Histoire de l'infanterie française*, Vol. 4, p.305. The first edition of this work was *Histoire de l'ancienne infanterie française* and its Vol. 4, p.18 has more details on this little-known campaign.

stood at 279,610 according to the King's notes in his desk, about 163,000 for campaigns (119,250 infantry 43,990 cavalry) and 116,370 in garrisons (100,000 infantry and 16,370 cavalry).

Louis XIV was optimistic. He went to Flanders again and, in late February and early March, had his troops simultaneously invest the fortresses of Luxembourg, Namur, Mons, Ypres and Ghent. Ghent surrendered on 9 March, Ypres on 25 March; this had a rather discouraging effect on the allies who now increasingly sought a negotiated settlement of the conflict. Louis XIV also wished an end to hostilities, but not just yet. He wished to gain more points at the negotiation table so the other sieges became more like blockades to drag out military operations to tire the enemy. Following the siege and capture of Ghent, the King stated that William of Orange hesitated to attack him because "my army is large and my troops in a very good state." He was then at the head of some 60,000 men with 7,000 pioneers in Flanders to keep the allies apprehensive. He then left for Versailles leaving command of that army to the energetic Marshal Luxembourg.[13]

Meanwhile, in mid May the Sun King was back in Flanders, this time ready to negotiate peace treaties. The allies too wished to negotiate. They saw that there was no way they could decisively beat the numerous French army, invade part of France and force the Sun King to humble himself into a beggar's peace treaty. On the contrary, he now had many cards in his diplomatic deck and was willing to sacrifice some of the less important ones such as the Sicilian adventure. On 10 July at 11 in the evening, France and the Netherlands signed a peace treaty. This was done by diplomats at Nijmegen and couriers galloped out.

On 14 July, Marshal Luxembourg received the news near the villages of Saint-Denis and Casteau at about nine in the morning. He knew that William had arrived in his camp the night before so did he know? Yes. He and the Duque de Villahermosa had previously been notified, but unofficially. Both armies were facing each other, the French had about 40,000 men and the allies about 45,000, part of which was Spanish under Villahermosa. Both allied commanders were upset by this news since they had the advantage; they had received unofficial news only and they resolved to fight. At about noon, the allies attacked and there was especially heavy fighting for the control of the village of Casteau at the cost of about 4,000 casualties in each army. Both sides claimed victory, but it was a draw. Dutch, Spanish and British historians usually felt that William of Orange having the advantage since the French could not pursue the siege of Mons after such a struggle. A fine theory except that pursuing the siege was hardly likely: the war was over![14]

The Rhineland front had been something of a face-off between the two armies opposing with several small, but no great engagement, which was less the case in the Pyrenees. Marshal de Navailles advanced into Spain and besieged the fortress of Puycerda that capitulated on 28 May. Holding on to it was out of the question. Instead, Navailles all its fortifications were blown up and levelled what

---

13 *Lettres, instructions et mémoires de Colbert*, Pierre Clément, ed. (Paris: Imprimerie impériale, 1869), vol. 6, p.343.
14 Quincy, *Histoire Militaire*, Vol. 1, pp.591–595. Rousset, *Histoire de Louvois*, Vol. 2, pp.514–515–532; Nimwegen, *The Dutch Army and the Military Revolutions 1588-1688*, pp.509–510.

The battle of Saint-Denis, 14 July 1678. The fighting for the village of Casteau is shown in the distance. The mounted officers in the foreground appear to be Spanish, as they wear red sashes. Detail of a print after Romeyn de Hooghe. (Courtesy Rijskmuseum, Amsterdam. RP-P-OB-79.316)

had been one of the keys to Catalonia. Hostilities ceased gradually thereafter; Spain signed the treaty of Nijmegen on 17 September and the Holy Roman Empire on 5 February 1679 as well as Sweden and Brandenburg.

France had gone to war in 1672 to humble the Dutch who came out of the struggle reinforced, but Louis XIV had then raised the stakes by greatly expanding the army, forcing the allies to do the same. Nevertheless, the French army had prevailed following the evacuation from the Netherlands. It had lost Turenne and Condé, but the allied commanders were not as talented and often had command cohesion problems. On the whole, the Sun King could be satisfied by the treaties, which ceded to France all of Franche-Comté and the fortresses of Bellegarde in Roussillon, Aire, Bailleul, Bavay, Bergues, Bouchain, Cambrai, Cassel, Condé, Fribourg, Saint-Omer, Valenciennes and Maubeuge. Louis also gave back a number of places that were not considered essential. The logic was that there would be as few French enclaves as possible in Spanish Flanders and vice versa. This way, French troops could be better grouped within the *Pré-carré* plan.[15]

---

15 Bély, Bérenger and Corvisier, *Guerre et paix dans l'Europe du XVIIe siècle*, p.354. France gave back Maastricht and the principality of Orange to the Netherlands, Ath, Binche, Charleroi, Courtrai, Ghent, Limbourg, Leuw, and Oudenade Saint-Ghislain to Spain, Lorraine to Duke Charles V.

5

# The Sicilian Adventure

Discontented by its Spanish rulers, the large city of Messina, the capital of Sicily with some 120,000 inhabitants, broke into a fierce revolt from July 1674. The revolt overcame or chased out most Spaniards by August except for those in Fort Santissimo Salvatore at the harbour's entrance, who repulsed all attempts to take it. Hearing of this, Louis XIV saw an opportunity to occupy Sicily, which would give French naval power a great advantage as a base to control the central Mediterranean at Spain's expense.

A first step was taken in sending to Messina Admiral de Valbelle with six ships of the line, three fireships and two transports loaded with military supplies and food. On 27 September 1674, the French squadron arrived at Messina to the cheers of the population; French guns and gunners joined the Sicilians, which resulted in the capitulation of Fort Santissimo Salvatore. Valbelle went back to report on Sicily and sailed for Messina again with the Marquis de Vallavoire accompanied by about 20 elite officers with five infantry companies on board to provide military and combat training to the Sicilian militias raised during the uprising. Valbelle's squadron came in sight of Messina on 1 January 1675 to find a large Spanish fleet of 22 sailing warships and 19 galleys blockading the city. In no way intimidated, Valbelle attacked, broke their line and got through to Messina's harbour without much fighting while the Spanish fleet prudently sailed away. On 3 January, after 38 days of Spanish blockade, a triumphant entry was given by the starving population to the French, who came with plenty of food.

Elsewhere in Sicily, the cities of Palermo on the northern coast, Taormina, Catania, and Syracuse on the east coast remained under the Spanish standard held up by about 3,500 Spanish soldiers in all of Sicily. But it was said that if Louis XIV would send sufficient aid, the whole Sicilian population would rally to his troops. The Duc de Vivonne was now brought into the Sicilian operation. He was a lieutenant general in the army, vice-admiral of the Ponant (Mediterranean) fleet, general of the galley fleet and now appointed viceroy of Sicily. An army expeditionary corps with more warships would go to Sicily under his command.

The expeditionary corps that was sent comprised about 3,400 infantry consisting of a battalion each of the Picardie, Piédmont, Louvigny, Crussol and Provence infantry regiments with 255 men of Lhéry's cavalry regiment.

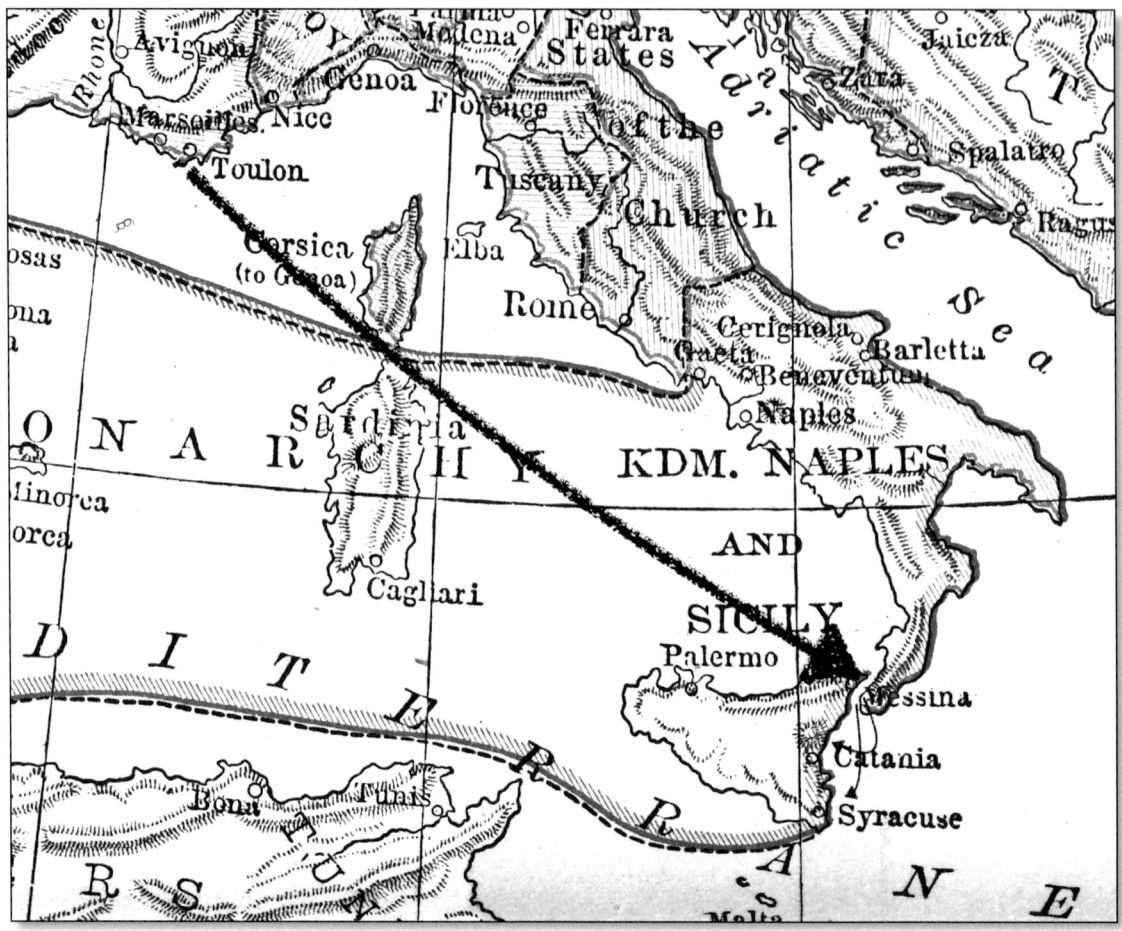

Spain's domain in the Mediterranean in the seventeenth century included Sicily. This map shows that Madrid's reach included Sicily; its most important harbours, Messina and Syracuse, had the potential of controlling access between the eastern and western Mediterranean, if provided with powerful naval fleets. This was a prime reason for Louis XIV's intervention in 1674, when troops and ships were sent from Toulon and Marseille. Map from Ridpath's 1880s *Cyclopedia of History*. (Author's photo)

These troops arrived at Messina in May 1675 and again received with joy by the city's inhabitants. Vivonne and his officers set up his vice-regal government in Messina and enlisted Sicilians to form local regiments to serve with the French troops. The objective was to 'liberate' the rest of the island, but Vivonne had to face supply problems and did not move swiftly. At length, he finally sailed to Agosta, which surrendered rather unexpectedly after a few cannon shots on 17 August. It was strongly fortified and Vivonne sent the regiments of Louvigny and Crussol with the cavalry to garrison it. Shortly thereafter, Vivonne learned that he had been promoted marshal of France.

Meanwhile, the Spanish court in Madrid was not about to give up Sicily easily. The connection with the island went back to 1516. To Louis XIV, although very interested in securing Sicily, it remained a secondary concern while it was of primary importance for Spain's rulers and very high up on their agenda. The Lisbon Regiment was immediately sent from Barcelona to Sicily with some cavalry and, in the months to come, more troops from Naples, Milan, Sardinia and other Spanish possessions. The Hapsburg

# THE SICILIAN ADVENTURE

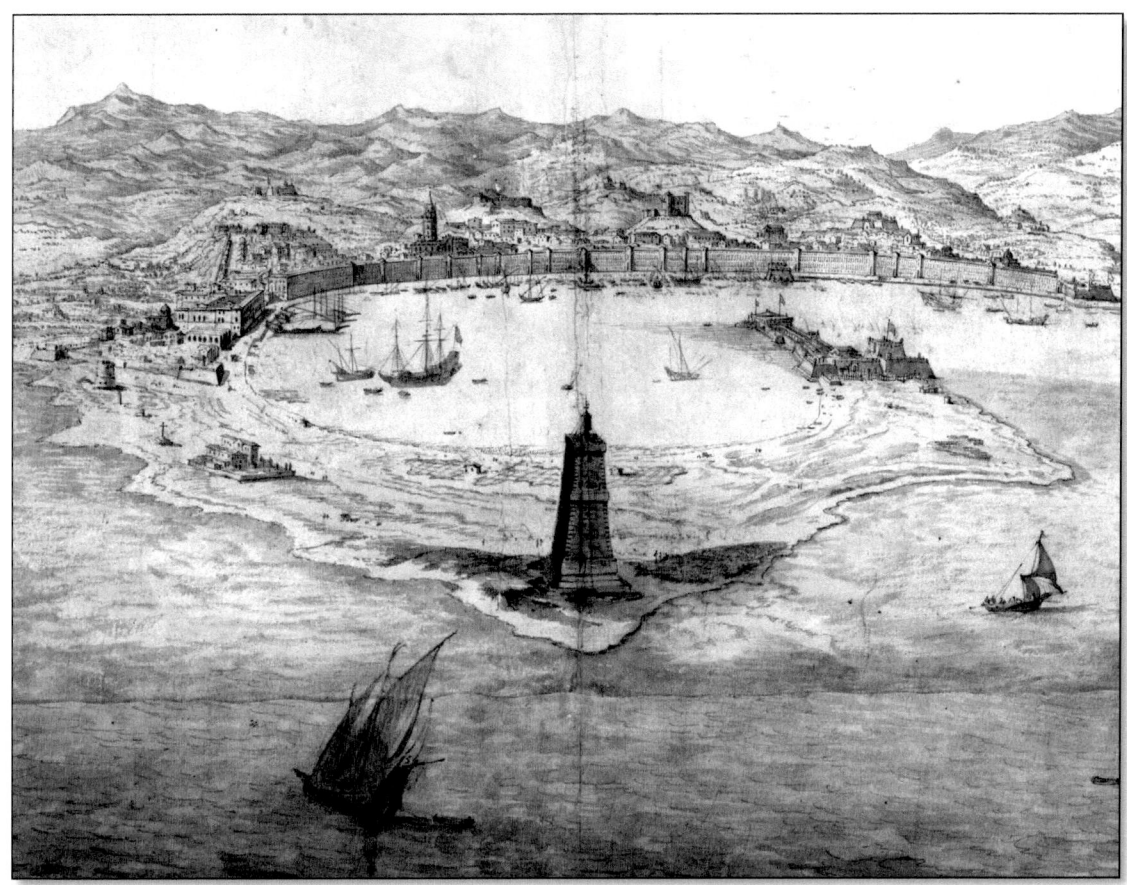

Messina, Sicily, 1664. The aspect of the city was essentially the same a decade later when the French army came to Sicily. Fort Santissimo Salvatore on the narrow peninsula (at right) commanded the harbour's entrance. The Faro (lighthouse) tower is in the foreground. Detail from a watercolour by Willem Schellinks. (Courtesy Rijskmuseum, Amsterdam, RP-T-00-415)

Emperor, in Vienna, sent 4,500 'German' troops via Trieste in mid 1675 and other reinforcements kept trickling in while local levies were raised.[1]

French naval superiority in Sicilian waters was already somewhat unstable. Toulon, the main French navy base in the Mediterranean, was far while the Spanish navy in the area could depend on Syracuse and Naples. The land forces on both sides were thus dependent on who controlled naval access to the island of Sicily. Initially, the arrival of strong French squadrons would secure the area, but when they went away, Spanish ships would be back blockading Messina, to be chased away when a strong French fleet arrived, usually with reinforcements and supplies. French naval power was seriously challenged when Dutch warships arrived to reinforce the Spanish. In Amsterdam, William of Orange saw a chance to curb French ambitions by sending a really strong naval reinforcement to Sicily under the command of Admiral de Ruyter as long as Spain would foot most of the bill; the court in Madrid readily agreed. On 8 January 1676, Ruyter was off Stromboli in northern Sicily with 19 ships of the line and was met by French Admiral Abraham Duquesne heading 20 ships of the line; the ensuing battle was

---

1   Émile Laloy, *La révolte de Messine: l'expédition de Sicile et la politique française en Italie 1674–1678* (Paris: Klincksieck, 1929–1931), Vol. 3, has several chapters on the Spanish government and its forces in Sicily p.341.

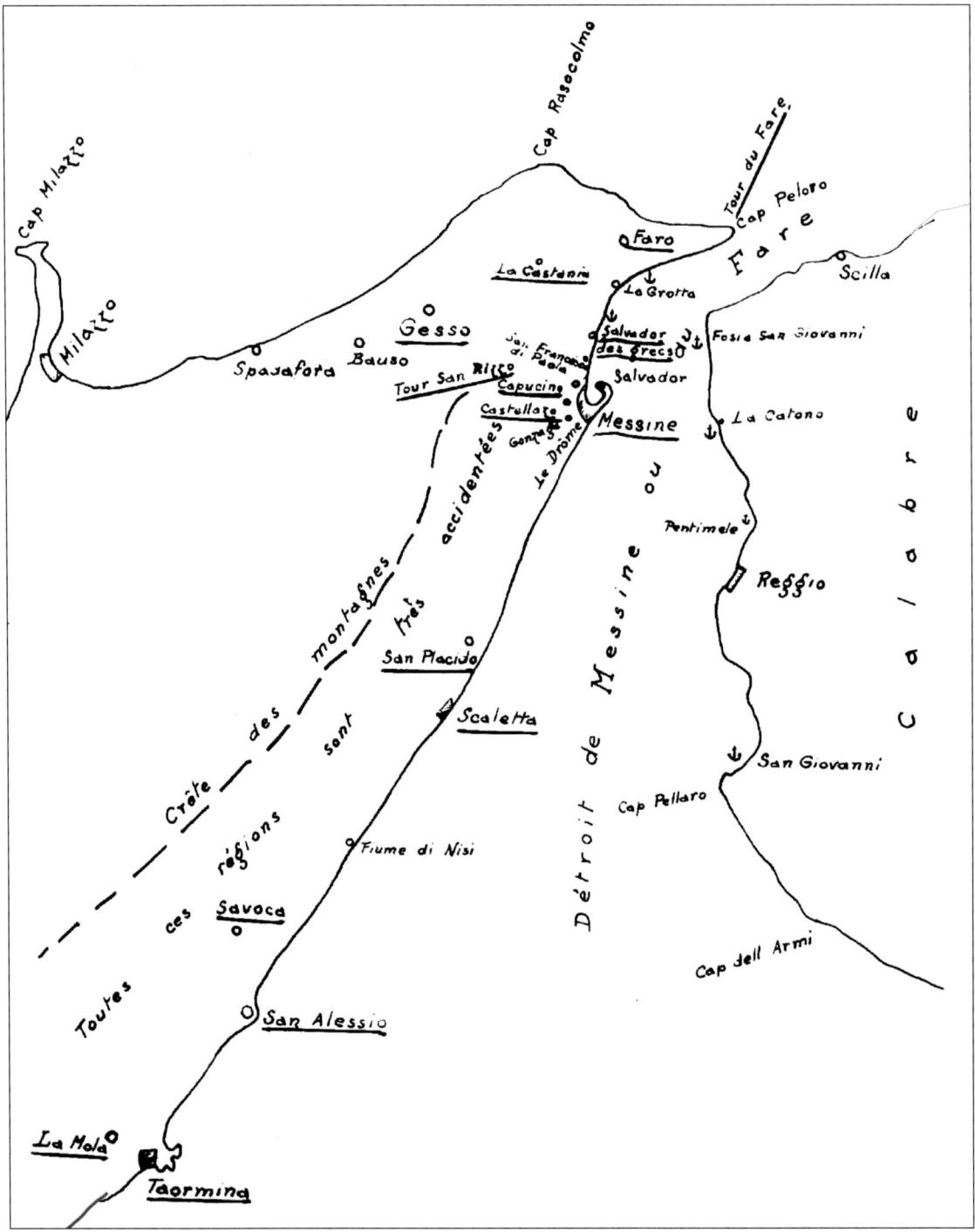

The French garrisons in northeastern Sicily, 1674–1678. The locations underlined had detachments of French troops during this period, although this would vary. Agosta is not shown and was south of Taormina. Sketch map after Cazeneuve.
(Courtesy Bibliothèque Nationale, Paris)

# THE SICILIAN ADVENTURE

Above: A view of Taormina taken from its nearby eagle's nest citadel of La Mola. One can only imagine the efforts of the French soldiers who climbed up and took it by storm in October 1677. Other lower hills also had forts, as this photo shows, as well as the ruggedly beautiful landscape of eastern Sicily. (Photo courtesy of Michelle Guitard)

Below: The siege and capture of Scaletta, Sicily, 25 October to 10 November 1676. This period print shows Scaletta's rugged terrain, typical of eastern Sicily, with the French galleys near the shore and the French bombarding its Spanish citadel. (Courtesy Library of Congress, Washington)

inconclusive. After refitting respectively at Syracuse and Messina, they battled again off eastern Sicily on 22 April 1676, Ruyter having 27 ships of the line (including 10 Spanish) and Duquesne 29. This time, the allied fleet retreated after Ruyter was severely wounded, and he died on 29 April at Syracuse. He was arguably the most famous and greatest admiral of the seventeenth century and his death a terrible, if short term, blow to the allies. His fleet ultimately went back to Amsterdam. What Spanish ships left were attacked by Duquesne on 2 June, four were destroyed and the remnants mostly huddled in ports.[2]

Duquesne's squadron and the galleys now had naval supremacy and in late June cruised off Syracuse looking to attack, but were recalled to Messina. In August 1676, the French forces in Sicily amounted to 5,800 infantry and about 900 cavalry. At that time, the Spanish had about 10,000 men including 1,000 cavalrymen. Thanks to the proximity of mainland Italy, supplies and reinforcements continued to arrive in Spanish Sicily. But the French had the edge thanks to superior naval forces. Some of the troops in Messina boarded Duquesne's ships and Vivonne's galleys. In early October, some 2,700 men including 1,200 marines led by Major General La Villedieu landed near Taormina, which was sited on difficult hilly terrain and defended by several forts. The French overwhelmed the curtain walls and the town was taken on 16 October, possibly by treason, but its eagle's nest citadel of La Mola that oversaw the whole region remained Spanish. It spite of being almost inaccessible, it had to be taken and, after being invested, finally fell a few days later. The French then besieged Scaletta from 25 October until it capitulated on 10 November.

The real prize, Syracuse, which Spanish General Castel-Rodrigo had reinforced, remained out of harm. The less numerous French troops had less territory to control, which permitted small offensive operations while the Spanish had to deploy their troops over most of the island to guard against possible attacks from French squadrons. However, from late 1676, the French expeditionary force on land was in a tactical stalemate. Its commander was too hesitant to take risks in a major attack while the Spanish were spread too thinly to take advantage of their superior numbers. Both sides could rely on men detached from navy ships, but these were only temporary reinforcements. The Sicilian militias on both sides were unpredictable as steadfast troops, especially as the islanders were independent minded and, by now, not overly enthusiastic about the French or the Spanish; many wanted to set up their own republic.[3]

By early 1677, the strength of the Spanish regular troops in Sicily had risen to 12,276 men according to musters of 30 March 1677, and 14,140 officers and men by 21 December. Meanwhile, French reinforcements were also sent consisting of Stuppa Jeune's Swiss Regiment of 1,700 officers which landed in Messina on 26 April 1677, and another 3,000 infantry in June. With the arrival of about 5,000 men, the French forces stood at about 12,000

---

2 Clonnard, *Historia organica de la infanteria y caballeria española*, Vol. 4, p.442.
3 Cazenave, *La Campagne de Sicile 1674–1678* (Brest: École de guerre navale, session 1935–1936, typescript) via BNF, Gallica, pp.44, 52–53.

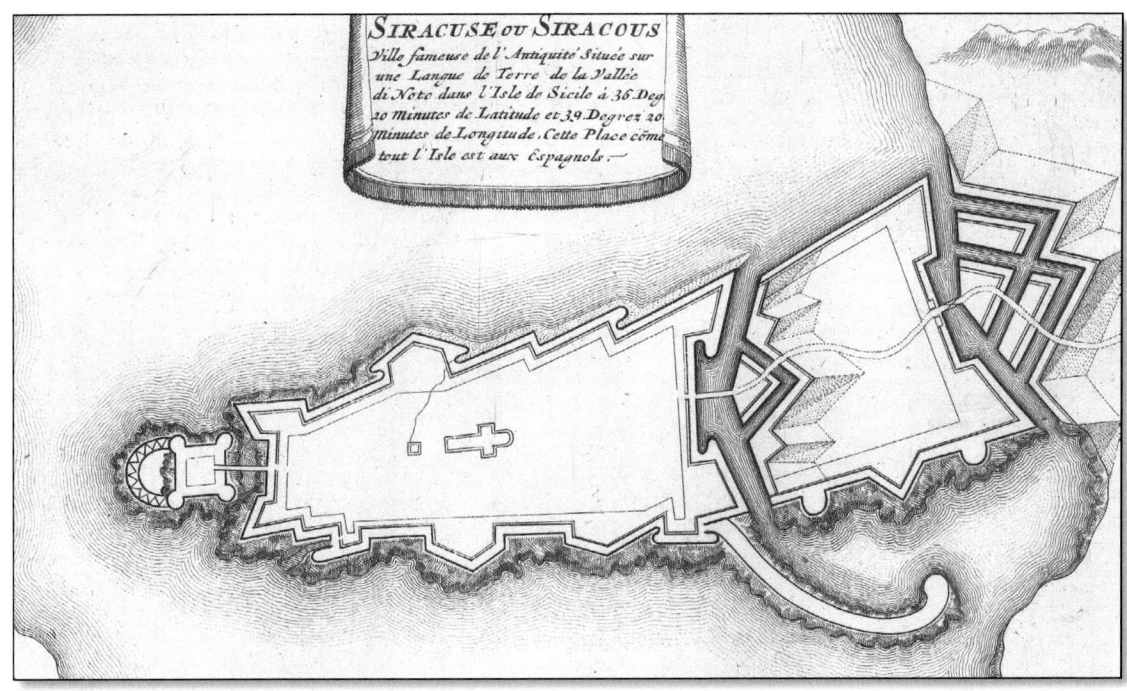

Syracuse, Sicily, late seventeenth century. Marshall Vivonne planned three attacks on Syracuse, but could not carry them out. Castle Maniace, built from 1239, was the city's citadel and the curtain walls were built in the sixteenth and seventeenth centuries over earlier structures going back to the eighth century BC. Syracuse was attacked many times in its long history and owes its fame to the military mechanisms invented by Archimedes, a leading scientist of antiquity, during its siege by the Romans in 213–212 BC. From a 1726 print after N. de Fer. (Courtesy Rijksmuseum, Amsterdam, RP-P-OB-83.036-162)

army troops, 1,500 Sicilian auxiliaries with 2,000 naval marines and 1,300 galley marines. With such forces and naval superiority everyone expected that the French army would soon set out to battle the Spanish and conquer the island, but nothing happened. The King had urged action and Vivonne worked on a highly "secret plan" to attack Syracuse during June, but the arrival of Duquesne signalled to the Spanish that something was up and they again reinforced Syracuse and also Catania. Instead hurrying up, Vivonne sat in Messina and could seemingly not decide what to do next.[4]

In late August 1677, Vivonne sailed towards Syracuse for another attempt at occupying this important harbour. On board the ships and galleys were 1,500 elite troops picked from amongst the best soldiers in all regiments. Once in view of Syracuse, he revealed his hitherto secret plan on how to take the city to his naval officers, who largely disagreed with it; meanwhile, the sea was getting rougher so bombardment became impossible while the troops on board became sick with a mysterious fever, and had to be landed at the plain of Mascari where many died. Thus Vivonne had no more success than previously, which can be partly attributed to his hesitant nature. He then returned to Messina to cope with a plot by some discontented Sicilians.

---

4   Rousset, *Histoire de Louvois*, Vol. 2, pp.446–447; Cazenave, *La Campagne de Sicile*, appendix I.

There was discontent in France too. Louis XIV now saw that his dreams of Sicilian and Mediterranean domination were in peril. Louvois was politely but firmly displeased with Vivonne's way of doing things with the troops; due to sickness and desertion, the strength of companies was generally low and he even had to write Vivonne several times to consolidate and reorganise his forces. Thus, from 1676, the French expeditionary force was in a tactical stalemate. Its commander was too hesitant to take risks in a major attack while the Spanish were spread too thinly to take advantage of their superior numbers. Vivonne finally attended to it, and by November 1677, the French forces in Sicily had been reorganised into 138 companies of 50 men each, posted as follows:[5]

> Forza: 1 company of the Normandie Regiment, 4 of the La Marine Regiment.
> San Alessio: 1 company of the Normandie Regiment.
> Savoca: 3 companies of Royal-Marine.
> Scaletta: 3 companies of Royal-Marine.
> Gesso: 12 companies of the Champagne Regiment and 2 Swiss companies.
> Messina: 17 companies of the Crussol Regiment, 17 companies of Louvigny, 12 of Schomberg, 16 of Vivonne and 4 Swiss companies.
> Taormina and La Mola: 12 companies of the Picardie Regiment, 13 of Provence and 2 Swiss companies.

To these 6,900 men could be added 1,500 Swiss and about 500 men recruited in Messina, so that Vivonne had about 9,000 regulars to which about 1,000 Sicilian volunteers could be added for a total of 10,000 troops. At that time, there were about 16,000 Spanish troops in Sicily. Far to the north, William of Orange had convinced King Charles II of England to join the Netherlands in the fight against France by a treaty of alliance formally signed at the Hague on 10 January 1678. French spies and diplomats had warned in December 1677 that this was about to happen. It radically changed the strategic situation in the Mediterranean. The British Royal Navy warships joined with the Dutch and Spanish in that area would have great naval superiority with some 59 ships of the line against at most 30 French at Messina and Toulon. Even if the 21 Spanish ships were considered mediocre, the 20 British and 18 Dutch now sailing into the Mediterranean were state-of-the art line warships equal to anything the French navy had. Against such superiority, communications between France and Sicily could no longer be sustained and the French expeditionary corps would be trapped and eventually forced to capitulate. It was not a good prospect just as all parties desired peace negotiations to take place. The potentially humiliating loss of the French forces in Sicily would undoubtedly have a negative effect on the bargaining chips available to the Sun King to sign an honourable peace treaty.[6]

---

5   Laloy, *La révolte de Messine*, Vol. 3, pp.316–317.
6   Laloy, *La révolte de Messine*, Vol. 3, p. 130; Cazenave, *La Campagne de Sicile 1674–1678*, pp. 57–58. According to Cazeneuve, the French contingents sent to Sicily were in 1675: January, 300 infantry; May, 3,180 infantry of Picardie, Piémont, Crussol, Louvigny and Provence regiments and 255 horsemen of Lhéry's regiment. 1676: May, 800 infantry of Schomberg's regiment and 250

Meanwhile, in Sicily, things were not going well on land either. The reinforced Spanish were slowly gaining ground. In December 1677, Taormina's French garrison was evacuated. In the last days of the year, Louis XIV, pressed by Louvois, reluctantly bowed to common sense and agreed to evacuate the French forces from Sicily. It was, at best, a dubious bargaining chip in the peace negotiations; Louvois had realised that perhaps the only European power that really wanted Sicily was Spain and that it was time to get out of there. The withdrawal had to be performed with the greatest secrecy so everyone would safely be out as quickly as possible. Vivonne was recalled and replaced by Marshal La Feuillade, who arrived at Messina on 3 February and announced that the whole French force was mustered at once to go out for a speedy attack so as to not alarm the Spanish. He quickly loaded the French fleet with all the troops, artillery, ammunition and supplies, and all ships and galleys sailed on 15 March having withdrawn Messina's guard sentries. Other French garrisons evacuated from Agosta on 21 February 1678. Once at sea, the French fleet sailed west and reached Toulon in March. The 8,000 troops fit for service from Sicily were immediately sent to Catalonia where they were the decisive factor that resulted in the capitulation of the fortress of Puycerda on 28 May.

As for the hapless Sicilians, they were left "holding the bag" with no allies anywhere, four years after their uprising hoping to form their own republic. Their Spanish masters were back in force. The Sicilians were left, Racine sadly related, in the hands "of the tyrannical government of a nation that never forgives." Indeed, because it was true. A general amnesty had been promised to all by the Spanish, but once they were secure again in Sicily, they reneged and its inhabitants came under every vengeful measure that an evil government can think of.[7]

---

foot dragoons of Audijos' regiment; August, 3,000 infantry of Picardie, Champagne, Piémont, Normandie and Provence regiments; September, 800 infantry of Normandie and Royal-Marine, 550 horsemen of the Monbas and Chevalier Duc regiments. 1677: April, 1,700 infantry of Stuppa jeune's regiment; June, 700 infantrymen (unit unknown); October, 140, Flemish prisoners. 1678: 120 infantry from Piémont regiment. Total: 14,200 men of which 7,900 returned to France.

7  Racine, *Précis historique des campagnes de Louis XIV depuis 1672 jusqu'à 1678*, p.14. For a highly detailed account of what happened in Sicily after the Spanish came back, see: Laloy, *La révolte de Messine*, Vol. 3. Its last chapters certainly vindicate Racine's opinion of the Spanish.

# 6

# 1678–1684: Peace, Expansion and Ottomans

## Peacetime Military Activities

The war was over and the army was reduced to about 138,000 men by 1679. Nevertheless, military activity was going on, with the repair and construction of new fortresses to complete the fortification defence network at France's borders, for instance at Saar-Louis on the Saar River and at Huningen near Basel. Furthermore, the King was looking to have new allies and, in 1680, the Dauphin married Anne-Marie-Victoire, sister of the Elector of Bavaria. The following year, the 'Canal royal en Languedoc' (Royal Canal in Languedoc – now the Canal du Midi), whose construction had started in 1666, was completed. It was 30 feet wide and had 106 locks; its 64 lieues (250km) went from Sète on the Mediterranean to Toulouse, from which navigation could continue on the partly canalised Garonne River to meet the Gironde River at Castet-en-Dorthe that led to the port city of Bordeaux on the Atlantic. The army was partly involved in the canal's construction for engineering and labour. It was a man-made strategic waterway and one of the most extensive construction projects of the seventeenth century; it was was not only important for trade and commerce, but also vital for swiftly shipping military supplies, heavy ordnance and troops, taking 11 days from one end to the other instead of many weeks.[1]

In 1681, the King had not forgotten that the supposedly free and independent city of Strasbourg had been rather unfriendly to the French forces in Alsace during the war. That city was a prize he wanted because it controlled the Rhine trade by its strategic position and was thus just as important militarily because of its bridge, by which the Imperial army had crossed into Alsace in 1674. During peace negotiations at Nijmegen the King had obtained the strict neutrality and a certain control of the city. At the time he did not wish to annexe it, just neutralise it. In May 1681, the Strasbourg magistrates entered into a negotiation with Vienna to have 4,000 Imperial soldiers in its

---

1   Quincy, *Histoire Militaire*, Vol. 1, pp.671, 676.

## 1678–1684: PEACE, EXPANSION AND OTTOMANS

Entry of Louis XIV and the Queen with a large staff into the city of Strasbourg, 23 October 1681. Print after Gerlier. (Private collection. Author's photo)

garrison. When the Sun King heard about this, it was the last straw; no way would he let Imperial troops control the bridge or the city again. He resolved to annexe it. The city itself was unsure about what to do, so to end the debate the King mustered 30,000 men that accompanied Louvois to convince the Strasbourg citizens that force could be used if necessary. On 29 September, the King learned from Louvois that Strasbourg had made its submission to the inevitable, and the next day, Louvois with French troops entered the city. Surprisingly, on 23 October, it was the Sun King himself with the Queen and a large suite that entered Strasbourg to the salute of 265 cannons greeted by rather awed officials and inhabitants who were amazed the French royal couple would honour them with a visit to their city. This further secured Alsace as being part of the kingdom with Strasbourg as its capital.[2]

Since the 1678 Treaty of Nijmegen, there were constant incidents, many of them violent, concerning the frontiers of French and Spanish Flanders. According to Louis XIV, the Spaniards were doing all they could to contest and delay the fulfilment of the clauses of the treaty. The Spanish did not recognise

---

2  Quincy, *Histoire Militaire*, Vol. 2, pp.2–4, 7; Voltaire, *Le Siècle de Louis XIV*, p.211; Rousset, *Histoire de Louvois*, Vol. 3, pp.37–56; Bély, Bérenger and Corvisier, *Guerre et paix dans l'Europe du XVIIe siècle*, p.362.

Ensign, Royal-Comtois Regiment, c. 1680. The regimental colours had an orange field sprinkled with gold lilies and a red Burgundy cross. Print after Philippoteaux. (Courtesy New York Public Library, New York City)

that the County of Alost, the old town that was part of Ghent, and several other places, should go to France. Louis XIV replied that the Spaniards could keep Alost in exchange for the fortress of Luxembourg and that, according to the treaty, they should evacuate the garrison of Courtrai because it was too close to the French border. Things came to crisis proportions in late October 1683 when the Spanish took a few small castles with small parties of French border guards; not the sort of action that was likely to impress the Sun King, who immediately ordered Marshal d'Humières to besiege and take Courtrai, which was accomplished from 2 to 4 November followed by Dixmude, which surrendered without a fight.

In Madrid, Spain had declared war to France on 26 October 1683, so previous to Louis XIV's army's actions, and one can wonder why. According to Quincy, William of Orange had convinced the Swedes to send 14,000 men to Flanders to which would be added 16,000 Dutch troops. The Spanish court had enthusiastically seen an opportunity to humble the Sun King and thus started formal hostilities. It notably wished to regain the initiative in Catalonia and Flanders. Unfortunately for Spain, the Netherlands was not an autocratic state and when the powerful elected state councils learned of William's discreet diplomatic activities they flatly refused to have a war with France, so the military aid to Spanish Flanders collapsed. Sweden then also withdrew from the scheme.[3]

The French regular army did not expand greatly at that time. It had a strength of about 150,000 to 158,000 men in 1684, a respectable number that could meet any short term need insofar as organising field armies. Luxembourg was one of the key places Louis XIV wished to occupy. It was a redoubtable fortress situated on a rocky hill partly surrounded by the Alsitz River (a tributary of the Moselle) with four bastions and demi-lunes carved out of rock. Only the northern side, although very well fortified, could offer reasonable hopes for a successful assault. The French army led by Marshall de Créquy and General Vauban consisted of about 27,000 men divided into 35 infantry battalions, 41 cavalry squadrons and four artillery companies with 45 cannons and 15 mortars, which Vauban felt was not sufficient for the siege of such a work. The garrison led by the Prince of Chimay, which offered resistance "worthy of the highest praise", was some 5,000 strong including

---

3   Quincy, *Histoire Militaire*, Vol. 2, p.44.

# 1678–1684: PEACE, EXPANSION AND OTTOMANS

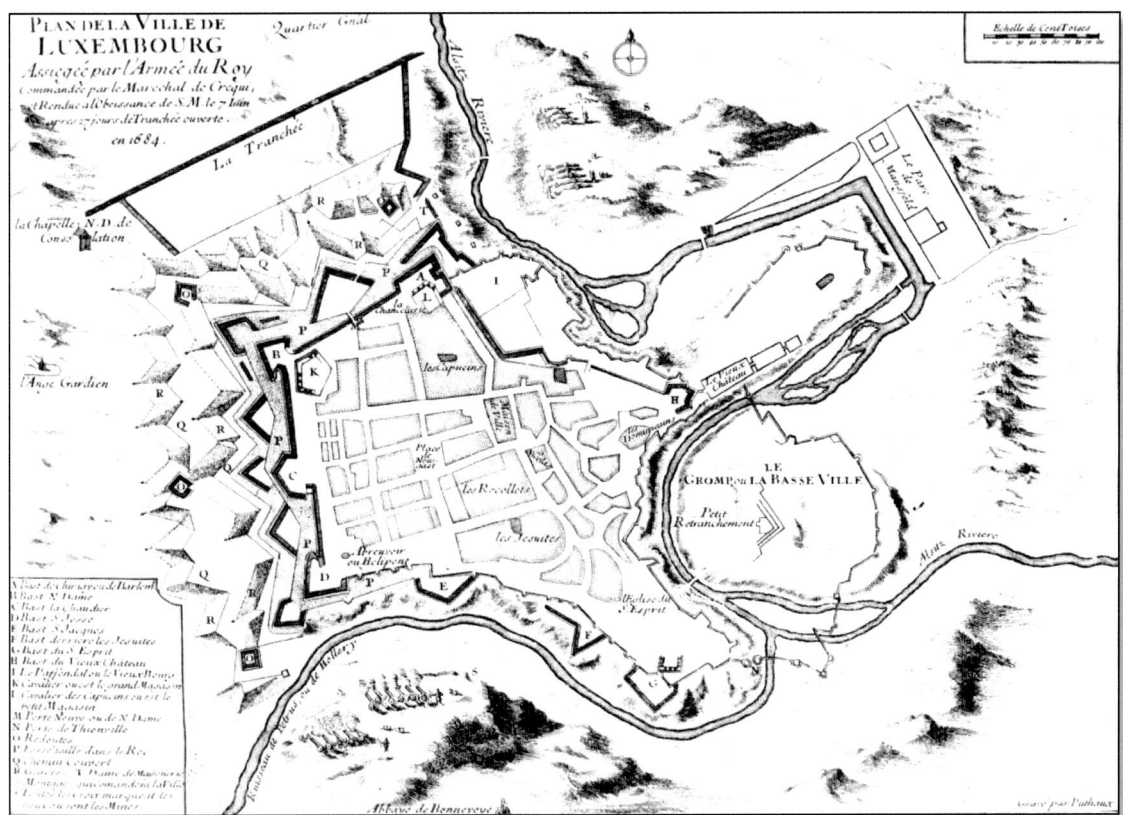

Plan of the city of Luxembourg, 1684. The plan shows the trenches of Marshal de Créquy's French army (upper left). In spite of elaborate fortifications, the north and west sides of the city were the most vulnerable. After a siege of 27 days, the city capitulated on 7 June 1684. Print after original plan. (Private collection. Author's photo)

about 600 town militiamen, none being especially thrilled at the prospect of a French occupation. There were skirmishes outside the city before the place was invested, and from about 10 May 1684 trenches were dug approaching the more vulnerable works on the north side, although their progress was punctuated by many sorties. On 19 May, the French captured the Marie redoubt after intense fighting; the Berlaimont redoubt was evacuated due to heavy bombardments two days later. Although suffering heavy casualties, the French army persisted and, by the end of May, had advanced up to the main curtain walls. Fearing the outrages on the population that would likely result from a general assault, the Prince of Chimay called for a ceasefire to negotiate a surrender. The fortress formally capitulated on 7 June and its remaining 1,300 infantrymen, who were mostly Spaniards or Walloons, and 500 Croatian cavalrymen, came out drums beating and colours unfurled, to be replaced by French troops. Vauban felt that had the garrison been stronger, all its fortifications could have been fully manned and the siege "might have taken six months." The fighting during this siege was very intense and the casualties were estimated at 2,700 for the garrison and more than 7,000 for the French. Créquy followed up with the occupation of Trier for the purpose of destroying its fortifications.[4]

---

4   Musée de l'Armée, Paris, library Ms Y1722, state of the army in 1684; Philippe Henri de Grimoard, *Recherches sur la force de l'armée Française* (Paris, 1806), p.55; Quincy, *Histoire Militaire*, Vol. 2, pp.54–86; Clonnard, *Historia organica*, Vol. 4, pp.443–444; Gilles Boué, 'Luxembourg, Siege of

In Roussillon, Marshal de Bellefond led a mixed force of regulars with Roussillon and Béarn militiamen and Miquelets over the Pyrenees in March 1684, sometimes marching through snow. Once they crossed, they engaged the Spanish at Ter on 12 April led by the Prince of Bournonville, who was overwhelmed by the French and withdrew into the fortress of Gerona. The French started digging the trenches on 22 April, but their assaults in the following six days were all repulsed. Bellefond concluded the place was too strong for the force he had and withdrew. It was indeed a very formidable fortress that had previously been besieged in vain 23 times. Bellefond went on to take Cap-de-Quiers and Campredon a few weeks later. Thus, the Spanish troops in Catalonia were put on the defensive by Bellefond's vigorous and short campaign.

At the negotiating table, the Spanish stubbornly refused to concede anything to Louis XIV, but the Dutch did not want another war just then and would not help the court in Madrid. The Elector of Brandenburg and Emperor Leopold I in Vienna were totally absorbed by their own eastern opponents so no assistance was likely from there nor from England. The situation was none too reassuring in Catalonia either because the French army there might have withdrawn from a long siege at Gerona, but was certainly a much more dangerous force than its Spanish opponents. King Carlos II of Spain finally ratified a truce of 20 years with France on 20 September 1684 that ceded Luxembourg and its province as well as Courtrai and Dixmude.[5]

## Ottoman Invasion, Ottoman Equation

The empire of the Ottoman Turks undoubtedly had a large if relatively secret place in the Sun King's mind, and also in Louvois' geo-strategic visions. No one could really tell, but their standing army, apart from camp followers and non-combatants, was said to number some 296,000 men without counting garrisons in other distant domains that would likely raise the total to some 350,000 soldiers.[6]

For the French army, the Ottoman armies were vitally important because they were the neighbours of France's most powerful opponent: the Germanic Holy Roman Empire, whose main portion was Austria with its capital, Vienna, the place of residence of its emperor. Just to the east and south were countries that made up part of the Ottoman Empire: much of the Balkans, Serbia, Romania, Bulgaria, Greece further south, and it just went on. The

---

(April–June 1684),'*Ground Warfare: An International Encyclopaedia*, Stanley Sandler (ed.) (Los Angeles: ABC-CLIO, 2002), p.515. Quincy gives a very good and detailed account of the siege of Luxembourg that interested readers should consult.

5   Quincy, *Histoire Militaire*, Vol. 2, pp.44–54, 85–86; Clonnard, *Historia organica*, Vol. 4, pp.444–445; Rousset, *Histoire de Louvois*, Vol. 3, pp.209–266.

6   *Etat abregé de la maison du grand seigneur, de ses revenus et le gouvernement civil, militaire et ecclesiastiques de cet empire*, c. 1660s–1680s. This is a large statistical chart of the Ottoman Empire with views of Constantinople (Istanbul) printed in French at the Library of Congress, Washington. The domains whose garrisons were not counted were those of Yemen, Habesch near Ethiopia, Laxa near Persia, Tripoli, Tunis and Algiers on the Mediterranean North African coast.

# 1678–1684: PEACE, EXPANSION AND OTTOMANS

Map of the Holy Roman Empire, second half of the seventeenth century. It was under military pressure by France on its western frontiers and by the Ottoman Turks on its southeastern border. (Private collection. Author's photo)

Austrians were sometimes joined in their resistance to the Ottoman Turks by other Slavic countries such as the Christian parts of Hungary, Transylvania and the then large kingdom of Poland. From the French point of view, whatever the military worth of all these nations, the question was, could the Ottoman armies keep a lot of Austrian and German troops standing on guard at their eastern borders? That was the "Ottoman equation". Or could the Ottomans actually invade them and thus upset the balance of power in Europe? There had been such a fear in 1664 and young Louis XIV answered the call for help by sending a French corps of 6,000 men that distinguished itself at St Gotthard (see Volume 1). Time passed, and if there had ever been warm French feelings towards Emperor Leopold I, they had evaporated, especially after he had sided with the Netherlands from 1672 and sent sizeable contingents led by good generals to fight the French. At that time,

Emperor Leopold I of the Holy Roman Empire, c. 1685. St Florian Monastery, Austria. (Author's photo)

the Ottomans seemed weaker so fewer Imperial troops were necessary to stand guard eastward. In the advent of a war on two fronts, one facing the French and the other the Ottomans, the relative size of the Austrian army mattered. On paper, it was some 80,000 men in the 1680s and 1690s, but the field armies had only about 27,000 men with the others being garrison and border troops.[7]

The very varied population of the Ottoman Empire was not a uniform monolith and there were rumours of sizeable uprisings from time to time. The eastern European domains right up to Turkey had predominantly Christian populations that carried on the heritage of the conquered Byzantine Empire. A sizeable uprising had been crushed in Bulgaria at the turn of the seventeenth century and, although drowned in blood, there would be more. So the Ottoman army was indeed very large, but what was its real capacity and efficacy during campaigns? In order to learn more about the Ottoman army, Minister of War Louvois organised a discreet information network from French diplomats and also French officers who had been in Austrian service. Reliable information was based on rumours and the tales of travellers. The Ministry of War's intelligence officials, however, did not attempt to make critical analysis and nor did they suggest any practical use of the information gathered. It had been assumed that, on the eastern borders, the Ottomans were weakening, but as the 1670s passed it became fairly certain that the Ottomans were not weaker, but becoming strong enough to mount a major offensive from the Balkans. Of course the Austrians knew this much better than anyone. Nevertheless, for the French, it was an explanation as to why Imperial troops were not as numerous in the Rhineland and Flanders towards the end of the decade and into the next.[8]

By unexplainable coincidence, the sultans in Istanbul nearly always planned their campaigns against the Holy Roman Empire when it was at peace with France. During the Dutch War, the French ambassador had encouraged the Ottomans to mobilise their forces against Austria before a peace treaty would be signed, but nothing major was done until 1681–1682 when central Hungary, then partly in revolt against the Austrian emperor, was occupied successfully by the Ottomans who chased out Imperial forces. It was still a somewhat local conflict until 6 August 1682 when the Ottomans

---

7   Patera, *Unter Osterreiches Fahnen*, p.25.
8   Cénat, *Louvois, le double de Louis XIV*, pp.183–184; Flamen Pavlov, *Bulgaria and Bulgarians: a brief history* (Sofia: Borina, 2009), p.59.

## 1678–1684: PEACE, EXPANSION AND OTTOMANS

The defeat of the Turkish army at Vienna, 12 September 1683. The foreground shows the Polish cavalry charging into the Turkish camp. Print after Johann Martin Lerch. (Courtesy Anne S.K. Brown Military Collection, Brown University Library, Providence, RI, USA)

declared war on the Holy Roman Empire. They planned a massive attack on Austria in 1683 with some 200,000 men or more. France was at peace, but the Sun King looked closely at this evolving eastern situation. There were reports reaching him that the Austrians did not have a large enough army and that the fortifications meant to protect their cities, including Vienna, were not as sophisticated as French fortresses. Fortunately for Emperor Leopold I, it took a long time for the Ottomans to muster their army, which gave him the opportunity to gather all the support he could to mobilise troops elsewhere in the Empire, and Pope Innocent XI called on all to defend Christendom. The Kingdom of Poland also saw the threat and joined the alliance because everyone in central and even in western Europe would have to bear the consequences of a victorious Ottoman invasion of Austria.

Louis XIV had an army in Alsace, bordering the Empire's domains, and let it be known that it would be available to join the Imperial forces to fight the Ottoman invasion, and that he would not enter into military operations against Spain and the Netherlands. In Vienna, Leopold I was none too reassured by this pledge to help. Politically, and this is also what Louis hoped for, the prospect of having large numbers of the French army – the best and most modern in Europe and led with fine officers – was not reassuring to the Holy Roman Emperor. Many rulers and people in western Europe would look to powerful France for salvation and thus the Sun King might become the actual leader of the coalition. Louis knew all this and was ready to become protector of the Holy Roman Empire and even crown the Dauphin as King of the Romans.[9]

Events would decide the issue of these fears and ambitions. The huge Ottoman army that made its way toward Vienna was impressive. Various accounts mention very high figures such as 300,000 men, but a safer number would be half of that or less. At his formal entry into Belgrade in May 1683, the Sultan's escort marching before him consisted of some 12,000 Janissaries and 4,000 *spahis* cavalrymen. Behind him and his two sons were 1,500 Bosnian lifeguards distinguished by their Albanian-style sabres, white linen coats with wide sleeves and red trousers. Then came a large, green and torn standard that had been taken from the Hungarians followed by a company of *heiduques* wearing a blue uniform with large silver buttons, their headdress garnished with plumes and armed with sabres and lances. The parade ended with 400 cavalrymen. By 14 July, the Ottoman army was in sight of Vienna and summoned its surrender. The military governor of the city, Count Ernst Rudiger von Starhemberg with a garrison of some 14,000 regulars and 8,000 militiamen refused, and the siege began. The Emperor had already evacuated with the court and part of Vienna's population, while the defenders hoped to soon see the promised large relief army. Duke Charles V of Lorraine, commander-in-chief of the Austrian forces, provided some assistance with his corps of some 20,000 men lurking outside Vienna. By early September, the garrison was still holding on, breaches had been made so an assault could be expected. On 12 September, the relief army of about 70,000 men led by King John III Sobiesky of Poland arrived at last and decisively defeated the Ottoman army.[10]

Once everyone in central and western Europe breathed a sigh of relief, the repercussions of what turned out to be a turning point for the Ottoman Turk

---

9 Voltaire, *Le Siècle de Louis XIV*, pp.214–215. Napoleon had the same ambition for his son and achieved it. But his reign was short because the allies won the final struggle, and the King of Rome became an Austrian prince.

10 Joseph von Hammer, *Histoire de l'Empire ottoman* (Paris, 1838), Vol. XII, pp.82–83. The *heiduques* (or haïdouk) were armed bands fighting Ottoman occupation in Hungary and the Balkans. This company had obviously rallied to their opponents. Voltaire, *Le Siècle de Louis XIV*, p.216; David Nicolle, *Armies of the Ottoman Turks 1300-1774* (London: Osprey, 1983), pp.32–33; Patera, *Unter Osterreiches Fahnen*, pp.22–23; John Frost, *Pictorial Modern History* (Philadlphia: Gillis, 1846), pp.202–205. Voltaire relates (p. 216) that when Emperor Leopold I came back to Vienna, the religious service giving thanks to God was ending, and in the sermon the presiding priest paraphrasing the scriptures: 'There was a man sent by God named John', meaning of course the brave and fighting king of Poland instead of the fleeing Leopold. The Emperor never quite lived it down until his death in 1705. By comparison, Louis XIV always worried his officers on battle days by his wishes to get closer to the action while at the same time knowing he was there as the ruler of France, not as a general of its armies.

Empire had to be considered in view of France's military and foreign policies. Was it the beginning of the end for the Ottoman equation and – the worst scenario for the French army – the decline of that empire? Certainly, the already loosely connected Holy Roman Empire was losing ground to a few emerging Germanic states. Austria would be strengthened and Brandenburg was rising. They could eventually devote more military resources to fight Louis XIV's army in a future war.

7

# The Business of War

## Money and Armies in the 1660s and 1670s

France may well have been the most prosperous nation in seventeenth-century Europe, but it also levied the most taxes on its population. It was well known as the garden of Europe thanks to its lush agricultural production which occupied a very large part of its population, commonly known as peasants. They were the base of the pyramid in France's complicated society and paid the most taxes and levies to, basically, the King and his royal government, the Church, the local lords and humble seigneurs (squires) who usually owned the land and, in towns, controlled the local governments. While a precise figure of what proportion went to military expenditure is all but impossible to determine, as explained in Volume 1, it is certain that much of that money went to maintain armies and that, because nobles were basically exempt from paying large amounts of taxes, the fiscal burdens of military establishments and wars were paid for largely from the meagre revenues of those who tilled the land. Shopkeepers and merchants in towns were also subject to those taxes, but often found ways to legally avert some of them, notably by serving in the local bourgeois militia (which we will delve into in Volume 4).[1]

While French peasants were always heavily taxed, the pressure became more acute in the reign of Louis XIII as his prime minister, Cardinal Richelieu, shaped the government into a centralised organisation. Royal officials such as intendants now had increasingly significant powers in fiscal matters in all provinces of the realm, but were often opposed by the nobility who feared for their privileges. France's involvement in the Thirty Years' War heralded

---

1 The *taille* was the main income tax with variable rates; noblemen were practically exempt since they only paid it for their non-noble earnings, which were often negligible or non-existent. It nevertheless brought in over half of the royal tax revenues at the beginning of the seventeenth century, but this decreased to a quarter by the reign of Louis XIV. While many managed to legally avoid it, even the worse off were not exempt as shown in the 1696 tax roll of Cuverville-sur-Yère (Normandy): the widow of Jean François, defined as a beggar, owed 2 livres, 10 sols, 6 deniers and the widow of Jacques Ferrand owed 12 sols, 6 deniers, as per: Archives départementales de la Seine-maritime, C2095, transcribed by Nathalie Champmartin. The salt tax, nicknamed *La Gabelle*, was another widely resented imposition. It had its own tax collection police nicknamed the *Gabelous* by the people, which is still heard in France for discreetly denoting customs or revenue officers.

hitherto unseen levels of royal taxes to keep armies of over 100,000 men in the field. These taxes, which provoked some peasant uprisings, easily surpassed Church tithes and annuities paid to local lords so that royal officials were increasingly the subject of resentment. After the 1659 treaty of the Pyrenees and the advent of Colbert as Louis XIV's finance minister, there was some relief in peacetime except for the short War of Devolution. Nevertheless, there were some revolts against taxes such as the uprising called the "Great Days of Auvergne" in 1665–1666 that, this time, was crushed by royal troops sent to the rebellious province in ways that would greatly discourage such outbursts and serve as a warning to others who might be tempted by tax rebellions. Some nobles and officials of the province of Auvergne had been at the root of the exploitation of the peasantry, which was not unusual anywhere in the realm; as a royal official put it, local justice was rendered by men "without honour" nor remorse.

The young Sun King was aware of the exploitation of the most humble folk in his kingdom, and the events in Auvergne gave him an opportunity to do something about it. He surely knew he would not stop all abuses, but he could signal that he would not tolerate abject conduct. This had the advantage of promoting his royal justice and applying it to all, be they the meanest peasants or the haughty nobles in the provinces. So he added a new twist to repression. Once order had been reestablished, he sent royal judges to inquire as to the causes of the "Great Days" and, if they found that his royal powers had been abused by local officials and nobles, to prosecute the suspects. After reviewing some 12,000 complaints, the tribunals found the poorest in the countryside terrified by a small number of gentlemen and condemned to death or exile the most outrageous culprits, who were mainly noblemen. The courts thus achieved the King's objective in proclaiming that he was the source of all justice in the eyes of the people and that he was not about to tolerate another Fronde from the nobles. They would serve their king loyally; there was no other option. Most importantly, royal taxes would be levied to whatever level was necessary to finance the armies.[2]

"Louis Dort" (Louis sleeps), a satirical print showing Louis XIV taking a nap, c. 1700. He is warmed by the golden sun's rays and surrounded with bags full of gold "Louis d'or" specie – a play on words in France. At lower left is a battle scene, meaning the money was spent on wars. Print after Pierre Bonat. (Courtesy Library of Congress, Washington)

---

2   Pierre Goubert and Daniel Roche, *Les Français et l'Ancien Régime, la société et l'état* (Paris: Armand Colin, 1984), pp.310–312. Many towns and the province of Brittany were exempt from the *taille*. Another way to escape it, especially later in the reign, was for wealthy individuals to buy a venal royal office such as sub-delegate to a provincial intendant. Other royal revenues came from customs duties or other indirect taxes. Provincial and town taxes were used to maintain roads and hospitals while parts of these revenues also went into royal coffers. Feudal taxes took many forms such as levying a proportion of a harvest against the use of a lord's windmill. For more details see: Marcel Marion, *Dictionnaire des institutions de la France aux XVIIe et XVIIIe siècles* (Paris: Picard, 1923) and Voltaire,

In this, once he took power in 1661, the King established a *Conseil royal des Finances* (royal board of finances) presided by himself, Marshal Villeroi (the elder) as its largely honorific chancellor and Colbert who was its comptroller-general and the actual minister of the economy. The Sun King was a good listener to the opinions of his officials and the sole decision maker as to what was allowed to be spent. Louis did not change the basic revenue system so that it continued to press mainly the rural commoners. Furthermore, the tax system was not equal throughout the realm since, by ancient customs or treaties, some provinces or towns had higher taxes while others had a lighter burden. What this burden amounted to is seemingly impossible to determine precisely, but about 25 percent to 35 percent of a person's earnings seems most plausible. While this may appear advantageous when compared to today's levels in western Europe and North America, it must be pointed out that, in the seventeenth century, there were no national systems paying for all citizens' basic healthcare, education, social services and extensive communications networks and infrastructure as we understand them today. For instance, royal subsidies might be paid to religious orders to maintain hospitals as long as they took care of military personnel and the "king's engineers" who were usually army or navy officers also would oversee infrastructure constructions such as roads, canals, windmills and even provide plans to build churches. In the France of Louis XIV, as in other countries of the era, it seems that what went back to the citizens was modest; the bulk of the money went to the military on land and sea – possibly as much as four-fifths of revenues. Fiscal pressure on governments invoked other ways to raise money; for instance, the sale of tobacco was a royal monopoly from 1673. Goods were taxed in transit within the kingdom. Thus, French towns often had tax collection posts at their gates. The government, however, was not subject to taxation and royal officials issued passports listing tax-exempt goods intended for the King's service. From our delving into French archives, these passports overwhelmingly concerned all types of military supplies. All in all, revenue was about 120,000,000 livres in 1661 rising nearly threefold to some 331,000,000 livres in 1715. This is what it took to sustain a French army of hitherto unseen high numbers of officers and men. The basic population of France, however, remained at about the same level (some 20 million souls) during this period.[3]

---

*Le Siècle de Louis XIV*, Vol. 2, chapter 30. See for specific cases *Lettres, instructions et mémoires de Colbert*, Pierre Clément (ed.) (Paris: Imprimerie impériale, 1864), vol. 1, p.ii.

3  "Notice sur les surintendans, contrôleurs-généraux, et autres chefs de l'administration des finances", *Collection des meilleurs dissertations, notices et traités particuliers relatifs à l'histoire de France*, E. Leber (ed.) (Paris: Dentu, 1838), Vol. 7, pp.466–467, 474–478. The figures are given simply for an idea of proportions, they are notoriously varied. The organisation of the government was refined in September 1665, details of which are given by the minutes of a royal council in *Lettres, instructions et mémoires de Colbert*, Vol. 6, pp.369–391. Besides to the unfathomable proportions of national revenue that went to the War Ministry that were evoked in the first volume of this study, we add Jean-Philippe Cénat's recent calculation in his 2015 *Louvois* (p.65) at being never less than a third in peacetime as much as 65 percent in war years. That may be plausible for only the War Ministry, but we feel it was substantially higher because as we previously stated, much money for military purposes was not identified as being for the army.

In all these numbers, one should bear in mind that the general fiscal situation for individuals as well as for European nations was then very different to what is familiar in western economies in our own twenty-first century. At that time, there was practically no inflation, and indeed sometimes there even occurred some slight deflation. This explains the unchanged rates of military pay for a very long time without major grumbling from the ranks, but it also had a huge effect on the state of national wartime economies, not only in France, but also on its opponent countries. This was tied to the very modest growth of European economies at 0.1 percent as well as the slow demographic rise of European populations at 0.5 percent between 1700–1820. In France as elsewhere, the one opportunity to have extraordinary if mostly short-term economic activity was to have a war. However, as growth and inflation were practically at a standstill for many decades, the "new money" for the government could only come from increasing tax revenues and borrowing to pay for the greatly increased expenses for its armies. While kings could envisage enrichment through the conquest and annexation of territories, bankers and business leaders were heartened at quick profits thanks to money lent, and increased production of arms and supplies for armies; officers and soldiers were attracted by the prospects of substantial bounties and prize money, besides outright pillage. Meanwhile vast numbers of humble subjects in the kingdom were tempted to join the armed forces and partake in raising their meagre living by prize and pillage, as cartoons of soldiers and sailors holding bags of gold doubloons luringly showed. The risks were great, kings might lose territory instead, lenders might be ruined, many soldiers might die in their attempt at self-enrichment and just a few make fortunes, but just enough officers did build handsome estate houses while some common soldiers might at least have more comfort to entertain the illusion. This lust for gain and glory through war certainly benefited enlistment in order to escape a relatively unchanging and unpromising civilian lifestyle.[4]

What did actually change in France from the 1660s was the advent of far more efficient central control of the kingdom's finances and tax revenues. The Sun King imposed swiftly and forcefully his vision of orderly government with the dismissal and imprisonment of Finance Minister Fouquet, and by abolishing the post of colonel general of infantry. Holding high office in the government was still a path to self-enrichment, but never to previously seen levels. The lion's share of the nation's budget went to the army, followed by the navy. Colbert at Finance and Louvois at the War Department were the two most important ministers that basically created modern government departments as we know them today, with sizeable bureaucracies that imposed a high level of scrutiny insofar as how money was collected and spent. The discretionary powers of local governors evaporated and their prestige was now tied to being advocates of the Sun King; they continued to enjoy a high military rank with comfortable revenue and all the honours due to their rank as long as they applied the policies of central power. Louis XIV did not forget that barely a decade had passed from the times when part of France's nobility was involved in the Fronde revolts. By his control of the kingdom's finances and army, nobles

---

4   Thomas Piketty, *Le capital au XXIe siècle* (Paris: Seuil, 2013), pp.134, 160, 177

wishing to succeed had to curry his favours and, once appointed, be utterly loyal and deliver efficiently. To make sure that they would, intendants and their commissaries (their subalterns), were now everywhere scrutinising budget expenditures and reporting any unusual event to department heads that might, if serious enough, come to the attention of the minister and the King himself. Most of all, as seen above, the collection of revenue was more efficient in that it went directly into royal coffers with fewer commissions to collectors. Central budget cycles were much more predictable in that revenues were relatively stable and thus surpluses or shortfalls could be addressed by more coherent planning. Conversely, expenditures monitored closely revealed if approved expenditures were actually being spent at a pace to meet delivery dates. This was important because it showed efficiency or else; if the money was not spent, it meant that the objectives of the government's programme were not being met. The official response from the royal court to observations or complaints was usually in a tone of concern in the name of the King, sometimes from the King himself, calling for action or else be disgraced.

## War as a Profitable Venture

Another aspect of raising money to finance military activity regarded war as a profitable venture. The most obvious benefit of a victorious war was increased territory and thus more tax revenues into the royal treasury. The 1667–1668 War of Devolution had effectively confirmed this by the transfer to the crown of France of part of Spanish Flanders including some of its most prosperous cities. Following that war, Louis XIV sought to raise a much larger regular standing army in peacetime that would hover at about 150,000 to 200,000 men, which was two to three times its strength before the war. A robust economy was necessary to fund such forces. Finance Minister Colbert was an ardent promoter of mercantilism, sometimes called *Colbertisme* in France, which fostered the royal government's intervention to protect local business with customs duties on imported merchandise while investing in local production of goods and services for the home market and also vigorously promote their export. The positive trade balances would be invested locally thus rapidly creating prosperity.

## The Sun King's Military-Industrial Complex

During the 1660s, the French economy greatly benefited from these policies, which largely concerned military aspects. Both the government and individual regiments were involved in the procurement of arms in the reign of Louis XIV so that it is not certain exactly how much and what was produced. Known early orders record, for instance, the Royal and the Foix infantry regiments ordering muskets at Charleville in 1687–1688. Weapons that had previously often been imported were increasingly made locally from the 1660s. Indeed, today's French arms industry, which is still one of the world's most important, was created from the 1660s thanks to Colbert's policies approved by the King, and by the early eighteenth century had become Europe's largest arms producer. It was now exporting weapons to allies, notably Spain, levels of production in the several arms factories surpassing 100,000 firearms a year.

Another new industry was the manufacture of cloth for an army that would henceforth wear uniforms. Not only were uniforms made locally in France needed, but the demand, as for everything else for the army, multiplied enormously. Tens of thousands and eventually, hundreds of thousands of men needed to be clothed. For army uniforms, there was not at that time a central government organisation supplying uniforms to the army. Instead, regimental commanders usually mandated one or more of the unit's officers to negotiate terms with a clothier, often in Paris, with whom a contract was passed specifying what was needed, when and where it would be delivered to the regiment and at what cost, always a delicate part since a percentage of profit had to be made from the total sum, which came from the clothing deduction in the NCOs' and soldiers' pay. Contrary to common belief, colonels and captains might lose money in these and other supply transactions since the men's pay was so low. They could only make it up if they had a bonus or pillaged. Clothing issue periods could vary and do not seem to have been steady until the 1680s, but an average of sorts was two years for wool cloth garments and less for other items. The repercussion boosted manufacture in many provinces and towns outside Paris. A 1709 cloth maker in Darnetal who supplied Paris clothiers had over 500 employees. Hats often came from Caudebec (Normandy). A lot of the grey-white cloth was made in the province of Berry and at Lodève (Languedoc). The city of Lyon was the specialist until the late twentieth century for making lace with silk and other materials as seen in the contracts and supply lists of the period.[5]

Large permanent armies could no longer gather enough food off the land they passed through as in former times. An army of 60,000 officers and other ranks actually required up to 90,000 daily rations of bread, wine and meat. The difference was because officers had more than one ration and many support staff also had to be fed. Feeding troops on campaign became an enormous logistical challenge. War Minister Louvois was very worried about this and in 1671, as unprecedented numbers of troops would soon be assembling to invade the Netherlands, he confided to Vauban that "when we have to think of 50,000 mouths [to feed] coming to the same place for five or six weeks", it was the organisation to feed them that haunted him. Being a talented and powerful administrator, he solved it by creating a more centralised food industry with government support through a corps of commissaries that produced the enormous number of daily rations required. Only through a sophisticated network of bakeries and transportation managed by private or government officials could this be done. Louvois had *magazins* (warehouses) built to store the goods. Having a few warehouses was not a novelty, but having a large number of these organised into an integrated system was a new concept. In 1672, as the French armies

---

5 Jean Chagniot, *Paris et l'armée au XVIIIe siècle* (Paris: Economica, 1985), pp.266–273 reveals some of the many Paris military outfitters and their web of suppliers in the provinces. On officers' revenues, see Hervé Drévillon, *L'impôt du sang* (Paris: Tallandier, 2005), p.396.

were marching into the Netherlands, there were seven large warehouses built in northern France and in the Cologne area filled with a six-month supply of 200,000 daily rations amounting to 36 million rations. Just for bread, which loaf of one and a half pound was the main staple, many factory-sized bakeries were built that employed thousands of workers to make and ship the great quantities needed. Some of this bread was *biscuité* (double-cooked like biscuits) so it could keep for at least two months. Louvois insisted it should be issued every day, but in some instances, it took longer. In 1677, Vauban wrote to Louvois that the troops he was with had not received their rations for three weeks. They were obviously reduced to marauding local inhabitants to survive and this weakened the soldiers' discipline. However, this system with the warehouses as its lynchpin appears to have generally worked quite well, taking into consideration that supplying an army moving through the countryside was no simple matter.[6]

France had a large population of horses that had been bred for many generations mainly for farm work and for pulling wagons and carts. Breeding needed to be improved and the supply of good riding horses for an expanding army was also addressed early during the King's personal reign. In 1665, Colbert created government breeding farms that became eventually the famed *Haras Nationaux* (National Studs) that Louvois also encouraged; foreign stallions were imported to upgrade as well as increase breeding and they were spread across the county. Efforts were made to breed a good pulling horse for carriages. Progress in breeding was made especially in Alsace and Lorraine, but fell short of the great numbers needed so the importation of horses from Switzerland and Germany continued. Thoroughbred horses, especially appreciated by army officers, came of age at that time thanks notably to the Haras du Pin at Le Merlereaux (Orne) that became the most celebrated of France's national stud farms, with fine horses also being bred in Normandy and Navarre. In conclusion, there can be no doubt that the influx of royal funds into local industries and agriculture to purchase military supplies, horses and food was a great benefit to the economy and created much employment.[7]

If a powerful army, in wartime, campaigned outside its own national borders and kept opponent forces out, the economic benefit was thought to be even greater since it would control and tax enemy territory to defray part of its expenses. Meanwhile, the national territory would not suffer the ravages of war and thus remain productive with populations confident in their own safety. The King and his ministers undoubtedly espoused such notions and did not hesitate to invest in creating or upgrading an enormous web of fortifications which required large numbers of soldiers assisted by numerous mobilised militiamen who were all paid to provide countless garrisons.

France was an autocratic state and its economy's ultimate goal was not to amass capital, but to provide money for its rulers to pay for a greater nation-state. At that time, that mostly meant paying for wars and the lion's share

---

6   Rousset, *Histoire de Louvois*, Vol. 1, pp.248–249; Cénat, *Louvois*, pp.65–67. The hard biscuit bread would be broken up in a hot soup or stew in a pot that usually had rations for six or seven soldiers.
7   *The Book of the Horse*, Brian Vesey-Fitzgerald (ed.) (London: Nicholson & Watson, 1946), pp.84–85; Denis Bogros, 'Les chevaux de la Cavalerie française à la fin du XVIIe siècle', *Histoire, économie et société*, XV, 1996, pp.105–112.

went to the army. And the bill went up as years passed. As seen above, the French army stood at some 180,000 in 1672. Five years later, it comprised some 300,000 men of which 230,000 were infantrymen, reduced by 20,000 later in 1678 since the war was ending.[8]

# Infantry Pay

A surprising and effective way to fund armies was to reduce the pay of members of the armed forces. In the sixteenth century, a professional infantryman could be paid, say, four florins a day while a skilled worker such as a mason would pocket less than three. To the military pay was added booty from plundering or ransoming towns. This level of income decreased from about 1590 and especially from the Thirty Years' War when starving and desperate peasants took lower pay to become infantrymen. According to Voltaire at the time he wrote his *Siècle de Louis XIV* in the mid eighteenth century, the soldier's pay of five sols a day had not changed since the reign of King Henri IV. During Louis XIV's reign, basic soldier's pay was equivalent to that of a common unskilled labourer. Company officers below the rank of captain also saw substantial reductions in pay over the years. Early in his reign, the Sun King with his ever present sense of order decreed the pay of officers and men belonging to infantry regiments recruited in France on 20 December 1663 to be as follows:

Captain: 75 livres per month
Lieutenant: 30 livres per month
Ensign: 22 livres 10 sols per month
Sergeant: 10 sols per day (approx. 15 livres per month)
Corporals: 7 sols per day
Anspessade: 6 sols per day
Soldier: 5 sols per day (approx. 7 livres 5 sols per month)

He also ordered that it would be regularly paid and it was, which was a notable improvement over past practices. If it was not and War Minister Louvois heard about it, his wrath could be great and consequences catastrophic for the guilty. When on campaign, about half of the basic pay of captains and lieutenants was added so that they received 110 livres 10 sols and 45 livres respectively. Another source of some small revenue for the captains was the deduction of the "usual sol" per day from the soldier's pay for clothing and weapons. If the captain's company mustered the regulation 50 men, he received three soldiers' pay (15 sols) as a bonus. When the standard was raised to 60 men from 12 June 1671 and 20 October 1675, the captain received five soldiers' pay (25 sols). Louvois was opposed to any deviations such as captains retaining more money than allowed. Officers caught in the act could face very severe sanctions. In September 1684, a guilty captain was jailed while the soldier who had

---

8   Arnault Skornicki, *L'économiste, la cour et la patrie* (Paris: CNRS, 2011), pp.39–53, 78–79; BMA, Ms A1b, 1626, 'Tiroirs de Louis XIV'; Maxime Weygand, *Histoire de l'Armée française* (Paris: Flammarion, 1938), p.150.

A regiment of infantry receiving its pay, late seventeenth century. The soldier's pay may not have been high, but for most of the reign, it was regularly paid. (Private collection. Author's photo)

reported the abuse was allowed to immediately leave the army with a month of the captain's pay as a bonus. To encourage emulation and good behaviour, bonuses were occasionally granted. On 1 September 1663, the King reviewed 8,900 infantrymen at Metz. The next day, he cashiered four captains whose companies were "very bad" and rewarded 20 others publicly for their "very good" companies with bonuses of 100 and 150 *Louis d'or* each, which worked out to about 1,100 to over 1,600 livres, a handsome bonus.[9]

This sum would have been just as welcome in 1700 and even in 1800. The reason was that money was extremely stable in value from the late seventeenth century to the middle of the nineteenth century. There was practically no inflation in France and Britain between 1700 and 1820, the worse hikes being of only 0.2 percent to 0.3 percent compensated by a negative fall of only −0.2 percent. Thus, the value of military pay retained its value and did not need to be raised. Therefore, the skilful use by military authorities of cash bonuses and moneyed "gratifications" became morale boosters for ambitious officers and men in search of fortune and glory.[10]

---

9   Voltaire, *Le siècle de Louis XIV*, pp.534–535; R. Carré de Verneuil, *L'armée en France* (Paris: J. Dumaine, 1880), pp.187–189; Bély, Bérenger and Corvisier, *Guerre et paix dans l'Europe du XVIIe siècle*, pp.239–240; *Lettres, instructions et mémoires de Colbert*, vol. 9, pp.476–477. The units reviewed at Metz were 29 companies of Gardes-Françaises, 14 of Gardes-Suisses, 700 men of Turenne's Regiment, 700 of La Ferté-Senneterre, 300 of the Duc d'York Irish and "the two royal regiments".

10  Thomas Piketty, *Le capital au XXIe siècle* (Paris: Seuil, 2013), pp.171–175. An example given in that, since the early eighteenth century to the first third of the nineteenth century, £30 sterling (and its equivalent in France) was an individual's medium annual revenue that would suffice to live humbly, but correctly, whereas about up to 20 to 30 times that amount was needed to have a comfortable and elegant lifestyle with some servants.

# 8

# French Line Infantry

## Raising Standards by Central Authority

During the early 1660s, the King took forceful steps to create a truly formidable infantry. He started at the top by becoming its colonel-general and appointing officers that had at least a year's service in the infantry before obtaining a commission. With a wilful minister such as the Marquis de Louvois, there was no way that even mute opposition would be tolerated for long because, in his plan, the King's will and desires knew no obstacles. For the army general and the infantry in particular, as it was the "Queen of Battles", the vision of its improvement and how to achieve it was similar for both the King and his minister. For all his faults, the brilliant qualities of Louvois could not and still must not be minimised. He obviously had a real passion for making a great army and managing it. With the support of his royal master to which he always deferred – occasionally after a vigorous discussion – he created the first really large and integrated army in modern times. All arms of the service were important, but the key to meeting the objective lay with having the best infantry anywhere.

Thus, a stream of instructions and orders came out of the Ministry of War as well as updated manuals such as De Lamont's *Les fonctions de tous les officiers de l'infanterie depuis celles du Sergent jusques à celles de Colonel* (Infantry officers' functions from those of sergeants to colonel) becoming often reprinted best sellers. Not only was the royal guard to henceforth become the army's true elite by unrivalled military prowess, but the Régiment du Roi – the King's Own Regiment – was created in 1663 with the specific mandate to be the line infantry's model unit. By all these measures, a really national infantry emerged, which had a hitherto unseen level of control by the King and Minister of War Louvois. The result was that, for a time, the French line infantry was the best in Europe.

## Organisation

When Louis XIV became a child king in 1643, the infantry formed the bulk of the army that, like other armies of the time, had many variations insofar

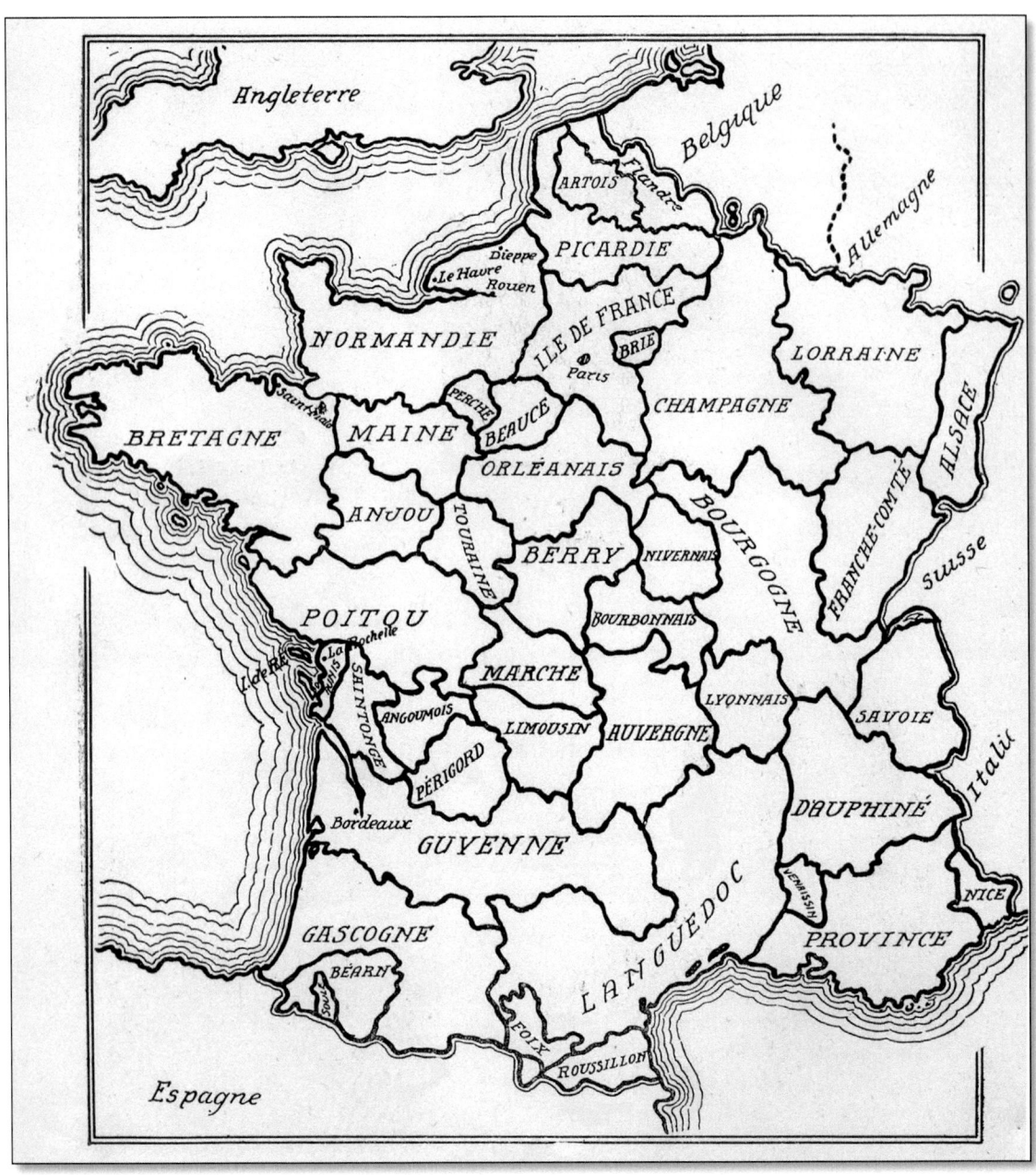

Map of France's provinces during the seventeenth and eighteenth centuries. Many regiments in the French army bore the name of a province, which was sometime a favoured recruiting area. (Private collection. Author's photo)

as the strength of regiments. Most units were raised when a war started and disbanded when it ended. A shifting minority of infantry regiments remained on the French peacetime establishment. The most senior were the six *vieux corps* (old corps) as they were nicknamed consisting of the Gardes-Françaises, Picardie, Champagne, Piémont, Navarre and Normandie regiments. They were followed by the next six most senior *petits vieux* (little old) Chappes, Rambures, Bourg-L'Épinasse, Sault, Vaubécourt and Beaumont regiments whose names, unlike the *vieux*, changed with succeeding colonels except for Rambures who became Ile-de-France in 1636 with several others that also took the provincial names of Auvergne, Lorraine, Angoumois and Touraine.

# FRENCH LINE INFANTRY

A line of musketeers and pikemen, mid seventeenth century. These figures, shown in action, are based on the engravings of soldiers depicted in Lostelneau's *Le Mareschal des Batailles* (Paris, 1647). Print after JOB. (Author's photo)

At the time, most of these regiments, at least those with provincial names, appear to have had 20 companies.

In 1643 the nation was at war and the line infantry numbered, on 14 May, some 131 regiments which included six German, five Swiss, two Irish, two Lorraine, one Scottish and one Italian on the foreign establishment. Two Polish and a Catalan corps joined them in 1646–1647. These were followed by disbandments and new regiments raised from 1648 and into the 1650s. By 1658 and the battle of the Dunes, the army had 103 line regiments of which many were disbanded once peace was convened with Spain. Only 33 remained in 1662 and 31 the following year, Of the remaining regiments, only the *vieux* and *petit vieux* regiments had 20 companies, others having various strength levels, some with as few as four or even two companies. So the number of regiments was misleading as to the actual strength of the army. The number of battalions could give a better idea, but this too was not stable since some battalions might have more companies than others. By that time, battalions were divided into three *manches* (literally "sleeves" but really sections of several companies each, two of which were musketeers and the other of pikemen). From 1643 to 1 September 1715, regiments were raised and others disbanded nearly every year so there are sometime different figures advanced. One compiler calculates that the lowest number of infantry regiments was 29 in 1665–1666 with the peak being 298 from 1709 to 1711.

One senses that the King, once in absolute power and ably aided by Minister of War Louvois, was looking to build up a larger permanent force that would be the most efficient and impressive in Europe. The quick successes of the 1667–1668 War of Devolution certainly gave encouragement and he proceeded to augment the permanent army gradually. By early 1672, there were 59 line infantry regiments of unequal strength plus 350 independent and recruit companies. The six *vieux* corps with the du Roi, Royal, Dauphin, Duc d'Anjou and La Reine regiments had 70 companies of 53 officers and men each, others had 33, 24, 20, 18, 17 and 16 companies each. Swiss regiments had much stronger companies at 200 men each, Erlach's Regiment for instance, having 12 companies and thus 2,400 men.[1]

By then many officers, NCOs and soldier in all regiments could contemplate a military career that had good chances of being permanent beyond the end of a war. Instead of massively disbanding nearly everyone, reductions since 1668 were being made by lowering the number of men in companies and keeping as many worthy officers and NCOs as needed to always have a strong permanent cadre of experienced infantrymen to train recruits when enlistments were up. While some soldiers wished not to serve more than the minimum four-year service period according to the royal order of 28 October 1666, it could be extended in wartime. Indeed, enlistment periods were actually variable insofar as they were an agreement between a captain and a recruit; how could authorities formally contradict recruiting captains when the army was desperate for recruits? Some volunteers were even enlisted on the promise that they could quit the service when they pleased while others agreed to a six-year enlistment, which was the number of years finally ordered in 1716, although even after that date some unlucky recruits were "enlisted forever"…! But perhaps the saddest cases were those that, in periods of famine, were starving and would agree to anything as long as they had bread to eat. On the other hand, other soldiers that remained for decades in the army could think that if they lived long enough, they would have a small but welcome pension and, if maimed, could rely on medical care as an invalid (see Volume 4).[2]

With regard to the number of men in the infantry, we have seen in Volume 1 that the figures varied wildly until the 1660s when they seem to have become somewhat less erratic. Even Colonel Belhomme's late nineteenth century figures seemed closer to a believable state of the army. From 1672 to 1711, he calculated that the infantry stood at:[3]

| | | | |
|---|---|---|---|
| 1672: 138,620 | 1683: 143,330 | 1697: 374,660 | 1706: 408,281 |
| 1673: 163,570 | 1684: 129,420 | 1699: 156,676 | 1707: 385,856 |
| 1674: 214,950 | 1688: 242,000 | 1700: 138,158 | 1708: 388,226 |
| 1675: 227,000 | 1690: 290,000 | 1701: 213,763 | 1709: 384,600 |
| 1676: 225,650 | 1691: 310,600 | 1702: 270,838 | 1710: 368,800 |
| 1677: 229,970 | 1692: 351,055 | 1703: 375,433 | 1711: 387,000 |
| 1679: 112,430 | 1693: 379,670 | 1704: 396,451 | |
| 1681: 112,942 | 1696: 381,220 | 1705: 390,598 | |

---

1 Quincy, *Histoire Militaire*, Vol. 1, p.312; Eugène Fieffé, *Histoire des troupes étrangères au service de la France* (Paris, 1854), Vol. 1, pp.165–166; J.J. Pattyn, 'L'infaterie française de Louis XIV', *La Figurine* (Brussels), Vol. 36 (1974), pp.32–38. The number of regiments given by various sources can vary.

2 Albert Babeau, *La vie militaire sous l'Ancien Régime* (Paris: Firmin-Didot, 1890), Vol. 1, p.69; Camille Rousset, *Histoire de Louvois et de son administration politique et militaire jusqu'à la paix de Nimègue* (Paris: Didier, 1864), Vol. 1, p.184; André Corvisier, *Le soldat, de Louvois à Choiseul* (Paris: PUF, 1964), Vol. 1, pp.105, 171–177 and notes of conferences by Professor Corvisier at the University of Ottawa.

3 Victor Belhomme, *Histoire del'infanterie en France* (Paris: Lavauzelle, 1892). The figures given are dispersed throughout volume 2 as are those in Maxime Weygand, *Histoire de l'Armée française* (Paris: Flammarion, 1938).

# FRENCH LINE INFANTRY

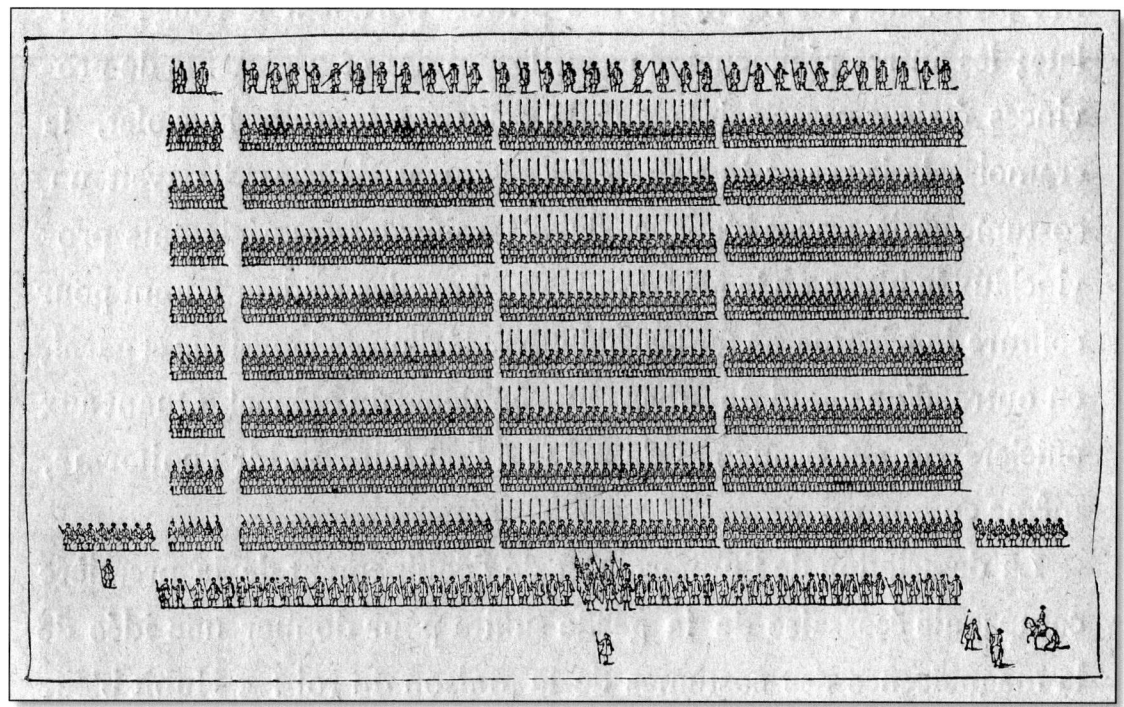

Infantry battalion of 17 companies aligned for battle, *c.* 1670-1679. There were 16 companies with 38 musketeers and 12 pikemen in each company. The 50 elite grenadiers company's soldiers were armed with flintlock muskets and carried grenades. The companies were aligned in eight ranks, the sergeants at the rear and the officers in front, three colours at the centre and drummers at each side. The centre with the pikemen formed the **corps de bataille**, the musketeers on both sides were the **manches** and the grenadiers were at the right of the battalion (seen at left when facing the unit). Print after Puységur's *Art de la guerre*. (Author's photo)

Other sources generally give lower figures. General Weygand's history gives 230,000 infantrymen in 1677 of which 50,000 were foreign and 24,000 serving in garrison battalions. The King's own notes dated 1 January 1678 list 119,250 infantrymen on campaign and 100,000 in garrisons for a total of 219,250. By 1691–1693, the infantry is 380,000 strong according to Weygand although Rousset calculated it was decreasing, which is confirmed by an "Estat" of 1696 that put the infantry's strength at 208,000 foot troops.

Colonel Belhomme's figures become suspiciously high again during the War of the Spanish Succession whereas General Weygand give a more credible 185,000 infantrymen in 1702, while Professor Corvisier figured the whole army to have been at about 350,000 men in 1706, nearly 60,000 men fewer than just the infantry as calculated by Belhomme. More figures could be cited, but the reader will understand that, in Louis XIV's reign as before, such statistics are always more approximate than precise. Furthermore, even with the strengths indicated above, there remains the question of effective strength, which affects not only the infantry but the whole army of any nation. Again, this can only be an approximate guess based on various bits and pieces of evidence.[4]

At that time, honour and precedence was very important in an officer's values and for decades there had been considerable bickering regarding such matters, seemingly ridiculous in our day, but all important three centuries ago. The worst dispute in the army concerned claims as to which of the *vieux* and *petit vieux* regiments had the privilege of parading first therefore having precedence over the next regiment. They all passionately claimed seniority due to having been raised at the same time. As such matters could reach near-crisis proportions, the King solved them in a rather shrewd fashion by three royal orders on 19 and 28 February 1666 and 26 March 1670. Since they all claimed seniority, he agreed they all were and that they would henceforth be the senior line unit successively every year in an orderly system that was called the *sémestre* (semester); this because the marching and parade priority order was really only applied when several of these *vieux* and *petit vieux* regiments were serving together on campaign during summer semesters.[5]

## Standardised Infantry Discipline

The Sun King loved an orderly process in anything he supervised. As a youth, he must not have been impressed by the rather slovenly looking and ill-disciplined soldiers of the mid seventeenth century led by equally haughty and pretentious officers who seemed to know little of the art of war while waving their noble genealogies to justify anything they did. At the time, this was more or less true in other European armies and passed for normal. In the past however, the success of better-formed troops in the Netherlands and Sweden seemed to have been partly due to good discipline and drills. In 1661, after he abolished the post of captain general of infantry and assumed its duties, he actively sought to make unprecedented reforms in the infantry. An early initiative was to have model units apart from the guard regiments. On 2 January 1663, the King created his own regiment, the Régiment du Roi (the King's Regiment) and made himself its colonel-in-chief. Its lieutenant colonel was Jean Martinet, an officer of humble background already renowned for his great knowledge in military matters and especially talented with regard to infantry organisation, drills and manoeuvres. Typically, when an untitled gentleman of capacity came to the King's attention, noble blood was not required to elevate him and Martinet proved to be the right officer for the task. Under his leadership, the Régiment du Roi was the first unit to be regularly drilled and put under strict discipline. The improvements were soon visible to all; even when on campaign, its camps were very well ordered and clean. As a result, the regiment became the model unit in the line infantry and Saint-Simon related the King's pride of "his" regiment. It was elevated to a status close to that of the guard regiments and, although a new unit, given as 6th

---

4 Grimoard, *Recherches sur la force de l'armée Française*, p.55
5 This system remained in force until the order of 19 February 1777 when a lottery assigned a fixed rank and a regimental number to these regiments.

in precedence within the *petit-vieux* regiments. In 1664, the post of colonel lieutenant was created in the regiment and went to the Marquis Dangeau, who had bought the commission as a venal post hoping the King would elevate it further to be a regiment of the royal guard. Louis XIV did nothing like that but pocketed the money. Dangeau passed the post on to the Duc de Nevers who gave up also, so that in 1670 Martinet, who was the real colonel all along, was finally appointed colonel lieutenant by the grateful King. Minister of War Louvois was his staunch supporter and guide.

Once Martinet had made the Régiment du Roi everyone's envy, Louvois tasked him with the bigger job of spreading the wide-ranging reforms to the whole line infantry. In October 1668, Martinet was named inspector general and sent to inspect all the garrisons in newly acquired fortresses in Flanders and Artois and report if the troops were in good order, "if they drilled well or badly", and to have officers satisfy his demands for improvements on such matters as repairing soldiers' weapons and clothing. He was further to rid the troops of *malingres* (troublemakers), that they should be well clothed, but not necessarily all in the same manner if not possible, well shod with a good musket of standard calibre and drilled frequently. To be sure the reforms were implemented, the King ordered that some officers from his regiment be posted in the garrisons and report on progress made every week. This is matter of fact in any army today, but it was quite new then that such things as drills were now imposed by central authority. The muted wrath was great amongst some officers who saw their power lessened, while their men resented being told what to do all the time because Martinet felt they should always be kept busy instead of lounging around. To be sure, he was obviously a severe and determined drillmaster. The inspector-general thus became rather unpopular in the army, but the tone was set and, as the future would show, his influence was great and timeless not just in the French infantry, but in all countries. Today, the *Oxford Dictionary* defines "martinet" as a "strict disciplinary" person. Of the many millions who use the expression, very few know it rooted back to one of the Sun King's favourite officers. He was also brave and met his end in 1672 during the siege of Doesburg in the Netherlands. But his heritage was outstanding.[6]

## Regimental Composition

The organisation of regiments was not and would not be standardised throughout the army during the Sun King's reign. Corps continued to have varying strength. Some regiments had one battalion and others had more, but some progress towards uniformity was made. Each regiment was led by a colonel assisted by a regimental staff. Then came a variable number of companies, each led by a captain, a lieutenant and an ensign with two sergeants, three corporals, three *anspessades* (lance-corporals), one or two drummers and the privates whose numbers varied. A company might have

---

6   Rousset, *Histoire de Louvois*, Vol. pp.206–210; Gabriel Daniel, *Histoire de la milice françoise* (Paris: Jean-Baptiste Coignard, 1721 and Amsterdam: Compagnie de Jésus, 1724), Vol. 1, pp.281, 285; Louis Susane, *Histoire de l'infanterie française*, Vol. 3, pp.204–206, 210–211.

Infantry musketeer, c. 1645–1650. This front view shows details of the dress, weapons and equipment of a musketeer, here holding a matchlock musket at the *Portez le mousquet haut position*. Print after Lostelneau's *Le Mareschal des Batailles,* Paris, 1647. (Author's photo)

as many as a hundred men in wartime, but a more common and realistic number was about 50 or 45 or sometimes less.

By the royal order of 28 February 1679 given at the behest of Louvois, the French infantry was separated and organised into two distinct entities depending on their service. The first and most numerous type consisted of the regiments that went on campaign whose basic tactical unit was the battalion. Regiments might have one or several battalion. Each battalion had 16 companies including that of grenadiers with each company mustering 45 men. The second type were the garrison troops whose basic unit was the company. There were garrison units that often were one-battalion regiments which would have a fluctuating number of companies, usually four including one of grenadiers of about 30 to 35 men each and there were also independent garrison companies. In 1684, the garrison battalions were transformed into regiments and each was given the name of a province. Some regiments might have both a campaign and a garrison battalion. On the whole, soldiers in the garrison companies had lower pay and their unit strength would fluctuate more than campaign regiments. However, campaign regiments did not necessarily have priority to stay on the establishment when wars ended and troops disbanded; about half of the infantry in peacetime was of the garrison type. Louvois' system remained until 1718 when all units would henceforth have the same war and peace establishments.[7]

During the 1680s up to the early 1690s, a campaign battalion's infantry company had a captain, a lieutenant, an ensign, two sergeants (one superior to the other), one to three corporals, one to three lance-corporals and a drummer, In theory, there were 23 musketeers, 10 pikemen and four to six fusiliers. The colonel's company might also have a fifer. The theoretical battalion composition was still supposed to be two-thirds musketeers and one-third pikemen, but these last were actually decreasing in number while fusiliers were being officiously and officially accepted onto the strength. During the 1690s the pikemen all but disappeared followed by matchlock musketeers as more flintlock muskets became available to arm the men. For their part, grenadiers were and had always been armed with flintlock muskets. Garrison companies had a captain, a lieutenant, two sergeants, a corporal, two lance corporals, a drummer, 33 musketeers and six fusiliers or 30 grenadiers. From 1691, an infantry battalion was to have 13 companies including one of grenadiers.[8]

Following the end of the war, the usual reductions in battalions were made. In December 1699, a battalion's 12 companies had 35 fusiliers each and its grenadier company had 45 grenadiers. Clouds of possible hostilities were soon thereafter apparent and a royal order of 4 October 1700 raised the number of fusiliers to 45 in each company and the grenadier company now had 50 grenadiers.

With the nation going yet again to war, this time to fight for the throne of Spain, the army had to be greatly augmented. In 1702, some 70 battalions of conscripted men of the royal militia were embodied and became the 2nd battalions of existing line infantry regiments. By a royal order of 25 May 1703, the militiamen were amalgamated totally with the veteran soldiers of their regiments. This was the first time in the annals of the French army that militiamen were legally (and somewhat forcibly) merged into regiments and henceforth considered regular soldiers. This raised the strength of battalions from about 500 to 800 men, but this was obviously not considered sufficient.

So, another 92 totally new regiments were created in 1702 with another 24 in 1705–1706. The Chevalier de Guignard, who was a veteran soldier and writer, commented later on the effect of the raising of these new regiments. He himself was a lieutenant colonel in Doigny's Regiment (which beame Thil's from 1704), of one of those raised in 1702. He related that the people who raised those new regiments were:

---

7    Victor Belhomme, *Histoire de l'infanterie en France*, Vol. 3, pp.22–23.
8    Pierre Carles 'L'infanterie du roi de France à la mort de Louvois', *Histoire, économie et société*, 1996, 15e année, no. 1, pp.57–73. Online at: <http://www.persee.fr/doc/hes_0752-5702_1996_num_15_1_1852>; Daniel, *Histoire de la milice française*, Vol. 2, p.535.

Infantry captain, mid seventeenth century. This captain is on duty mounting the guard, and therefore wears his gorget and holds his spontoon. Print after Collombon's *Trophée d'armes*, Lyon, 1650. (Author's photo)

… nameless adventurers without experience, who were awarded [colonel's commissions] on the pretext of raising regiments at their own expense; of which I can say, and even certify, that the King's intentions were very badly carried out, being certain that they have been infinitely more expensive to His Majesty than if he had paid three times the ordinary price [of raising a regiment].

The result instead was that while these upstart colonels thus gained a position in society, robbed the King's coffers with the complicity of some inspectors and, "even worse", further "pillaged" their own unfortunate officers and soldiers. Guignard further commented, so as to find some virtue in these levies, that there also had been other worthy commanders "of very rare merit and of distinguished capacity as seen by the good services that they and their regiments rendered wherever they served."[9]

The virtues and experience of some officers and men could not alter the fact that the stability, cohesion, steadiness and effectiveness was gravely reduced in the whole of French line infantry as never before. General Susane termed "this levy as the ruin of the infantry" and we feel it was close to the mark in the short term. Instead of incorporating recruits and new officers into existing regiments where they would be trained under veteran supervision, which had been at least partly done previously, the lure to save money won and a sort of "private sector" business had been created within the army. As seen by Guignard, some new colonels saw it as a fine way to self-enrichment with absolute and effective impunity, especially as treasury officials were overwhelmed with the demands of a wartime economy and skyrocketing expenses everywhere.[10]

The first casualty was France's "Queen of Battles" itself. For the new regiments, some 7,000 new officers had to be found. Logically, some experienced and battle-tested NCOs could have been commissioned and some officers promoted from older units to fill a substantial part of the new posts and provide a cadre. However, for NCOs, it was not in the overwhelming values of those times that their experience equated the qualities of gentile birth so, if sergeants were commissioned, they must have been few. Some officers came from other corps, but again probably not in great numbers since the new colonels, who were paying for the levy, certainly had their own candidates. Naturally, what these new colonels sought most of all in their new officers was their ability to persuade men to enlist in their regiments, which came ahead of whatever military knowledge

---

9   M. de Guignard, *L'École de Mars* (Paris: Simart, 1725), Vol. 1, p.611.
10  Susane, *Histoire de l'infanterie française*, Vol. 1, p.214.

# FRENCH LINE INFANTRY

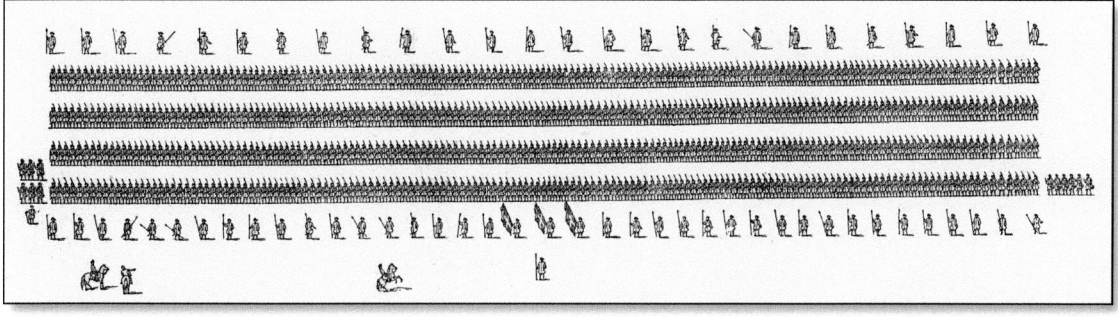

A battalion of infantry lined up in the early eighteenth century. The pikemen have vanished, as have the matchlock-armed musketeers, all those armed with firearms now have flintlock muskets. The line is reduced to four ranks. Officers in front, drummers at each side and sergeants behind the line. They are there to keep ranks aligned in battle and stop the flight of fusiliers who panic. Print after Puységur's *Art de la guerre*. (Author's photo)

Infantry corporal with shouldered musket, *c.* 1650. According to La Vallière, a corporal led a squad and was responsible for their knowing their duties as soldiers. Print after Collombon's *Trophée d'armes*, Lyon, 1650. (Author's photo).

they might have. The result was the arrival into the army of more or less noble gentlemen whose first military experience was probably when they put on their regiment's uniform.

Thus, during 1702–1703, the organisation of the new regiments weakened the effectiveness of the whole army. It was bad enough for the enlisted men who had little actual training from officers who generally were unfamiliar with military matters. However, at the end of their first campaign, the enlisted men would have become weathered soldiers in the field although still poorly trained for action. Their officers remained, on the whole, ignorant for much longer. This was not a good recipe for battlefield success when facing seasoned Austrian, German, Dutch and British soldiers who were led by good officers under such commanders as Marlborough and Prince Eugene.

Thus, the early years of the War of the Spanish Succession saw French infantry at its weakest in the Sun King's reign. In certain battles, some regiments where even annihilated and scores of their colours captured. For all that, the infantry was not ruined, but rather destabilised. In spite of discouraging losses, the good officers and men picked up the pieces and rebuilt it into a very sturdy and fearsome force. A royal order of 20 September 1710 even raised the establishment of each infantry company to 50 men each. By then, the French infantry was again on its way to being the finest in Europe.

Infantry officers drilling enlisted men, c. 1685–1690. The soldiers are aligned by an officer holding a cane. He is armed with a sword whose scabbard is barely visible behind the lower skirt of his coat. The soldiers hold their matchlock muskets, and their new waist-belts and shoulder belts with bullet pouches are clearly seen. Detail from a large brass medallion by Jean Régnaud and Pierre Le Nègre. (Musée du Louvre, Paris. Author's photo

## Regimental Officers and Enlisted Ranks

Every regiment had an *état-major* (regimental staff). A colonel was its supreme commander and patron who also "owned" the unit. This person could be the King, the Queen, other members of the royal family and grand nobles. The King also was nominal colonel-in-chief of his own units as well as those titled "royal" and all others with provincial or municipal titles although there were naturally exceptions. He was not the actual commander and a colonel was named by him to lead the unit. Other regiments had their noble gentry colonel's name, which would change when a new colonel was appointed. The colonels were supposed to actually lead their regiment, but that was often left to lieutenant colonels and majors for everyday duties. They expected to make a profit from various deductions (the "off-reckonings" in the British armies), but might not since a regiment was a risky business in more ways than one. The best-appointed regiments were usually those whose colonels had great revenues that they lavished on their regiments, the Villeroi family regarding the Lyonnois Regiment being a good example.[11]

---

11 See appendices for name changes. There were no official regimental numbers until 1762, when noble gentry colonel's names were abolished (except for a few princes and foreign units), and it

# FRENCH LINE INFANTRY

Majors and *aide-majors* were more concerned with daily administrative issues in the unit overseeing such things as lodging, feeding, pay, ammunition and disciplinary matters. On those last, French senior infantry regiments had *prévôté* which meant they were empowered to solve legal matters at the unit level and might have a squad of elite soldiers acting as provosts following the abolition of *pertuisaniers* (see below) in 1670. They were in charge of the marching and battle order of the regiment and supervised the drum major. Majors kept a muster of everyone in the unit amongst their many duties.

The rest of the staff was not made up of officers, but would include a surgeon with assistants, a chaplain – usually a priest from the Récolet Order, a drum major and several artisans.

Companies were led by a captain with subalterns being one or more lieutenant and ensign (also designated second-lieutenant). Captains were to know the duties of all in the company they led. They chose the sergeants, the *fourrier* (quartermaster sergeant), drummers and fifer. Lieutenants assisted the captains. All ensigns carried colours when all the companies had them, until the middle of the seventeenth century when it was felt sufficient to have a colour for each of the three wings of a battalion. So the ensigns were also called second-lieutenants thereafter.

Enlisted men in companies consisted of sergeants, corporals, *anspessades* (lance-corporals), drummers and privates, which could have the rank of musketeers, pikemen or fusiliers until around 1700 after which there were only fusiliers with the grenadiers that had been created in the later 1660s. There were also the *pertuisaniers*, an infantry function that vanished in 1670.[12]

Ensign, Poitou Regiment, early eighteenth century. White cross, quarters blue and red. Grey coat with red cuffs, gold buttons and lace. Print after Philippoteaux. (Courtesy New York Public Library, New York City)

## Sergeants

In 1669, Captain de Lamont described the function of sergeant in a book on the functions of infantry officers "from sergeant to colonel", which title gives

---

was not until the French Revolution that French regiments would be referred to by a number.

12 François de La Valière, *Pratique et maximes de la guerre* (Paris: Loyson, 1671). We have used the La Haye (The Hague) edition of 1693, pp.116–124.

an idea of the importance then granted to non-commissioned officers. The rank of sergeant was described as an honour that brought friends and esteem. It was to be carried out with suitable humility and wit when speaking while having utter discretion for sensitive matters privately reported. A sergeant's conduct was to be beyond reproach. He always had to be properly dressed, but without luxury or with an excess of ribbons "since this showed [a man with a] feeble soul and light [headed]." The sergeant was always have a nice sword, an "honest" bandolier, "a good hat, take care of his halberd, and avoid these reputations of drinker, smoker and women-chaser, which are things totally opposed to honesty, which prevents a sergeant from rising further." Such conduct would lead people to say that the sergeant, while being "truly a really brave soldier," was also "a drunkard, a bully, always attached to a whore's arse" or still a rogue that did not honour his company, which was worse because such a reputation could not be erased.[13]

Ideally, besides the required qualities mentioned above, Lamont advised that it was most important for the sergeant "to be useful to his captain" by assiduous performance of his duties, such as drilling the men while being strict but fair with them and keeping an ear on the company's morale, as well as discreetly reporting to the captain problems that might arise. It was important for the sergeant to see the officers often and the regimental major every day, to seek their advice while showing them utter respect, notably by taking off his hat when addressing them. A sergeant also had to know how to read and write, which was certainly a basic asset in an era when illiteracy was widespread. He thus could keep company accounts and write routine orders as well as read regulations to the company. The sergeant was thus a centre of life in the company that also had social extensions. He enjoyed better status being more literate and might well read news from home to illiterate soldiers, quite possibly in the company's canteen that was, very often in the French armies of the time, run by the sergeant's wife. NCOs also needed ways to increase their army pay.[14]

In seventeenth-century armies, the importance of sergeants could be expressed by their clothing as well as their armament. Early images suggest that some might wear their colonel's livery colours, but instead of having livery lace like drummers, would have more luxurious gold or silver lace and buttons. With the gradual universal adoption of uniforms in the army from the 1660s, infantry sergeants appear to have generally adopted the same regimental uniform as their men, but there is some evidence that this practice went on in a few units until the end of the seventeenth century and early eighteenth century.[15]

---

13 M. de Lamont, *Les fonctions de tous les officiers de l'infanterie, depuis celle du sergent jusqu'à celle de colonel* (Paris, 1669; we use the La Haye edition of 1693), p.12. Translation by the author.
14 M. de Lamont, pp.10–13.
15 Early records of naval and overseas troops also confirm different uniforms to the men, for sergeants. Before 1716, instead of grey-white coats like their men, galley troops' sergeants had scarlet coats, ship's marines blue coats, overseas garrisons in Acadia and Placentia (Newfoundland) also blue; sergeants in Canada and the West Indies had grey-white coats, but with scarlet cuffs instead of blue cuffs worn by their men.

## FRENCH LINE INFANTRY

Sergeant of the Provence Regiment, 1696. Originally the regiment's sergeants had all-scarlet uniforms. After high casualties amongst ithem, notably at Fleurus and Neerwinden, from 1695 their uniform was changed to grey-white lined and cuffed with red like the rest of the regiment. Detail from a print after Alfred de Marbot. Canadian War Museum, Ottawa. (Author's photo)

Sergeant of the Dauphin Regiment and corporal of the Lyonnois Regiment, early eighteenth century. The sergeant holds the Dauphin Regiment's distinctive halberd with its forked head; grey-white coat with blue cuffs, waistcoat, breeches and stockings, gold lace and buttons. The corporal's rank of Lyonnois is shown by the wool lace at his coat's cuffs; grey-white or white coat, red cuffs, lining, breeches and stockings, green waistcoat, yellow metal buttons and hat lace. Detail from a print after Alfred de Marbot. Canadian War Museum, Ottawa. (Author's photo)

In 1690 for instance, a clothing bill for a company of the Régiment du Roi mentions "very fine blue cloth" to make coats for two sergeants with ratteen material for their lining as well as red serge breeches and red stockings. The coats would be trimmed with gold lace and gold thread, probably to edge the cuffs and pocket flaps. Ratteen was also used to make cuffs. It was most probably red in this instance, which would result in the King's livery – he was the regiment's colonel-in-chief – but without the livery lace worn by drummers.[16]

According to its first regimental history, the sergeants of the Provence Regiment wore, from 1674 when it was raised, "red coats, waistcoats, breeches and stockings" until September 1695 when they started receiving white coats with red cuffs, white waistcoats, red breeches and stockings tied with silver buttons and hat lace. This was due to "the battles of Fleurus and Neerwinden where the regiment lost nearly all its sergeants", who made obvious targets for enemy fire probably now made more lethal thanks to the increasing use of flintlock muskets during the 1690s. It drove home the notion that "uniformity had to be total" in regiments apart from drummers who were less exposed, being usually behind the battalions. Vivonne's Regiment (Mortemart's from 1702) also had its sergeants dressed in red for a while longer until they changed to grey-white in 1703 following NCO losses at the battle of Eckeren. By then, it can be assumed that sergeants in nearly all units wore uniforms of the same hues as their men.[17]

### *Pertuisaniers*

During the early years of Louis XIV's reign, infantry regiments often had squads of soldiers armed with partisans, a polearm of Swiss origin that appeared in French armies during the later part of the fifteenth century. The soldiers so armed were called *pertuisaniers* and were considered elite fighting men. They were tasked specifically with the security of captains and senior officers in battle as well as escorting and defending the colours; they also were the most trustworthy soldiers and acted as provosts, like the military police

---

16 Uniform contract between Michel Rabinet, merchant, and Captain Charles Pasquet de La Vergne's company of the Regiment du Roi of 43 men and two sergeants, Poitiers, 28 October 1690. In *Revue Poitevine and Saintongeaise*, Vol. 11 (1894), pp.77–78. For 43 soldiers: 96 ells grey-white cloth for coat, 172 ells blue Lusignan material for coat lining, 32 ells fine blue Sommière ratteen cloth for cuffs and amadis, 43 ells of Falaize serge for blue breeches, 85 ells of strong linen to line breeches, coat pockets and buttonholes, 43 leather hides to make pockets of the 43 coats, thread and small buttons for the *amadis* of the 43 coats. Plus, for two sergeant: 5 ells of very fine blue cloth, 10 ells of Sommière ratteen for lining, 1 ounce of gold lace and two ounces of [gold] thread, 3 leather hides for the breeches pockets, 2 ells of red St. Lô serge for breeches, 45 pairs of stockings: 42 blue and 3 red. Plus: 4 ells of linen to line the sergeant's breeches and coat pockets, waist belts with brass buckles, 20 ells of black taffetas for cravats. Plus for the service of [Captain] Sieur de La Vergne: 2 ells of superfine grey blue [cloth], 7 ells of blue ratteen, 4 ounces of gold lace to put on seams, 1 3/4 ell of fine blue cloth for waistcoat, 2 ells of blue cloth for breeches, 2 ells of cotton material, 2 leather hides, 2 ounces silk, 2 ounces [silk] thread, 18 ells of very fine Holland linen for making shirts, 30 ells of very fine Rouen white linen for shirts and other things, 1 pair fine blue silk stockings. Plus, to make him a [civilian] coat and breeches: 2 2/3 superfine iron grey Meunier cloth, 2 ounces of narrow gold lace to put on seams, 5 ells of Sommières ratteen, 2 ells of lining linen, 6 ells of fine Lion bazin to make him a *chemisette* [nightshirt?].

17 Abbé du Houx, *Histoire du Régiment d'infanterie de Monsieur, créé sous le nom de Provence en 1676* (Bouillon, 1778), pp.xiii, 207.

# FRENCH LINE INFANTRY

Rear view of an infantryman and a *pertuisanier*, c. 1667. The grey-coated infantryman's equipment is shown, notably the bandolier with the some of the powder charge cylinders and match cord, a water gourd and a heavy-linen haversack. The *pertuisanier* on the right holds his distinctive partisan and wears a livery coat, in this case blue with red cuffs and lace for a royal or Guards regiment, but the coat could have been red, yellow, green, etcetera, with contrasting lining colour according to the livery of a colonel of a line regiment. Print after Philippoteaux from contemporary tapestries. (Anne S.K. Brown Military Collection, Brown University Library, Providence, RI, USA. Author's photo)

of modern armies. During the 1650s, there were eight per company although this was reduced to four by the early 1660s. The partisan itself was a quality weapon also carried by picked men of the royal guard, notably the Gardes de la Manche, the Gardes de la Porte and the Gardes-Françaises (see Volume 1). *Pertuisaniers* had higher pay and traditionally dressed in their colonel's livery, as, for instance those of the Lyonnois Regiment seen in 1666. The Sun King was not keen on these soldiers in his infantry. On 25 February 1670, after having seen "in the last wars" the few services they could give, he felt they would be "far more useful that these solders be armed with muskets or pikes" and thus ordered the captains to arm them as other soldiers of their companies.[18]

Although *pertuisaniers* were much less seen thereafter, they did not disappear totally. Some units that had squads of *gentilshommes du drapeau*

---

18 Étienne-Alexandre Bardin, *Dictionnaire de l'armée de terre*, (Paris: Corréard, 1850), pp.4383–4384; Comte de Chenel, *Dictionnaire des armées de terre et de mer* (Paris: Le Chevalier, 1863–1864), pp.977–978; BMA, Ordonnance du roi, 25 February 1670.

(gentlemen's colour guards) armed with partisans. Their equivalent were the *trabants* of Swiss and German regiments that continued to exist (see below). There was even something of an exception recorded. On 26 November 1672, the Sault Regiment greatly distinguished itself against Dutch troops and, possibly as result, was allowed to keep two brass guns and have *trabants* like Swiss and German regiments, a privilege that lasted for the rest of the Sun King's reign. These guards most likely wore the colonel's livery of the Créquy family to whom Colonel the Comte du Sault belonged.[19]

An infantry pikeman, mid seventeenth century. Well-outfitted with cuirass and tassets; the helmet is a morion transformed with upturned front and sides that, with its crest, gave it a popular neo-classical "Roman" look. Print after Solomon Savery. (Courtesy Anne S.K. Brown Military Collection, Brown University Library, Providence, RI, USA)

### Pikemen

In the 1640s, Lostelneau mentioned that a battalion of 256 men had 128 musketeers and 128 pikemen. The men were deployed eight ranks deep, each rank having 32 soldiers. This could have many variations in battle depending on what commanders ordered. By the 1650s, French line infantry regiments had two out of three soldiers armed with muskets and one-third armed with pikes, although this might actually vary. In 1656 for instance, there were far fewer pikemen so a royal order of 20 April stipulated that captains would be dismissed if they did not have enough pikemen in their ranks. Being a pikeman was less attractive to many soldiers because of the heavy helmet and armour they had to wear compared to musketeers so the problem obviously remained. On 25 July 1665, another royal order again mentioned that pikemen were to form a third of a regiment. The Sun King's mood favouring pikemen subsequently abated. A royal order of 20 June 1670 stipulated that henceforth, there would be 12 pikemen in newly raised companies of 50 men. Their official proportion continued to decline over the following decades. In an account of the 1693 battle of Marsaglia (Italy), it was reported that "apart from 10 or 12 campaign regiments, there was not a single pike in our army." They seem to have almost vanished by 1698 and were officially abolished on 1 October 1703.[20]

### Grenadiers

The use of hand grenades appears to have come to France via Austria, Spain or England. They were useful during assaults on besieged cities and might

---

19 Susane, *Histoire de l'infanterie française*, Vol. 3, p.154. *Pertuisaniers* squads also continued as local honour guards also called *hallebardiers*, as invalids that could not bear muskets and there were many in the galley fleet where they were guards of the prisoners on land and at sea.

20 Pierre de Lostelneau, *Le Mareschal de Bataille* (Paris: Sommaville, 1647), p.4; M. de Lamont, *La Fonction de tous les Officiers de l'Infanterie*, p.119; *Mercure Galant*, October 1693, p.298.

## FRENCH LINE INFANTRY

Infantry grenadier in action, c. 1695. Unlike most fusiliers at the time, grenadiers had a sling to carry their flintlock muskets. Print after Guérard. (Anne S.K. Brown Military Collection, Brown University Library, Providence, RI, USA. Author's photo)

scare horses during an enemy cavalry charge. Hand grenades were dangerous to handle and the few men who did handle them were obviously brave soldiers. During the July 1667 siege of Lille, Vauban perceived that they might be even more effective if the soldiers that handled them were clearly identified with a distinct status and trained to use them. The King agreed, and four elite soldiers in each company of the Régiment du Roi were given the additional duty of training to throw grenades. This represented 160 men as the regiment had 40 companies. The experiment proved very positive and, from 6 December 1668, the Régiment du Roi had a company of now officially titled 'grenadiers' whose pay was slightly higher and whose prestige would only grow. Candidates needed to be soldiers of proven bravery and calm in action, physically tall and strong so as to easily carry the heavy grenade pouch and to pitch grenades as far as possible. It was dangerous stuff, but effective, so having grenadiers was later extended to the six most senior line regiments. In 1670, 29 more grenadier companies were created in other regiments and, in 1671, all regiments now had them.[21]

---

21 "De l'institution des grenadiers", *Carnet de La Sabretache*, December 2005, p.142.

Infantry grenadiers, probably of foreign regiments, about to attack, early eighteenth century. Grenadiers first put fascines over enemy picket lines so assault parties could more easily step over them. The figures are armed with curved sabres and wear either red coats with blue cuffs or blue coats with red cuffs, all with light brown gaiters. All are wear caps of the cuff's colour ending in a tassel and with the same colour lining (but shown somewhat darker) turned up. From a manuscript copy of Vauban's work dated 1714, Fort Ticonderoga. (Author's photo)

Grenadiers had the same uniforms as the rest of the regiment, although a number of distinctive features quickly appeared. As early as 1676, it was preferred that they wore moustaches, which were becoming uncommon in the increasingly clean-shaven fashion of Louis XIV's era; this was to make them look fierce. They were issued with sabres or hangers rather than the common soldier's sword. Besides the grenade bag, slings – *grenadières* – were added to their muskets many years before other soldiers had them so they could sling their musket when pitching grenades. Another adaptation was wearing cloth caps, since hat brims might get in the way. Vauban mentioned seeing a "guard of 50 men, all wearing grenadier caps" when visiting Camaret in July 1694. These caps were usually the coat's colour with the turn-up of the same, or of the facing colour or else trimmed with fur. Some of these caps became ornate during Louis' reign, but many grenadiers also simply had hats later on and caps are hardly seen in early eighteenth century French prints.[22]

### Drummers

These men were "armed with a drum" instead of a musket or a pike. Their role was to signal various events and orders from a repertoire of rolls in daily life as

---

22 Quoted in *Vauban, un militaire très civil, lettres* (Lyon: Scala, 2007). Outlandish mitre-shaped and fur grenadier caps were soon seen in Prussian, British, Spanish and other armies.

# FRENCH LINE INFANTRY

Infantry grenadier, late 1660s. Note the sizeable pouch for his grenades. Engraving in Manesson Mallet, *Les Travaux de Mars*, 1672. (Anne S.K. Brown Military Collection, Brown University Library, Providence, RI, USA. Author's photo)

Infantry officers and men marching, *c.* 1685-1690. The officers are shown carrying their spontoons and wearing *Mousquetaire*-type swords held by a shoulder bandolier. They have the sash, which was white, around the waist. The enlisted men hold their matchlock muskets over the shoulder and their *Mousquetaire*-type swords are in scabbards held by waist-belts, a new arrangement introduced from 1684. The shoulder belt holds a bullet bag. From a large brass medallion by Jean Régnaud and Pierre Le Nègre. (Musée du Louvre, Paris. Author's photo)

well as in battle. Be they part of a garrison in a fortress or on campaign in a camp, the deep and loud sound of their drums regulated daily life for everyone who could hear it. Every morning before the sun came out, one or more drummers of the night guard would, at the "point of the day" when the sun was about to emerge, beat *La Diane*, which was the wake-up call and signal that another day was starting. This was followed by *L'Assemblée* (the assembly) after the soldiers had woken and dressed, signalling unit inspections or drills. After the morning drum roll calls for inspections, breakfast and routine orders, the troops moving from one place to another would pack up, fold their tents, form their units and march on to the various calls of the drummers. In a garrison, the first sound of the day that many inhabitants of a fortress city heard was the drummer's call of *La Diane*. It was followed by churches who rang their bells at sunrise while the city's gates were opened and would later ring at various times of the day as clocks and watches were then quite uncommon. Many more drum rolls might be heard during the day, notably *Le Ban* that announced the public reading by an officer or an official of royal or municipal regulations and, occasionally, public sales and sentences for those guilty of crimes. By early evening, everyone would hear *La Retraite* (the retreat) that warned one and all that the city gates would be closed at sunset followed by *l'Ordre* (the order) once they were shut and locked up. There were other drum calls such as *La Prière* (the prayer) or *La Garde* (the guard) and, when the enemy was in sight, the alarmist *La Générale* (the general call) to muster. All these drum calls would be the same in an army camp out in the field. As can be seen, drummers (with occasionally fifers) were essential to an army's everyday life. On the rare occasions that a full-scale battle occurred, they would

## FRENCH LINE INFANTRY

French infantry, early eighteenth century. From the left: Du Roi Regiment fusilier, Picardie Regiment officer holding its colour and Limousin Regiment fusilier. Picardie's regimental colour was a white cross on a red field. Print after Lienhart and Humbert. (Private collection. Author's photo)

be at the sides or at the back of their battalions beating the appropriate signals as directed by senior officers.[23]

Influenced by nineteenth- and twentieth-century literature and cinema, people commonly think that drummers in bygone armies were very often teenage boys. Not so in France's royal armies. While reliable data appears at the end of the seventeenth century and muster rolls are consistent from 1716, the statistical analysis by Professor Corvisier of masses of such documents leaves no doubt that boy drummers were very few. Those that were appear to have usually originated as *enfants du régiment* (children of the regiment) who were the sons of soldiers making up about two percent of the enlisted soldiers in 1716 and even less later, the average being only one and half

---

23  Guignard, *L'École de Mars*, Vol. 1, pp.228–237 and Vol. 2, p.625.

Top left: a fusilier, *c.* 1684. He is aiming a quite long-barrelled musket and is equipped with a small ammunition pouch. Engraving in Manesson Mallet, *Les Travaux de Mars*, 1684. (nne S.K. Brown Military Collection, Brown University Library, Providence, RI, USA. Author's photo)

Above: infantry fusilier, early eighteenth century. Print after Watteau. (Private collection. Author's photo)

Left: an infantry soldier on a march, early eighteenth century. Note the sword used as a cane. Print after Watteau. (Anne S.K. Brown Military Collection, Brown University Library, Providence, RI, USA. Author's photo))

percent. As children, many were apparently introduced to playing drums, but it appears that very few persisted and simply enlisted as soldiers. Prints of the period show drummers as adult men presumed to be well over 16 years old. Whatever their age, they were very visible wearing their ornate uniforms in the livery colours of their colonel, be it the King's or the Prince's and the noble gentlemen that led them.[24]

**Private Soldiers**

The lives and duties of private soldiers need not be explained in detail. Theirs was a mixture of standing guard as sentries, drills and battalion manoeuvres when not marching from one place to the other. No literary skill was required therefore many were illiterate, as were great numbers of peasants and labourers in that era. Indeed, when off duty, some might earn a few welcome pennies as labourers. They had to be physically fit with a sharp mind to get through a rough life as soldiers. They knew they were the bulwark of the infantry, knew they had to be brave facing the enemy and hoped they had good generals to lead them on battlefield. When one studies the Sun King's wars, the common soldier's amazing fighting record in all circumstances is admirable. Even later in the reign when defeats could discourage conscripted men with a summary military experience, they did not waver and, in the end, prevailed.

---

24 André Corvisier, *Le soldat, de Louvois à Choiseul*, Vol. 2, pp.767–770. This is one of the most important works on the French army ever, and an extraordinary example to all. In the English language, the closest such outstanding study we have seen, although less extensive, is Andrew Edward Cormack's *'These Meritorious Objects of the Royal Bounty', The Chelsea Out-Pensioners in the Early Eighteenth Century* (London: author, 2017).

# 9

# Foreign Mercenary Troops

In all ages, but especially in the seventeenth and eighteenth centuries, European nations resorted to hiring mercenaries to serve in their armies. These troops were recruited following previously agreed-upon conditions. For instance the authorities in Swiss Cantons would permit a senior Swiss officer to make a "capitulation", which was a type of contract outlining obligations between, say, the King of France and a colonel to recruit foreign men for a defined period of service with the French armies. Although the French army long had mercenary units, their numbers had been unstable and very few were kept in peacetime. During the early part of Louis XIV's reign, foreign regiments continued to be raised and disbanded when hostilities ended. Following the 1659 peace with Spain, very few were left and, from 1661 when the King assumed personal rule, none were raised until Furstenberg's (German) regiment in March 1670, Royal-Italien (Italian) in March 1671, five English regiments in April 1671, four Swiss regiments in February 1672 and more thereafter including three Walloon regiments. Some were disbanded, but most were henceforth part of the permanent establishment of the French army of which they formed an increasingly substantial part. In early 1672, of the 176,000 men in the army, some 30,000 were foreign mercenary soldiers. This came to one soldier in five being a foreigner. Five years later, the number of foreign mercenaries had gone up to some 50,000 men in an army of 230,000 so the proportion of Frenchmen to foreigners remained about the same. In 1690, there were over 60,000 foreign troops in an army that was nearly at 300,000 men, or about one in five.[1]

The internal organisation of foreign regiments was generally similar regarding officers and enlisted men and their duties as for French line regiments. Some might have the title "royal" but it was an honorific appellation. Foreign regiments were administered according to the terms of the contract they had with the French government and were fully expected to turn a profit to their colonels/owners. Regiments had equivalents of the *prévôté* to address legal issues internally in their own language according to their nation's legal customs.

---

1   Quincy, *Histoire Militaire*, vol. 1, pp.311–312; BMA, Ms A1b, 1626, 'Tiroirs de Louis XIV'.

## FOREIGN MERCENARY TROOPS

Eugène-Maurice de Savoie, Duc de Carignan, c. 1670. He was made colonel general of the Swiss troops in 1657. Initially Comte de Soissons, he became Duc de Carignan in 1662, lieutenant general on 15 April 1672 and died on 6 June 1673 in Germany. He was the father of the famous Prince Eugene of Savoy (1663–1736), the great general of the Austrian imperial troops. (Courtesy National Museum, Stockholm. No. 15842)

The Swiss in particular came to form the most important contingent. It has been rightly stated by Corvisier that "they formed an army within the army" with its own elite corps: the Cent-Suisses and the Gardes-Suisses of the royal guard. They further had their own colonel general of Swiss infantry who was the representative of the army's Swiss troops to the King of France. While there were many Swiss units raised and disbanded in the earlier seventeenth century, it was from 1671 that truly permanent Swiss regiments were raised. In 1676, Swiss infantrymen already amounted to some 25,400 officers and men including 3,000 Cent-Suisse and Gardes-Suisses, the rest belonging in six line regiment and 40 independent companies of 200 men each. The establishment of Swiss regiments was traditionally much higher, hovering at some 200 men per company led by five officers. This also meant there were fewer officers in Swiss units for the same number of enlisted men; one for every 40 Swiss as compared to one for every 16 French. Company captains obviously had more responsibilities and thus more prestige, that

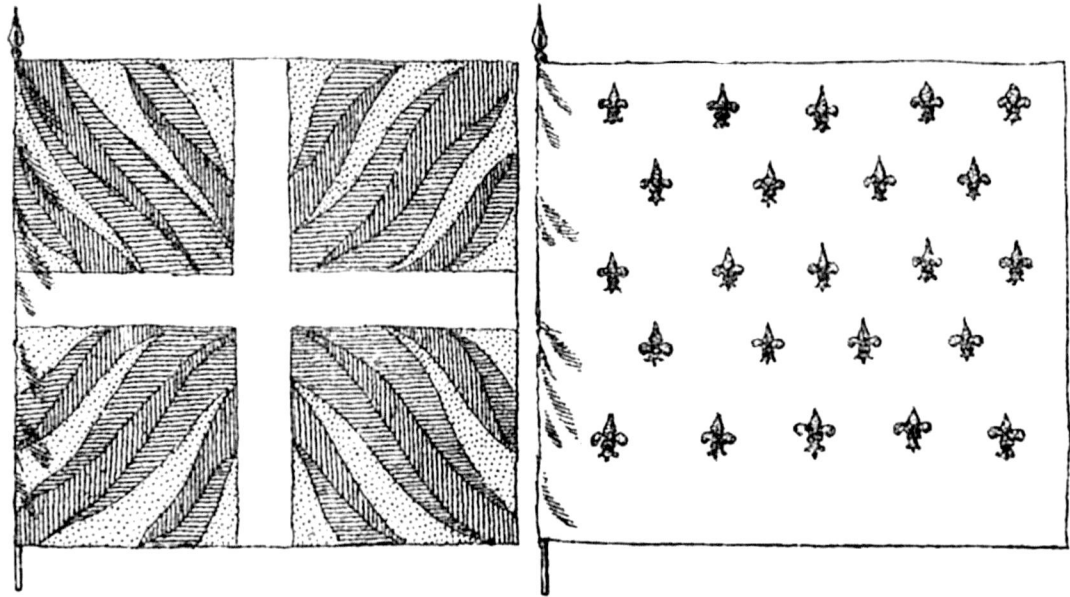

Regimental colour of the May (Swiss) Regiment and colonel's colour of Greder's (Swiss) Regiment, early eighteenth century. Yellow, blue and red for May; white with gold lilies for Greder. (Courtesy Rijksmuseum, Amsterdam. RP-P-OB-84.205)

was exemplified by the long-standing tradition of having their very own bodyguards called *trabans* (see below). The officers overwhelmingly originated from families that had contributed generations of officers to the French service, and Swiss royal guards officers often became field officers in a Swiss line infantry regiment.[2]

These Swiss units, along with other foreign units, were generally not disbanded (except for many independent companies) when peace came in 1678. By 1701, there were nine Swiss line infantry regiments, eight at 2,400 men each and the ninth, Pfyffer, with 1,800. Adding 3,700 men in the two the guard units brought up the total to 24,700 men. Thus, nearly half of the 54,350 Swiss mercenaries serving in European nations were in the French army. When they enlisted, their bounty was one-third higher than that of a French recruit and their pay was higher, but subject to their unit's "capitulation" agreement with the French government. Most were recruited in Catholic cantons of Switzerland, but Protestants were also admitted and had chaplains of their faith.[3]

Amongst the mercenary foreign troops, the Swiss were renowned as very brave, disciplined, steadfast and reliable soldiers so they were expensive troops. Minister of War Louvois at a meeting with the King told him that, with all the gold that the Swiss had received from the kings of France, a paved road could have been built between Paris and Basel. Colonel Pierre Stuppa was also present and he interjected: "Sire, that may be true, but if we could gather all the blood that the men of my nation have shed in the service of Your Majesty and his royal predecessors, it could also fill a canal going from Paris to Basel."[4]

---

2   André Corvisier, *Les hommes, la guerre et la mort* (Paris: Economica, 1985), p.201.
3   P. de Vallière, *Treue und ehre Geschichte der schweitzer in fremden diensten* (Nuremberg: F. Zahn, 1912), pp.316, 346. The Netherlands had the next largest contingent at 11,200 men, Spain had 6,400, Savoy 4,925, Austria 4,800, Poland 2,000, Rome (Papal State) 200 and Prussia 125.
4   Eugène Fieffé, *Histoire des troupes étrangères au service de la France*, Vol. 1, p.x.

Plate 1

(L–R): Conti Regiment, *pertuisanier*, c. 1660–1670; Lyonnois, sergeant, 1666; La Reine Regiment, drummer, c. 1661–1675

(Illustration by Ed Dovey, © Helion & Company)

*See Colour Plate Commentaries for further information.*

Plate 2

**(L–R): Douglas Scottish Regiment, fusilier, 1672; infantry musketeer back view, c. 1673–1680; Vierzet Walloon Regiment, field officer, 1679**

(Illustration by Ed Dovey, © Helion & Company)

*See Colour Plate Commentaries for further information.*

Plate 3

(L–R): Montroux Italian Regiment, sergeant, *c.* 1690–1702; Stuppa Swiss Regiment, fusilier, *c.* 1690–1695; Condé Infantry Regiment, drummer, *c.* 1685–1695
(Illustration by Ed Dovey, © Helion & Company)
*See Colour Plate Commentaries for further information.*

Plate 4

**(L–R): Rouergue Regiment, fusilier, *c.* 1695–1700; La Mark German Regiment, fusilier, *c.* 1702; Orléannois Regiment, officer, 1699**
(Illustration by Ed Dovey, © Helion & Company)
*See Colour Plate Commentaries for further information.*

**(L–R): Viverais Regiment, sergeant, *c.* 1705; Franclieu Regiment, drummer, *c.* 1707–1705; Royal-Roussillon Regiment, fusilier, early 18th century**

(Illustration by Ed Dovey, © Helion & Company)

*See Colour Plate Commentaries for further information.*

Infantrymen, mid 17th century. These two musketeers and a pikeman are based on a print after Lostelneau's *Le Mareschal des Batailles* (Paris, 1647). The pikeman is at the *Pique en défense contre la cavallerie* (pike in defence against cavalry) position. At this time pikemen made up half of the infantry battalions. Print after Marbot. (Canadian War Museum, Ottawa. Author's photo)

Infantry musketeers, 1660s. Watercolour after Lucien Rousselot. (Courtesy Yves Martin collection and photo)

Plate 8

Infantry pikemen, 1660s. Watercolour after Lucien Rousselot.
(Courtesy Yves Martin collection and photo)

Plate 9

Infantry musketeers, 1670s. Watercolour after Lucien Rousselot.
(Courtesy Yves Martin collection and photo)

A pikeman at the siege of Cambrai, 1677. From his armour edged with a gold border, he might be an offcer or a NCO. Detail from a mural painting made between 1677 and 1680, in the dining halls of the Invalides in Paris. (Author's photo)

Plate 11

Infantrymen on campaign, 1670s. From the uniform colours, these appear to be foreign troops in French pay. Some details are rather odd and are probably the result of later restorations. Detail from a mural painting done between 1677 and 1680 in the dining halls of the Invalides in Paris. (Author's photo)

Plate 12

Troops in camp, 1670s. Several pikemen are in the foreground, those wearing helmets might be Swiss. Painting at the Musée Condé, Chantilly. (Author's photo)

Plate 13

A possible officer's coat, 1680s. Blue with red cuffs and lining, gold lace and buttons. What appear to be the sleeves of a waistcoat are in fact just lower false sleeves. (Courtesy Royal Army Museum, Stockholm. AM.017482)

Plate 14

Pikemen of Stuppa's Swiss Regiment, 1680s and 1690s. Watercolour by Herbert Knotel. (Anne S.K. Brown Military Collection, Brown University Library, Providence, RI, USA. Author's photo)

Plate 15

Infantry pikemen, 1680s and 1690s. Pikemen in French infantry regiments had generally abandoned helmets and tassets by the last quarter of the 17th century. Watercolour after Lucien Rousselot. (Courtesy Yves Martin collection and photo)

Plate 16

Right: infantry soldier, probably belonging to the Régiment du Roi, 1690s. Pipe smoking was widespread in the army. Print after JOB, from a contemporary image. (Private collection. Author's photo)

Left: infantry sergeant, probably belonging to the Régiment du Roi, 1690s. Print after JOB, from a contemporary image. (Private collection. Author's photo)

Plate 17

Right: a soldier with some chickens, a pan and a long spit, 1690s. Probably the squad's cook. Note the several clay pipes on his hat. Print after JOB, from a contemporary image. (Private collection. Author's photo)

Below: fifer of a gentlemen's regiment, 1690s. These regiments were named after their colonels and their drummers and fifers wore the colonel's livery, in this case red lined with blue. Print after JOB, from a contemporary image. (Private collection. Author's photo)

Below: drummer wearing the royal livery, 1690s. He would belong to a royal or a provincially-named regiment, perhaps Languedoc or Berry. It was the practice to paint drum cases the same colour as the coat. Print after JOB, from a contemporary image. (Private collection. Author's photo)

Infantry musketeers, 1690 and 1695. Both are still armed with matchlock muskets and plug bayonets. Tricorn hats are coming into fashion. Watercolour after Lucien Rousselot. (Courtesy Yves Martin collection and photo)

Plate 19

Infantry musketeers, 1695 and 1700. One (at right) still has a matchlock, but with a socket bayonet. The other is a fusilier. Watercolour after Lucien Rousselot. (Courtesy Yves Martin collection and photo)

Plate 20

Infantry fusiliers, 1700 and 1705. Watercolour after Lucien Rousselot. (Courtesy Yves Martin collection and photo)

Plate 21

Left: infantry fusilier, *c.* 1705–1710. Fully equipped in marching order, with his accoutrements and ammunition pouch and his haversack for all his belongings. Watercolour by R. Marrion. (Private collection. Author's photo)

Right: captain, Piémont Infantry Regiment, early 18th century. He wears a white or grey-white coat with black cuffs, gold lace and buttons, red stockings, gilt gorget below the neck and holding his spontoon indicating he is on duty. Captains had gold edging lace on the coat. The Piémont Regiment's officers and NCOs had a tradition of having black cuffs to match the black regimental colours, adopted in mourning of beloved Colonel General de Brissac killed in 1585. Watercolour by R. Marrion. (Private collection. Author's photo)

Plate 22

Infantry fusiliers, early 18th century. At left, a fusilier of the Saint-Germain-Beaupré Regiment, *c.* 1705; at right, a fusilier of the Hainault Regiment, *c.* 1710–1715. Watercolour after Lucien Rousselot. (Courtesy Yves Martin collection and photo)

Plate 23

The Rouergue Infantry Regiment, early 18th century. Gaiters, which were made locally by unit, became popular during the War of the Spanish Succession. Watercolour after Lucien Rousselot. (Courtesy Yves Martin collection and photo)

Plate 24

Drummers of the Lyonnais, Dauphin and Boufflers regiments, early 18th century. The King allowed Lyonnais' drummers to wear the green livery of the Villeroi family, which they did until 1734. Print after Lucien Rousselot. (Private collection. Author's photo)

Trophy of colours associated with the Bussy-Rabutin family, reigns of Louis XIII and early Louis XIV. The exact identity of the regiments is uncertain, but it could be associated with the Bussy-Rabutin Infantry Regiment which fought at Rocroi in 1643. The quarters of the large infantry colours to the right have stripes in the red, white and blue hues of the family coat of arms. An orb at the centre of the cross which bears the motto *Concussus Surge* (I strike). Another panel has a generally similar colour, but the bars are slightly wavy, a red star laid on red flames is at the centre of the cross with a different and indistinct motto. The flags are set in a pseudo-Roman scene. Ceiling mural painting at the Château de Bussy-Rabitin, Burgundy. (Author's photo)

Plate 26

Left: ensign, Limousin Regiment, early 18th century. The regimental colours had orange, green and red quarters. Grey coat with red cuffs, gold buttons and lace. Print after Philippoteaux. (Courtesy New York Public Library, New York City)

Right: ensign, Royal-Vaisseaux Regiment, c. 1705. The rendering of a ship at the centre of the colour identifies the regiment – "Vaisseaux" in French is ship of the line – which is a reminder of its maritime origins. Print after Philippoteaux. (Anne S.K. Brown Military Collection, Brown University Library, Providence, RI, USA. Author's photo)

Plate 27

Right: ensign, La Sarre Regiment, early 18th century. White cross, quarters black and dark red. Grey-white coat with blue cuffs, red waistcoat, gold buttons and lace. Print after Philippoteaux. (Courtesy New York Public Library, New York City)

Left: ensign, La Reine Regiment, early 18th century. The quarters were 1 and 4 green, 2 and 3 black, the cross had gold lilies and crowns. Grey coat with red cuffs, blue waistcoat, silver buttons and lace. Print after Philippoteaux. (Courtesy New York Public Library, New York City)

Plate 28

Ensigns, Bourbon Regiment, early 18th century. Grey-white coat, red cuffs, lining, waistcoat, breeches and stockings, silver buttons and lace. All white colonel's colour. Regimental colour: white cross with blue, red, grey and brown quarters. Print after Delaître. (Private collection. Author's photo)

Plate 29

Left: regimental colour of the La Couronne, early 18th century. Blue field, a white cross with a large gold crown with red lining at its centre. (Anne S.K. Brown Military Collection, Brown University Library, Providence, RI, USA. Author's photo)

Left: regimental colour of the Dauphin Regiment, early 18th century. (Anne S.K. Brown Military Collection, Brown University Library, Providence, RI, USA. Author's photo)

Left: regimental colours of the Duc d'Anjou Regiment, early 18th century. Quarters: 1 and 4 yellow and red, 2 and 3 blue and red, border red, yellow, blue. (Anne S.K. Brown Military Collection, Brown University Library, Providence, RI, USA. Author's photo)

Right: regimental colours of the Bretagne Regiment, early 18th century. Quarters: 1 and 4 orange, 2 and 3 black. (Anne S.K. Brown Military Collection, Brown University Library, Providence, RI, USA. Author's photo)

Right: colonel's colour of the Royal-Bavière German Regiment, early 18th century. Several foreign units had saintly figures on their colonel's colours. (Anne S.K. Brown Military Collection, Brown University Library, Providence, RI, USA. Author's photo)

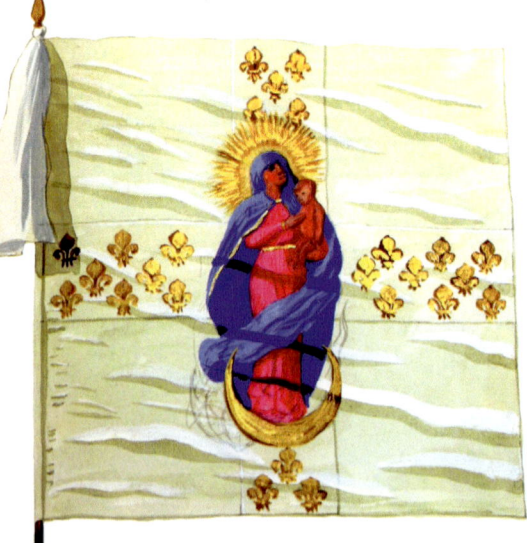

Left: regimental colours of the La Mark German Regiment, early 18th century. (Anne S.K. Brown Military Collection, Brown University Library, Providence, RI, USA. Author's photo)

Plate 31

Below:
Regimental colours of the Belzunce Regiment, early 18th century. Said to have been taken in Flanders during 1706. (Courtesy Rijksmuseum, Amsterdam)

Regimental colours of the Barrois Regiment, early 18th century. Said to have been taken in Flanders during 1706. (Courtesy Rijksmuseum, Amsterdam)

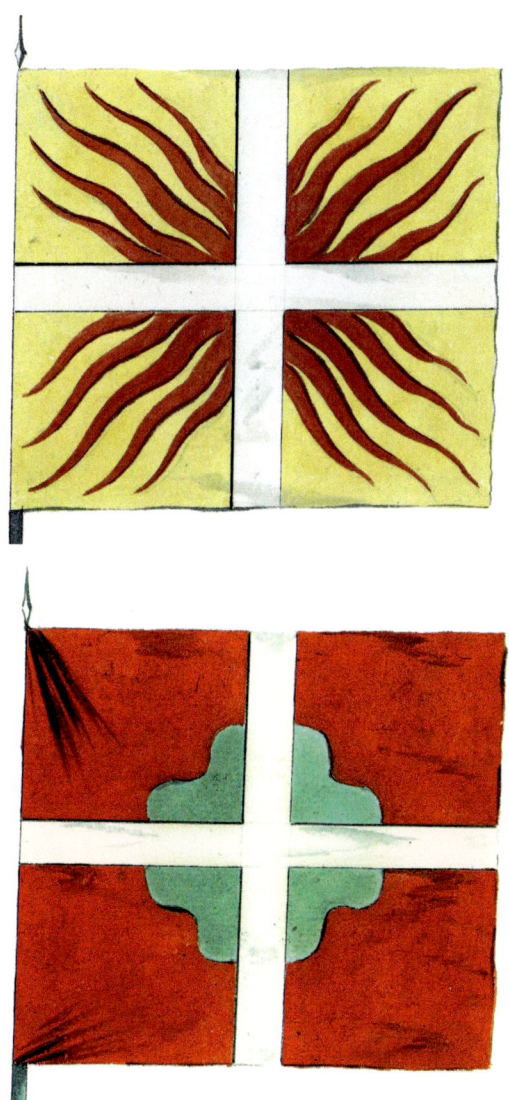

Above:
Regimental colour, Greder's German Regiment early 18th century. Print based on a colour at Geneva's Musée d'Art et d'Histoire. The field has red triangles and chevrons with small white trianges and white and light green bars, the centre badge has a blue field with gold crown, lilies and wreath with red ribbon and crown's cap. (Private collection. Author's photo)

Regimental colours of Brendlé's Swiss Regiment, early 18th century. This colour is said to have been taken in Flanders during 1706. (Courtesy Rijksmuseum, Amsterdam. RP-P-OB-84.205)

## Plate 32

Right: Regimental colour of the Périgord Regiment, early 18th century. Said to have been taken in 1706. Other illustrations show the points of the quarters pointing up and down. (Courtesy Rijksmuseum, Amsterdam. BI-B-FM-071-62)

Left: regimental colours of the Berry Regiment, early 18th century. Said to have been taken in Flanders during 1706. (Courtesy Rijksmuseum, Amsterdam. BI-B-FM-071-77)

Left: regimental colour of the Houdelot Regiment, early 18th century. This colour is said to have been taken in 1706. Green, red and yellow for Houdelot's. (Courtesy Rijksmuseum, Amsterdam. BI-B-FM-071-75)

Right: Regimental colours of the Sourches Regiment, early 18th century. This colour is said to have been taken in 1703. The regiment then served in Flanders. (Courtesy Rijksmuseum, Amsterdam. BI-B-FM-071-7)

# FOREIGN MERCENARY TROOPS

Left: Lieutenant General Johann Jakob von Erlach (1628–1694), *c.* 1690. He was the first commander of the Erlach Bernese Regiment in the French army from 1671 to 1694. He also became brigadier in 1671, major general in 1678 and lieutenant general in 1688; he converted to the Roman Catholic, faith thus losing his titles and citizenship in Bern, but was then welcomed by Fribourg as a patrician. Print after P. Favre. (Anne S.K. Brown Military Collection, Brown University Library, Providence, RI, USA. Author's photo)

Above: Colonel Jean Rodolphe Salis-Zizers (1610–1690), *c.* 1670. Colonel of the Salis Regiment, rose to major general in the French army. Print after portrait. (Private collection. Author's photo)

Left: Colonel Albert von Manuel (1640–1701). Officer in Erlach's Regiment, he succeeded General Erlach in its command during 1694 and led it with distinction in Catalonia. Print after a 1672 portrait. (Private collection. Author's photo)

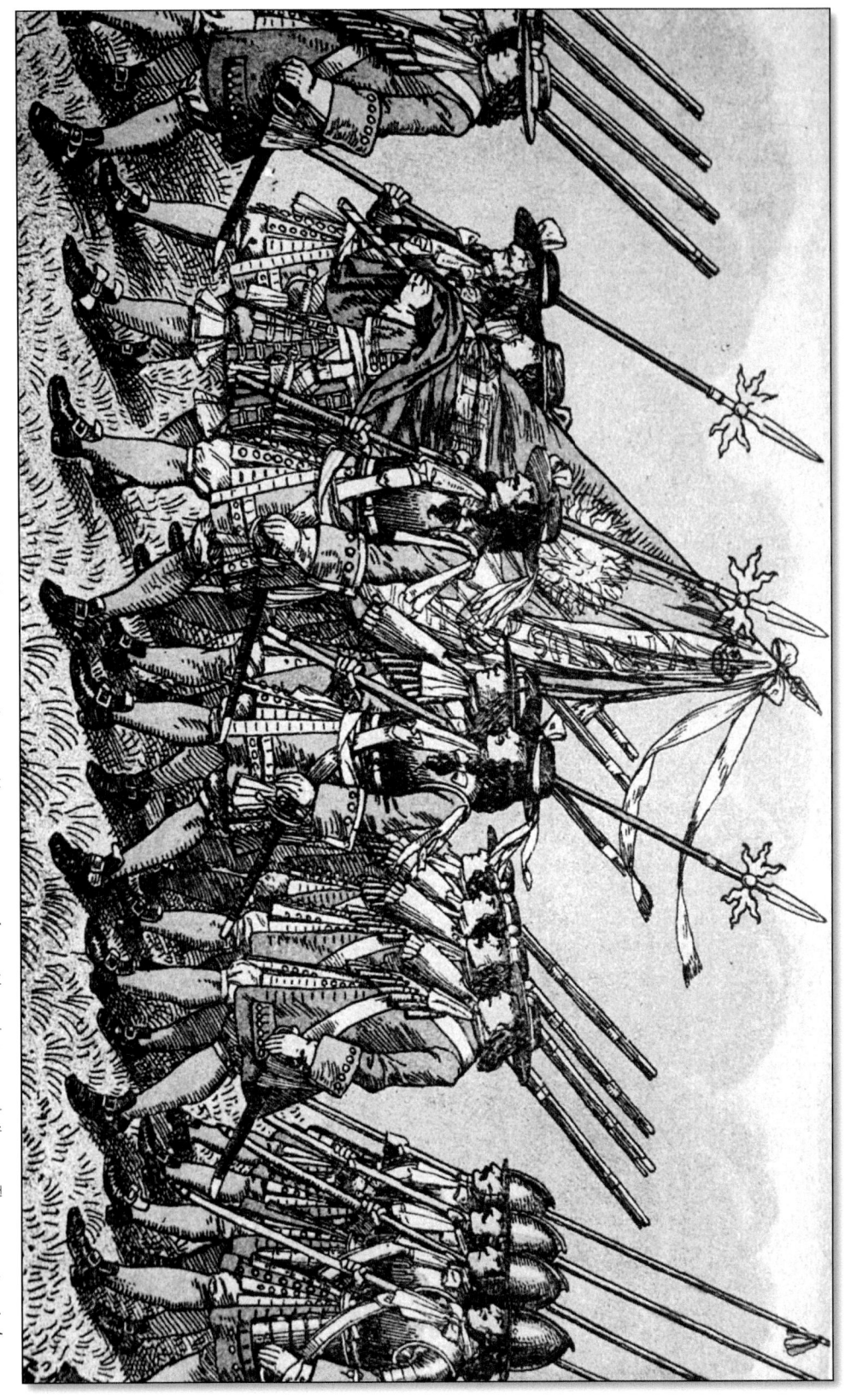

Soldiers of Erlach's Swiss Regiment, 1670s. At centre, a regimental colour held by an ensign and escorted by sergeants or *trabans* with musketeers and pikemen. The sergeants or *trabans* would have worn all red coats probably laced with silver, the musketeers and pikemen grey coats with red cuffs and all with red stockings. The colour had a blue field with a white St Andrew's cross, gold sun (left) and crossed swords (right, not visible), crowns and lilies at top and bottom (not visible). Print after Lederey. (Anne S.K. Brown Military Collection, Brown University Library, Providence, RI, USA. Author's photo)

## FOREIGN MERCENARY TROOPS

Sergeant, Erlach's Swiss Regiment, 1680s. This regiment's sergeants wore all-red coats and polished steel cuirasses. In the background behind the main figure, two more men drill soldiers wearing grey coats with red cuff and stockings. Print after Walter Meier Thalwil. (Courtesy Anne S.K. Brown Military Collection, Brown University Library, Providence, RI, USA)

Right: drum of a Swiss regiment. eighteenth century. Swiss units usually had their drums painted with the emblematic wavy flames as in this example, with red and pale yellow or yellowish cream white flames and hoops. These were traditionally of the commander's livery colour. Of the Swiss regiments, the closest would be Brendlé's which had red and yellow flames on its colours. (Musée de l'Armée, Paris. Author's photo)

Above: pikeman of a Swiss regiment, *c.* 1672. Swiss pikemen in French service kept wearing steel helmets and tassets attached to the bottom of their breastplates, a practice abandoned by French pikemen. Detail from a print in Mallet's 1872, **Les Travaux de Mars**. (Anne S.K. Brown Military Collection, Brown University Library, Providence, RI, USA. Author's photo)

Right: Swiss pikeman and musketeer, 1695. The original caption includes: "They only serve in the infantry, but render good services especially in sieges." Print after Guérard. (Anne S.K. Brown Military Collection, Brown University Library, Providence, RI, USA. Author's photo)

# FOREIGN MERCENARY TROOPS

Officer's gorget for a Swiss regiment of the French army, early eighteenth century. Silver with gilded royal monogram and crown. Print after J. Hilpbert. (Private collection. Author's photo)

The Swiss troops had a few other peculiarities when compared to French or other foreign troops. As noted above, officers had *trabans*. It was an enlisted man's rank mostly peculiar to Swiss and German infantry regiments, which, in German, meant a guard. They were the loosely approximate equivalents of *pertuisaniers* in French infantry regiments that were abolished in 1670. *Trabans* were not affected by this and they remained in Swiss units until the end of the eighteenth century. *Trabans* (sometimes spelt *Drabans*) were said to be originally the guards of the company's pay chest and evolved into being the guards of captains. In battle, their duty was to be near their captain. Every Swiss company had four *trabans* armed with partisans or halberds. They were also visually distinctive in that, according to Daniel, "… the [*trabans* wore] … the livery of their colonels like the drummers and fifers" rather than the regimental uniform.[5]

Although grenadiers appeared in the French infantry in the later 1660s, the Swiss did not have them until 1691. That year, Pierre Stuppa proposed to the King that Swiss regiments should also have grenadiers; the King agreed and 20 of the best soldiers with a sergeant in each company were chosen in each company to form grenadier companies led by elite officers in each regiment. Conversely, pikemen in Swiss regiments lasted slightly longer than

---

5   Daniel, *Histoire de la milice françoise*, Vol. 2, p.226; Baron de Zurlauben, *Histoire Militaire des Suisses* (Paris: Desaint, Saillant and Herissant, 1751), Vol. 1, pp.236–237. Zurlauben added that *trabants* in Swiss independent companies wore the captain's livery.

Colonel's colour of Greder's German Regiment, early eighteenth century. Furstenberg's (also German) had a similar colonel's colour. White strewn with gold lilies, gold sun and letters on blue ribbon lined red, blue globe strewn with gold stars, silver band with gold stars. (Private collection. Author's photo)

in the French infantry, the last finally exchanging their pikes for flintlock muskets during 1703–1704.[6]

German regiments were usually recruited in the states of allied princes and were generally made up of Catholics. There was a variable number of regiments with about half a dozen being a good average at the end of the seventeenth century. In 1691 Alsace had 26 companies, Zurlauben 22, Surbeck 18, Greder 14, Liesler 10 and Yoël (Danish) 14 – this latter was actually on the German establishment although its colonel was the natural son of the King of Denmark. German establishment companies stood at about 100 men although this could vary. In 1691, these regiments mustered 458 officers and 10,000 NCOs and privates. German soldiers had a reputation for being very faithful, loyal and quite brave. They were very well drilled and in battle, their salvos were remarkably steady and effective.

Italian regiments came from various states in what is now unified Italy. Royal-Italien was raised in Florence, Parma and Modena during 1671 and others later. By about 1690–1691, Royal-Italien mustered 16 companies of 100 men each. Recruited in Piémont were Royal-Monferrat at 18 companies of 50 men, Santena at 20 of 50 men, Montroux at 16 of 100 men, Thouy and

---

6    Baron de Zurlauben, *Histoire Militaire des Suisses*, Vol. 1, pp.323–324.

## FOREIGN MERCENARY TROOPS

Above: ensign of Sparre's German Regiment, early eighteenth century. The regiment colour has a blue field with gauge gold lilies and a white cross. The uniform was grey with blue cuffs, waistcoat, breeches and stockings, gold buttons and buttonhole lace, gold hat lace and white puma border. Print after C. Boode. (Anne S.K. Brown Military Collection, Brown University Library, Providence, RI, USA. Author's photo)

Above: ensign, Alsace German Regiment, early eighteenth century. The regimental colours had 1 and 4 green, 2 and 3 brown quarters. Blue coat with red cuffs, silver buttons and lace. Print after Philippoteaux. (Courtesy New York Public Library, New York City)

Left: Royal-Italien Regiment, ensign, early eighteenth century. The uniform was brown with red cuffs, gold buttons and lace for officers. The colour was red and brown with gold lilies on the white cross. Print after Philippoteaux. (Anne S.K. Brown Military Collection, Brown University Library, Providence, RI, USA. Author's photo)

Royal Savoie at the same strength, Nice at 12 companies of 100 men. One of the lesser known is Perri's, from Corsica, raised in 1693 at 16 companies of 50 men each, disbanded in 1682, raised again in 1690 and participating in many campaigns. All Italian units were considered good fighting troops.[7]

There were Walloon units recruited in present-day southern Belgium at various times in the French army. In about 1690, there were five: Famechon raised in 1677 and Solre, Rebecque, Poitiers and Mérode dating from 1688. The strength of Walloon regiments amounted to 399 officers and 5,900 NCOs and men distributed in 118 companies of 50 men each. Their colonels were from the Walloon gentry and they had a good reputation in combat.[8]

Mercenary regiments from Great Britain served in the French army before 1678. The best known is the Douglas (Scottish) Regiment that entered French service in 1633 as Hepburn's until 1637 when led by Lord James Douglas and his family's successors. It served in Italy, Flanders and in the King's army during the Fronde and the war with Spain that ended in 1659. Briefly repatriated to England during the War of Devolution, the regiment was quartered at Rye until October 1667 when it went back to France. The regiment then had 15 companies of 100 men each plus about 100 officers and staff. It was a distinguished unit on campaign and lauded by Marshal Turenne. It left the French army's establishment in 1678 and was incorporated into the British army that year. In 1685, years after it had left French for British service, Louis XIV granted pensions and bonuses to its officers for the regiment's outstanding conduct at the siege of Trier. By contrast, Monmouth's English Regiment was noted in 1677 by Louvois as "being so badly disciplined that it destabilises the whole army where it is by its bad example", while it was feared that the Royal-Anglais Regiment "will never be good."[9]

There were also a number of much more obscure Scots units that may have been recruited, but not formed during 1643. Campbell's raised on 20 June 1653 served in Catalonia before being merged into Royal-Irlandais on 6 January 1657, which seems to indicate that this officially Irish unit mustered a lot of Scotsmen. The same may be true for Hamilton's raised in 1671, supposedly "English" according to Susane, which is suspicious because it was raised by George, Earl of Hamilton and Abercorn, a Scottish peer. It served in the Netherlands and in Germany until 1678 when merged into Furstenberg's German Regiment on 10 March 1678. Still later, in 1692, some 150 Scots officers arrived in France following the crushed revolt in the Highlands and fought with French troops in many engagements thereafter.[10]

---

7   Xavier Poli, *Histoire Militaire des Corses* (Ajjacio and Bastia, 1900), pp.10–85 gives a detailed account of Corsican regiments.
8   Jules Brenne, 'Un régiment du Nord, Isenghien-Wallon 1697–1717', *Revue du Nord*, Vol. 50, juillet– septembre 1968, pp.417–433, gives details on the organisation and services of this unit.
9   *Calendar of State Papers*, (London: HMSO, 1866), Vol. 219, pp.506, 522. It left Rye "to the great satisfaction of the people there, whom they abused shamefully, notwithstanding the civility and courtesy shown in quartering them for the most part in private houses. The officers are most to blame, having encouraged them in their baseness.", Lawrence Weaver, *The Story of the Royal Scots* (London: Country Life, 1915), pp.21–33; Rousset, *Histoire de Louvois*, Vol. 2, p.277.
10  On Scots in France during the reign of Louis XIV, see notably: Stephen Wood, *The Auld Alliance* (Edinburg: Mainstream, 1989), pp.56–59; Francisque-Michel, *Les Écossais en France, les Français*

Finally, the great majority of Irish troops are not represented in this volume, but will be in Volume 3. Apart from some short-lived units in the earlier seventeenth century, Irish soldiers in France were not mercenaries. They were refugees that came in large numbers from 1689 and whose survivors formed peculiar military establishments alongside and within the French army. Unlike mercenary soldiers, they could not go back to their native land. They eventually settled and amalgamated into French society.

The Irish mercenary regiments that existed between 1643 and 1664 were the result of various recruiting ventures from Irish officers wishing to provide France with soldiers from 1635 during the Thirty Years' War. This was an era of civil wars and religious strife in Ireland compounded by the ambivalent attitude of the British Parliament; thus many mercenaries were recruited, but often were not allowed to go to France. There were two peak periods leading to the actual formation of Irish mercenary regiments: 1635–1639 and 1652–1653, this last period being actually part of an exodus encouraged by Cromwell giving full freedom and authority to any officer who was with the Irish to raise as many men as they wished to go and serve foreign princes. As a result, a flow of Irish soldiers arrived in France during 1653 and were incorporated into existing units or formed into new regiments. The 1655 treaty of alliance between England and France naturally cooled the prospects of recruiting further mercenaries in Ireland. In all, it is estimated that about 10,000 served in France between 1635 and 1664, about half of them from 1643.[11]

Lord George Douglas, Earl of Dumbarton (1630–92), c. 1670. He was colonel of Douglas's Scottish Regiment from 1653 to 1688. The regiment was in the French army's foreign establishment from 1653 to 1666 and from late 1667 to 1677. Print after portrait. (Private collection. Author's photo)

en Écosse (Paris: A. Franck, 1862), Vol. 2, pp.366–367 and chapters 35, 36 and 37.
11 Pierre Gouhier, 'Mercenaires irlandais au service de la France 1635–1664', *Revue d'histoire moderne et contemporaine*, XV, octobre-décembre 1968, pp.672–690. This excellent study from primary sources is much recommended for this topic.

# 10

# Infantry Weapons

Infantrymen of the Sun King were armed with a variety of weapons that, except for swords, defined their duties in battle.

## Swords

Of all the weapons a soldier carried, only the sword was common to all, be they officers, NCOs or enlisted men. Indeed, the sword was the insignia of a man-at-arms, no matter what his rank was in society or in the army. It was indeed an attraction for a lowly young peasant to join the army and have the cheap infantry sword issued to him more as a status symbol than as an effective weapon. Before and during the Sun King's reign, there was legislation in France forbidding commoners to have swords. It was a privilege of noblemen, gentlemen and all members of the armed forces.

A sword could kill, but it was not the main weapon for that purpose. Indeed, there were severe penalties imposed by Louis XIV on anyone using it in duels and, while it did not totally vanish, duelling with sword (or pistol) was greatly reduced during his reign. On the battlefield, it seems to have been something of a last resort weapon like other edged weapons (except bayonets) that slowly lost their efficacy during the seventeenth and early eighteenth centuries.

Of the types of swords, rapiers would have been common up to the 1650s when the elegant *à la Mousquetaire* (musketeer) type appeared and became the universal sword in fashion for the following century. This type of sword featured a single-branched brass hilt with a *pas-d'âne*, as the double curved projections bellow the grip is called, and a brass-dished bilobate counterguard. The sword's blade was double edged and about 70 to 75cm long. The guard was nearly always of brass for French private infantrymen and could be mass produced relatively cheaply. The swords issued to sergeants were of better quality with their hilts being usually gilded and the blades sometimes featuring engravings. At the other end of the scale, officers had as fine quality swords as they could afford, for it was equally the noble example of a gentleman.

Grenadiers had a stronger version, sometime with a curved blade and sometimes not, that made it a better fighting weapon. It was often rightly

# INFANTRY WEAPONS

A bove: infantry soldier's sword hilt, second half of the seventeenth century and early eighteenth century. This was the basic universal style, called *à la Mousquetaire* (Musketeer), used in the French and eventually all European armies. This plain but solid brass hilt has a brass grip. The blade was usually of a low grade steel. Former C. Ariès collection. (Courtesy National Historic Sites, Parks Canada)

Left: "Soldier on Guard", 1670s. Although he is well dressed with plumed hat, shoulder knot and a decorated shoulder sword belt, he is a corporal or private musketeer since he wears a shoulder bandolier with hanging powder bottles. Various edges weapons are crudely shown. Print after Gaya's 1678 *Traité des Armes*. (Author's photo)

defined as a sabre, but also then commonly called an *épée forte* (strong sword) that was generally similar to a cavalry sword (see Vol. 3) and, indeed, interchangeable with heavy cavalrymen that carried such swords. It was wielded, usually with success, by infantry grenadiers in assaults and quickly became one of their distinguishing features.

Foreign troops might also have musketeer-type swords and also *à la Wallonne* (Walloon) swords that were sturdier with several branches to their iron guards. French infantry NCOs usually had gilded hilts. As for officers, they carried swords of the musketeer type.[1]

---

1   For swords, interested readers will want to consult the authoritative and beautifully illustrated work by Michel Pétard, *Des sabres et des épées* (Nantes: Éditions de Canonnier, 1999), vol. 1 which covers the Ancient Régime. Regarding luxury, the Sun King once commented on the diamonds decorating the sword guard of the noble owner of one of the kingdom's greatest vineyards, who is said to have replied 'Sire, they are only rocks of my vineyard.'

## Polearms

The *armes d'hast*, as polearms are called in French, were the various sorts of pikes with unusual names used by infantrymen. In seventeenth century armies, polearms were common weapons and the main one for many soldiers was the pike. In the middle of the century, up to half and certainly a third of a battalion's soldiers were pikemen. They carried swords and most of all, the long pikes that could be 18 feet (5.84m) long, until 1686 when they were reduced to 13 feet (14 for Swiss infantry); grouped in the centre of the battalion, they formed a lethal-looking monolith between musketeers at their left and right as they marched into battle with pikes eventually levelled to charge or counter cavalry. The rising importance of firepower and the general introduction of bayonets during the second half of the seventeenth century saw the gradual decrease and final demise of pikes as an effective weapon. By 26 June 1688, a royal order specified there had to be 10 pikemen per company. The official introduction of socket bayonets from 28 November 1689 sealed their disappearance and pikemen were not mentioned in the royal order of October 1691 regarding the composition of infantry companies. They were officially recognised by an order of 1 October 1692 at six per company, but one wonders if many regiments had them at that time or for much longer thereafter. They were not mentioned at the 1698 Compiègne review and, finally, were officially abolished on 1 October 1703.[2]

Pikes were not the only polearms in armies of the time. Sergeants were armed with halberds. They consisted of a pike about 2.10m high with the head having a fairly wide blade at the top, under which was an axe blade on one side and a small horizontal wavy blade on the other side. This type of halberd head was slowly replaced during the Sun King's reign by another small wavy blade replacing the axe blade side. Most halberd heads appear to have been plain, but some surviving examples have engravings.

The officer's weapon was the *esponton*, or spontoon or half-pike to be carried by all infantry company and regimental officers. During the seventeenth century, some officers procured for themselves increasingly short spontoons, too short for the taste of Louis XIV who specified in a royal order of 1690 that this polearm was to be between 2.27 and 2.60m high. The spontoon's head was a spear that was often decorated with fine engravings and might also have some gilding. Generals and staff officers did not carry spontoons. Nevertheless, these remained, with swords, as infantry regimental officer's official weapons until the last years of the reign when, as seen below, some exceptions were made, but not sustained thereafter.[3]

There were a few *pertuisaniers* and, in Swiss and German units, *trabans*, in each company who were elite soldiers that, as seen previously, acted as captain's

---

2  François Bonnefoy, *Les armes de guerre portatives en France, du début du règne de Louis XIV à la veille de la Révolution (1660–1789)*, (Paris, Librairie de l'Inde, 1991), Vol. 1, pp.26–27, 141.

3  Order of 10 May 1690 on halberds and officers' spontoons. Halberds and spontoons were finally abolished in the later 1750s and early 1760s. George Snook, *The Halberd and other European Polearms 1300–1650* (Bloomfield, Ontario: Museum Restoration Service, 1998). A short but very good work on the origins of many types of polearms.

## INFANTRY WEAPONS

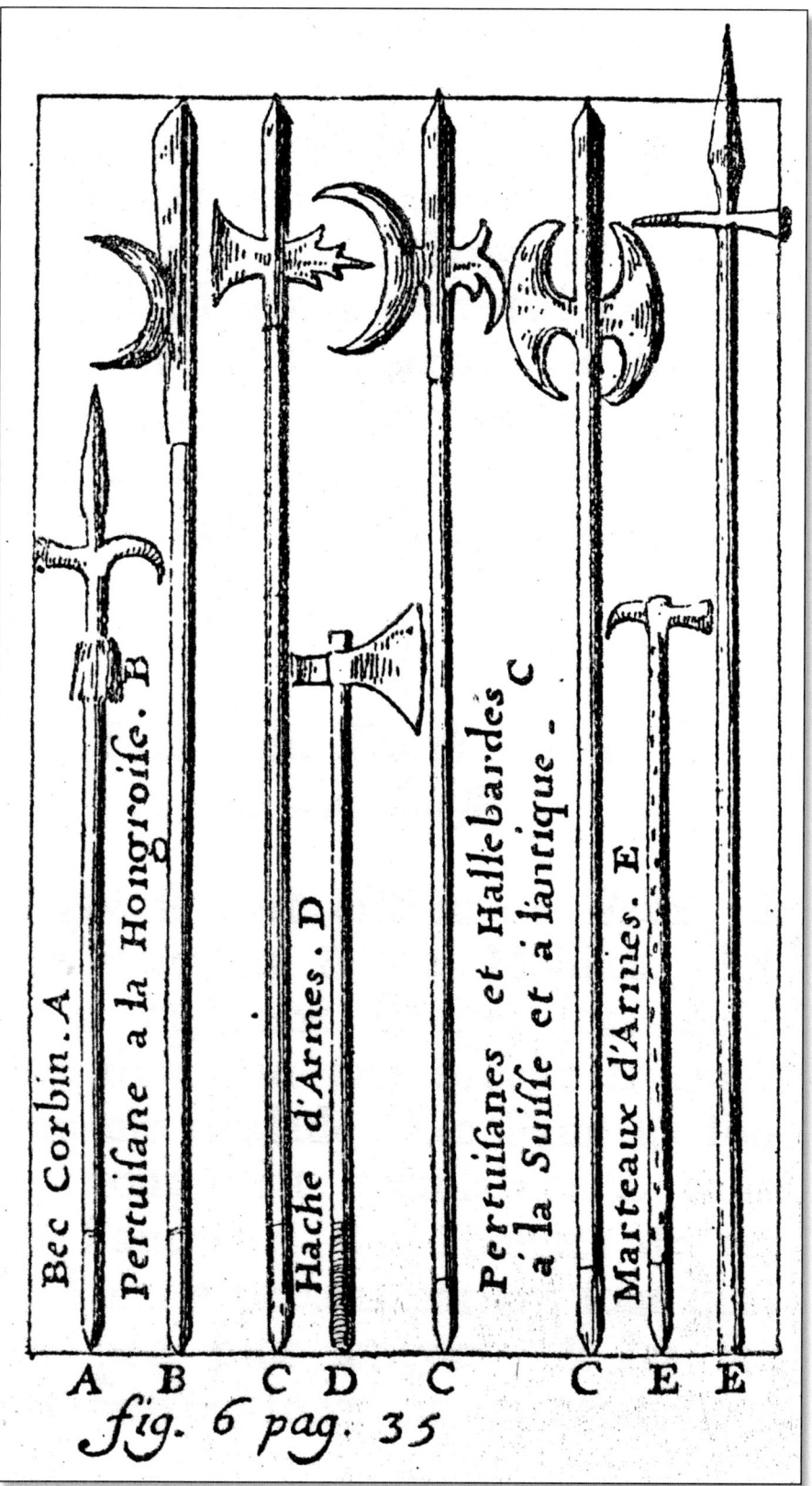

Various types of polearms used by French troops, seventeenth century. From left to right: the hammer-like "Bec de corbin", the Hungarian-style partisan, halberd, a war axe, "Swiss and Antique style partisans and halberds", short and long war hammers. By Louis XIV's reign, the halberd was the only commonly used weapon and carried by infantry sergeants. Print after Gaya's 1678 *Traité des Armes*. (Author's photo)

Right: sergeant's halberd head, late seventeenth to mid eighteenth centuries. Steel, and stamped "T.BO…". Former C. Ariès collection. (Courtesy National Historic sites, Parks Canada)

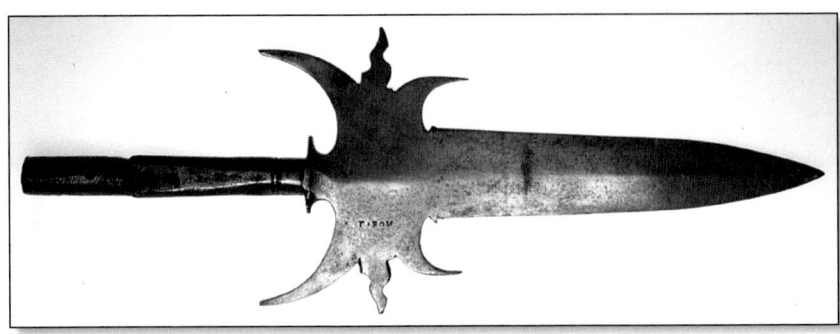

Below: a partisan and an infantry sergeant's halberd, mid seventeenth to early eighteenth centuries. (Museo Storico Nazionale di Artigliera, Torino. Author's photo)

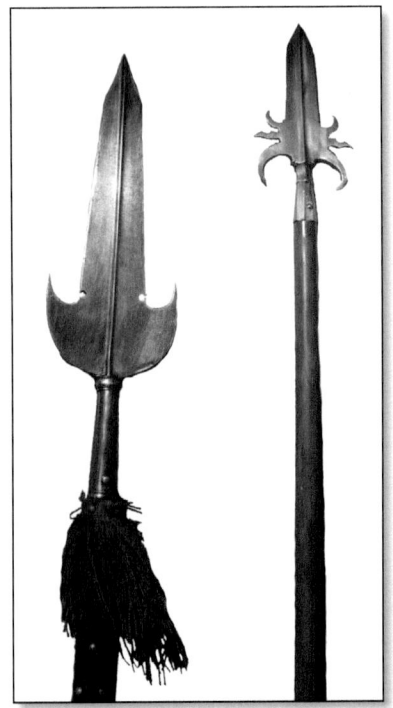

Right: both types of sergeant's halberd head in used during the second half of the seventeenth and early eighteenth centuries. Found by archaeologist at Fortress Louisbourg National Historic Site. (Courtesy Parks Canada)

Below: pike head for infantry colours, late seventeenth to early eighteenth century. (Musée de l'Armée, Paris. Author's photo)

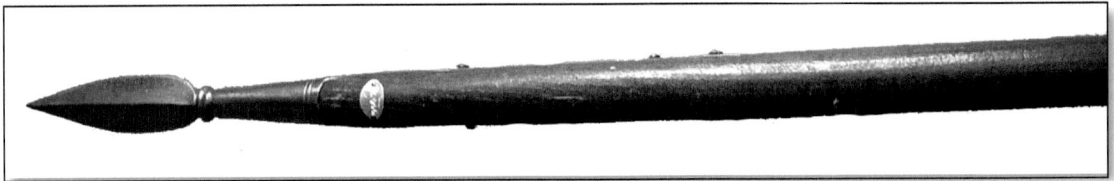

# INFANTRY WEAPONS

# THE ARMIES AND WARS OF THE SUN KING 1643–1715 VOLUME 2

Previous page: polearms carried by sergeants, *c.* 1670s–1680s. Type A was the most common halberd model carried by infantry sergeants, the pointed top as a long pique blade 12 to 15 inches long (French measure), one side having a form of crescent and the other "like a star" (represented by three wavy rays). Type B was a partisan. Type C was a "hache d'armes" (battleaxe blade fixed to a pole). Type D was a scythe blade. Type E was a "fourche" (fork), especially noted as arming sergeants of the Dauphin Regiment, which had two points up and a downward curved point that was "very good for attacks on outposts", and for hand-to- hand combat "when there was no time to use firearms." The sergeants shown wear the post-1683 swordbelt at the waist. In Maneson Mallet's *Les travaux de Mars*, 1684 Paris edition. (Anne S.K. Brown Military Collection, Brown University Library, Providence, RI, USA. Author's photo)

An infantry lieutenant. His spontoon is short, which was later frowned upon in the King's regulations. Print after Collombon's *Trophée d'armes,* Lyon, 1650. (Author's photo)

# INFANTRY WEAPONS

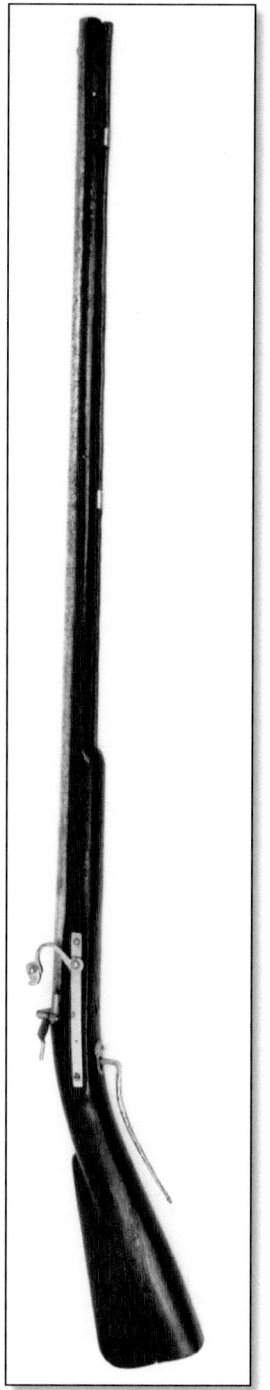

Above: a matchlock musket, 1660s and 1670s. In Maneson Mallet's *Les travaux de Mars,* 1684 Paris edition. (Anne S.K. Brown Military Collection, Brown University Library, Providence, RI, USA. Author's photo)

Right: soldier's matchlock musket, 1660s. This type of musket was the predominant weapon in the French metropolitan infantry. (Courtesy National Historic Sites, Parks Canada)

guards and provosts amongst their duties. As their name implies, *pertuisaniers* carried partisans. The partisan itself was a quality weapon whose pole was about six feet (1.94m) high or somewhat higher, often covered with velvet held by gilt nails, with a flat steel blade that was often elaborately engraved and might be partly gilded. *Trabans* were armed with partisans or halberds, but with heads of peculiar models. Generally, the spear was flat and wide like a partisan's or halberd's with both sides having axe-like blades. Partisans were abolished in the French line infantry in favour of muskets by the royal order of 25 February 1670. This did not apply to foreign units and *trabans* continued to be seen, particularly in Swiss units, for many decades thereafter.[4]

---

4   Baron de Zurlauben, *Histoire Militaire des Suisses*, 1751), Vol. 1, pp.236–237.

# THE ARMIES AND WARS OF THE SUN KING 1643–1715 VOLUME 2

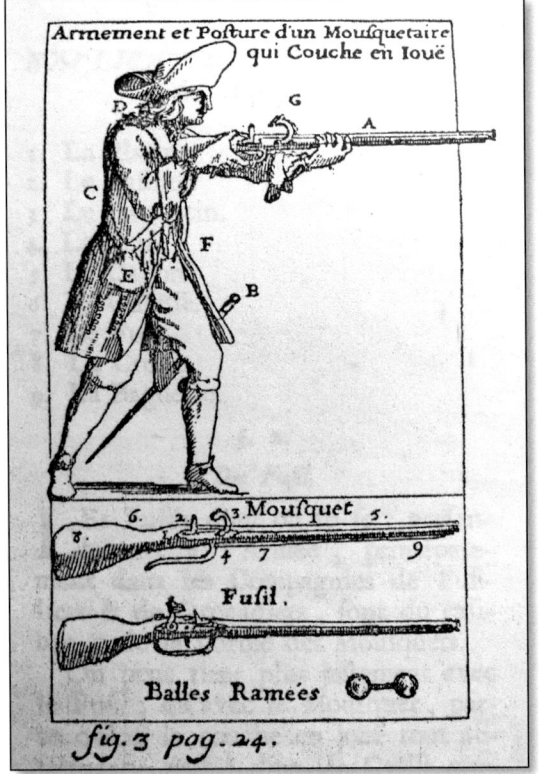 

Above, left: "Armament and posture of a musketeer [infantryman] presenting" during the 1670s. Besides his matchlock musket (A), he is armed with a sword (B) and is equipped with a bandolier (C) with charges hanging (F), and a ball bag (E) and a shoulder belt (D) for the sword. Below, crude renderings of a matchlock musket and of a flintlock musket. Print after Gaya's 1678 *Traité des Armes*. (Author's photo)

Above, right: the flintlock musket and its components, 1660s and 1670s. In Maneson Mallet's *Les travaux de Mars,* 1684 Paris edition. (Anne S.K. Brown Military Collection, Brown University Library, Providence, RI, USA. Author's photo)

## Muskets

Most soldiers were musketeers in that they were armed with muskets and their numbers kept increasing at the expense of pikemen in the last third of the seventeenth century. There was no question that pikes were proving less and less effective, but the most important debate early in the Sun King's reign concerned which type of musket would be the prevailing infantry weapon. Since the 1640s, flintlock muskets had appeared and gradually increased in popularity, especially since they were lighter and their mechanism was an improvement over the prevailing matchlock for military muskets. However, flintlock muskets were often a lighter calibre, which did not bode well for their lethal qualities as weapons. They were initially more likely to break and, perhaps most of all, they were at least a quarter more expensive than matchlocks. On 25 July 1665, its demise seemed to have been decided by the following order: "His Majesty wishes that the infantry be armed … one-third with [matchlock] muskets, the one-third with pikes, without any [soldier] armed with a flintlock musket, advising the war commissioners to break them on the spot and to see that the repeated orders on this matter be respected."[5]

---

5   Lamont, *La Fonction de tous les Officiers de l'Infanterie*, p.349.

# INFANTRY WEAPONS

Matchlock muskets in their various forms had long been the standard soldier's firearm in European armies. However, flintlocks had virtues too and their proponents pointed to their far more efficient firing compared to matchlock, that increased shooting speed because they required only 23 instead of 36 movements to load plus a better resistance in rain and bad weather. A standard calibre for military muskets was even more pressing and it was ruled to be 20 balls to the pound (16mm) for all army muskets on 16 November 1666. In France, the ball was the measurement rule, not the barrel's bore (as in Britain); from the late 1670s, 18 balls (16.5mm) to the pound was also used and became the prevailing calibre. The order of 6 February 1670 specified the length of the barrel at 3 feet 8 inches. For the flintlocks, Louvois and the King were not against innovations, but they were cautious. They started by allowing grenadiers to have flintlock muskets by the royal order of 30 April 1668 and this was followed by permitting four men per musketeer company to have flintlock muskets as long as they had the standard calibre. A fusilier regiment was created in 1671 and 13 independent companies of fusiliers were raised two years later. Although the efficiency of the matchlock was increasingly questioned, Louvois stalled the adoption of flintlocks due largely to the huge cost it would entail. A stop-gap measure was officially made by allowing six instead of four fusiliers per company in 1688. But there were still only about 17 fusiliers to about 83 soldiers armed with matchlocks in 1690. War had been declared by then, while the King's faith in matchlocks was now quite shaken. He might have sensed that his infantry's firepower was severely challenged and surely was not heartened to hear marshals Catinat and Luxembourg tell him that there were not enough good flintlock muskets available for all soldiers even if he made the decision to rearm. Meanwhile, France's opponents had largely invested in flintlocks and, at the battle of Steenkirk on 3 August 1692, French infantrymen were seen throwing away their matchlocks and pikes if they found a flintlock to equal the enemy's superior firepower. Two months later, the King did the best he could with what he had: he ordered that half of the infantry companies be fusiliers and the other half be armed with matchlocks. There were simply not enough flintlocks to go around for the rest of the war and it was only during peacetime on 15 December 1699 that, thanks to reductions in the strength of companies, flintlocks became officially the only infantry musket.[6]

Perhaps because of this half-century-long debate concerning matchlocks versus flintlocks, there were no regulation model or pattern muskets during the reign of Louis XIV and there would be none until the appearance of the infantry model 1717 musket. This may have been due to the various suppliers as well as because some colonels bought weapons for their regiments on their own. The important specifications were that, from 1666, all muskets have the same calibre and the same barrel length. Nevertheless a more French look evolved; the Germanic-looking stocks made way to more elegant, curved and lighter stocks and barrels, all being fastened by pins. The furnishings were also

---

6  Bonnefoy, *Les armes de guerre portatives en France*, Vol. 1, pp.46–50, Vol. 2, pp.696–697; Jean-Philippe Cénat, *Louvois*, p.202.

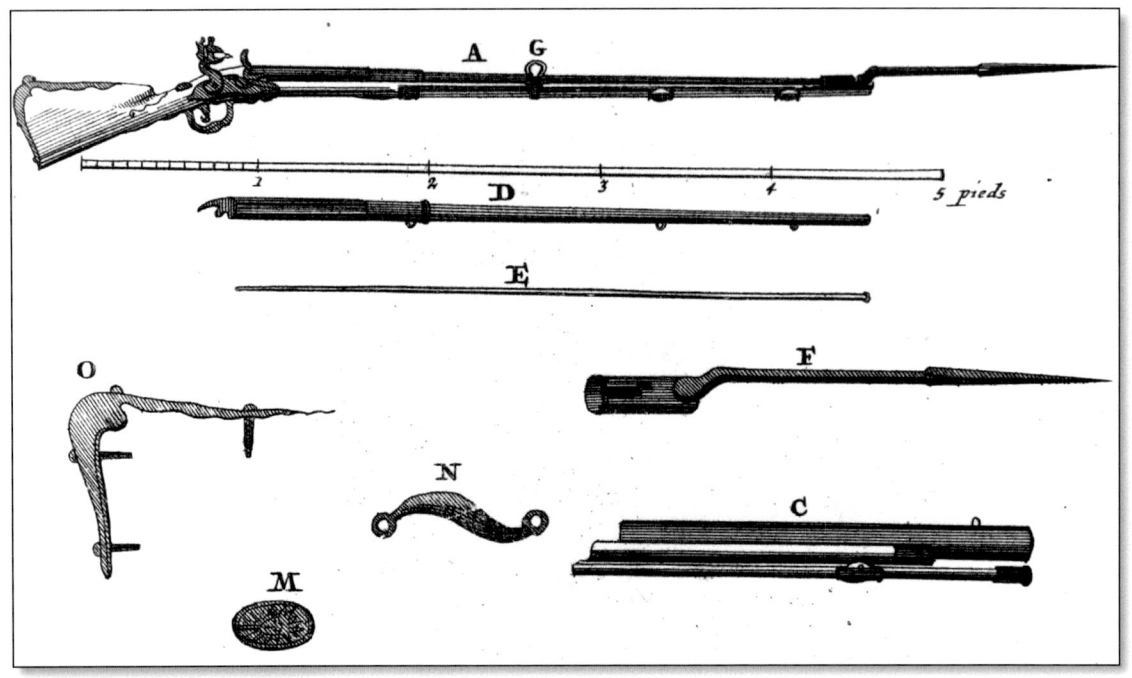

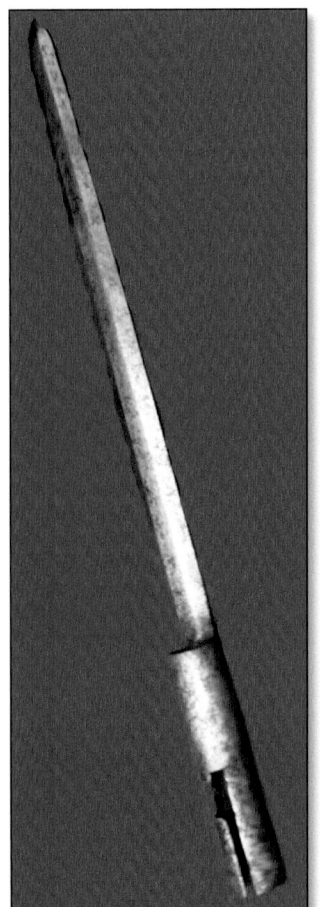
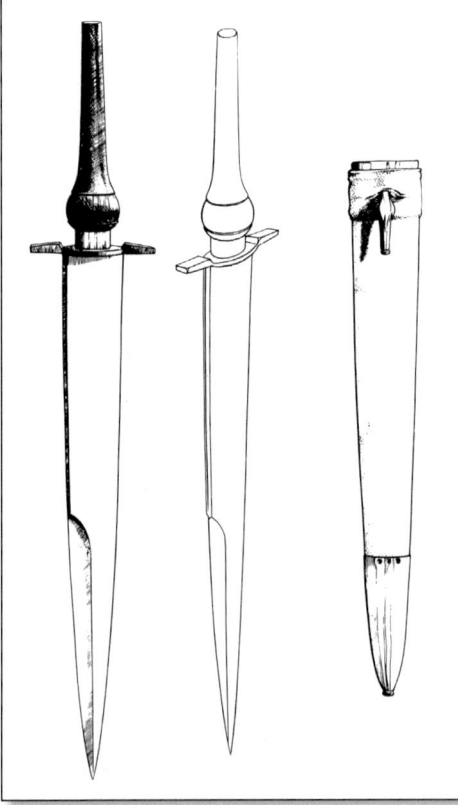

Above: flintlock musket with its socket bayonet, 1690s. The component parts are also illustrated. Print after Saint-Rémy's 1697 *Mémoires d'artillerie*. (Author's photo)

Far left: an early socket bayonet, end of the seventeenth century. This was one of the first types proposed. It has no branch and forms a complete blade. This and others, as well as equipment, were sent from France to Malta. (The Palace Armoury, Valetta, Malta. Author's photo)

Left: plug bayonet for a musket, second half of the seventeenth century. Note the narrow wooden grip so it could fit in the musket barrel. Drawing by Michel Pétard. (Courtesy National Historic Sites, Parks Canada)

inspired from the decorative arts of the Age of Louis XIV revealing the taste of *Le Grand Siècle* that became a worldwide benchmark. Apart from this, they were considered very efficient weapons.

## Bayonets

During the second half of the seventeenth century, military muskets increasingly came with bayonets so that they could be transformed into short pikes of about 160cm long for hand-to-hand combat. There initially was the knife-like and so-called "plug" bayonet whose narrow handle would be inserted into the barrel's muzzle. It had a fairly wide blade gradually coming to a point, was the standard model and the first type to be carried by the French infantry. This type of bayonet had the obvious disadvantage to annul any shooting while it was fixed into the barrel, but was still the common type used in armies up to the end of the seventeenth century. General (later Marshal) Vauban had considered the problem of having the possibility of firing the musket while keeping the advantages of having the bayonet on it. As a result, he is generally credited with the invention of the socket bayonet, sometime in the later 1680s. Vauban's invention, once known and accepted was slowly adopted in the army, presumably as plug bayonets wore out.[7]

Early socket bayonets had a very long branch of about 100mm with a triangular and gutted blade of about 240mm long. Another type had no branch, its socket becoming a blade beyond the muzzle. The more conventional bayonets with a long blade and almost no branch arrived in the early eighteenth century and it gradually became the favoured type in armies everywhere including the French army.

## Infantry Musket Production

From the 1660s, the steady rise in numbers of foot soldiers in French armies challenged the government and the manufacturing sector to produce hitherto unseen numbers of weapons for armies that, in wartime, would reach several hundreds of thousands of infantrymen. In the middle of the seventeenth century, most weapons for the army were imported. There were no sizeable arms factories apart from one at Saint-Étienne and craftsmen specialised in arms production were few. As the size of French armies increased, the government encouraged local arms production so that, from the mid 1660s, levels of production in France increased steadily. By 1675, Saint-Étienne had become the main producer and would be joined by Charleville in the 1680s and Tulle in 1691. By the end of the Sun King's reign, France was by far the largest arms producer in Europe.

Possibly the worst problem came at the outbreak and during the War of the League of Augsburg (1689–1698) when, largely because of previous

---

7 Bonnefoy, *Les armes de guerre portatives en France*, Vol. 1, pp.50–52.

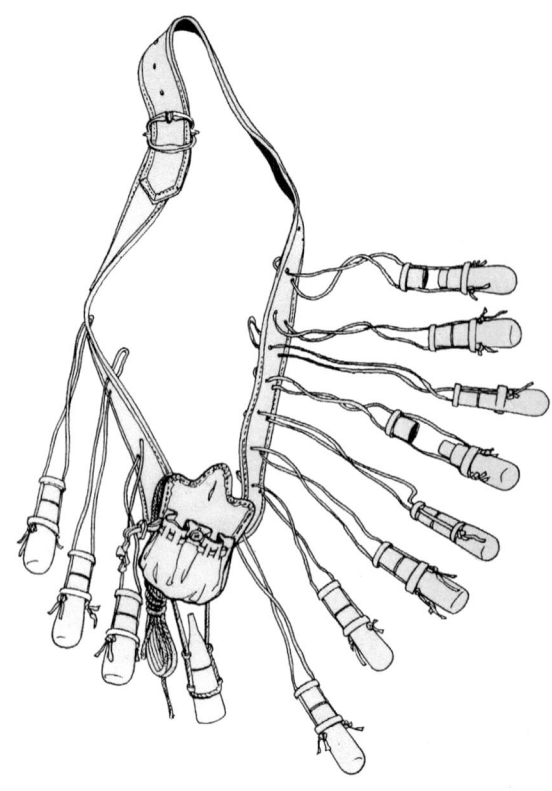

Bandolier with charges in wooden bottles, seventeenth century. Drawing by Michel Pétard. (Private collection. Courtesy of the artist)

budget restraints, the army found itself unable to provide flintlock muskets in sufficient numbers to rearm the whole army. If a nation does not invest enough in its arms industry, that sector of the economy cannot greatly increase its production. Just as today, arms production was a highly sophisticated industry. It could not turn around overnight to greatly multiply its production; larger facilities had to be created and, most of all, making and assembling such an item as a reliable musket flintlock required enough craftsmen. As seen above, in spite of producing at least 36,000 flintlock muskets in 1690 alone, the best that could be done even three years into the war was to hope that half of the infantrymen in the field would be armed with flintlocks. Part of the answer to the shortage lay in that the army already had up to 380,000 infantrymen in 1691. There would have been progress in the following years, but it was really only in 1699, once peace had been convened and the army reduced in numbers to about 140,000, that the immediate problem was solved.

At the outset of the eighteenth century, this technological lesson on the crucial importance of an effective arms industry had been learned. Even if national revenues were not as lucrative as in the past, there was obviously no hesitation in footing the inevitably large bills necessary to have a reliable and buoyant arms production in the kingdom that could meet the army's demand. When war was declared again in 1702, there were already about 185,000 infantrymen in the ranks and this rose to around 300,000 three years later. This time, the arms industry could meet the challenge. This was largely due to the efforts of Maximilien Titon, the director general of the King's arsenals. From 1665, he had built the main arms arsenal next to the Bastille castle in Paris, where some 15,000 or more reserve arms were stored. The royal arsenals had been emptied of all flintlocks to arm the new soldiers by June 1702, but he could report that the production of the two main arms factories at Saint-Étienne and at Charleville stood at 5,000 flintlock muskets per month for a total of 60,000 a year, and this rose to 70,000 in 1704. This production was only for the army because the navy and the colonial troops were being sufficiently supplied by arms at the Tulle factory. It is probable that, with smaller makers added, there may have been at least 10,000 more muskets produced above those at Saint-Étienne and at Charleville. With such production figures added to the muskets already issued, it was obvious all in the army would be armed with the best weapons of the day. Indeed, there would soon be more than enough.

As it were, France was now fighting for the throne of Spain and most Spaniards supported Louis XIV's grandson as their own King Felipe V. The

Spanish army was undergoing a massive modernisation programme put in place by the Spanish themselves with much help from French officials and senior officers. High on the agenda was the rearmament of the Spanish army and soon, France's arms factories were producing flintlock muskets for its allied Spanish army as well as other allies in what was an entirely new market. It was estimated in 1716 that over 100,000 arms had been sent to allies, mostly to Spain.[8]

# Arms Drill

The evolution of infantry tactics during the second half of the sixteenth century led to the creation of protocols or drills that were practised by infantry units. By the end of the century, the Dutch had taken the lead in this aspect of military sciences and, in 1607, the first illustrated drill manual in Europe appeared at The Hague under the title of *Wapenhandelinghe* sponsored by Count Johann II of Nassau. The 32 plates showing the musket drill and the 42 plates of the pike drill were illustrated by the master artist-engraver Jacob de Gheyn. It reflected that, at that time, half of a regiment was armed with muskets and the other half with pikes. The book was an instant artistic and military success. The following year, a French edition appeared and it was reprinted many times and still is. Its reach at the time quickly became European with German, Danish and English translations on the market by 1619. They were further plagiarised from 1609 in Frankfurt and Paris in 1614 as well as influencing Wallhausen's 1615 *Kriegskunst zu Fuss*, which also was published in French in 1615, 1620, 1621 and 1630 as *L'Art militaire pour l'infanterie*, and Hexham's 1637 *Principles of the Art Militarie* in England.

In France, Lostelneau's *Maréchal de bataille* that appeared in 1647 – Louis XIV was then nine years old – set the tone. Some 35 of its beautiful plates drawn and engraved by the author concerned musketeers and 13 were for pikemen, mirroring that regiments now had one-third of their soldiers armed with pikes; their proportion would keep diminishing in all armies during the following decades. While the plates were inspired by de Gheyn, the text had more in common with Wallhausen. This rather unwieldy and expensive work was soon copied by Jacques Collombon's *Trophée d'armes* published in Lyon in 1650 and reprinted 10 years later. The plates by C. Audran were crude, much smaller, did not show drill so much as simply various infantrymen by their rank, but the book was cheap and handy. This was the drill used by the French army during the War of Devolution. With the permanent army growing in size and more professionalism being stressed, a related version titled *Les Évolutions militaires* appeared in Lamont's 1669 *Les fonctions de tous les officiers de l'infanterie*, followed by the 1672 *Exercise général pour l'infanterie* that did not have plates by the Sieur d'Aigremont, a

---

8  Bonnefoy, *Les armes de guerre portatives en France*, Vol. 1, pp.187–199.

Infantry officer and pikeman, early 1680s. In Maneson Mallet's *Les travaux de Mars*, 1684 Paris edition. (Anne S.K. Brown Military Collection, Brown University Library, Providence, RI, USA. Author's photo)

royal engineer. It should be added that all the above were updated versions of de Gheyn's and Wallhausen's works.⁹

Pierre Giffard's *L'Art militaire françois pour l'infanterie* was the next notable drill book, which only appeared in 1696. It was a small handbook with 85 plates showing movements for musketeers, pikemen and also for officers and sergeants with their polearms. So far, all of these drill books published in France had been privately published with a seemingly favourable level of official approval. As the eighteenth century dawned, a lot of factors were changing on battlefields. Pikes had all but disappeared as an infantry weapon as had matchlock muskets in favour of flintlocks. This had changed the way battalions were made up, how they moved on battlefields and how their firepower would now be delivered. Infantry that had formed in 10 ranks in 1600 was now forming in five ranks by 1691 gradually changing to four by 1700. This brought about changes in battalion composition; they now had 13 companies instead of 17 (with grenadiers), which permitted older regiments to have four battalions instead of three. The rectangular formations with pikes at the centre had vanished in favour of battalions whose four ranks extended on a very wide front – they looked like ribbons on battlefield maps. This called for drill adapted to the new practices and quickly. Thus, the *Exercise de toute l'infanterie de France, et autres mouvemens réglés par la main de Sa Majesté le 2. Mars 1703* (Drill for all the infantry in France, and other movements regulated by the hand of His Majesty on 2 March 1703) came out under government authority. It had 44 rather basic plates all showing a fusilier of the Gardes-Françaises performing the various movements of the new manual at arms. It was not greatly different from the former one, but was solely devoted to all aspects of drilling with a flintlock musket. It remained in force for nearly half a century until replaced by the drill of 7 May 1750.¹⁰

---

9 *Les Évolutions militaires* was still being published in Lamont's 1693 edition at The Hague; D'Aigremont's drill appeared within François de La Valière, *Pratiques et Maximes de la Guerre*, pp.125–138.

10 Guignard, *L'École de Mars*, Vol. 1, pp.616–645; J.A. Houlding, *French arms drill of the 18th century* (Bloomfield: Museum Restoration Service, 1988), pp.3–13; Paul Martin, 'Les maniements d'armes et les Gardes-Françaises au XVIIe siècle', *Le Passepoil*, 1950, pp.1–3; Louis Susane, *Histoire de l'infanterie française* (Paris: J. Dumaine, 1876), Vol. 1, p.203.

## INFANTRY WEAPONS

Infantry musketeers, mid 1680s. In the 1672 edition of Mallet's *Travaux de Mars*, these three soldiers wore bandoliers and shoulder sword belts. In this 1684 edition, soldier "B" (lower left) is as in 1672, but the two others show the new sword belt worn around the waist with the bullet pouch attached, as well as a *pulverin* (small flask) for priming powder. A larger powder flask now hangs by a cord over the shoulder. (Anne S.K. Brown Military Collection, Brown University Library, Providence, RI, USA. Author's photo)

## Battle Lines

Armies lined up for battles in the Sun King's reign took on a tremendously impressive aspect, largely due to the introduction of uniforms, which gave the ranks in its martial beauty an absolutely unequalled appearance that would last until the middle of the nineteenth century when weapons technology began making giant strides in long range accuracy. Before that, however, one could contemplate two armies of, say, some 50,000 men each within sight of each other. The order of battle could be very wide with lines extending to, say, eight kilometres, the battalions marching in a few ranks, the men all in uniforms with their the three regimental colours fluttering, musket and bayonets like gleaming silver in the sun, a mounted officer here and there galloping, perhaps puffs of white smoke from a distant isolated skirmish. It was one of the most extraordinary things anyone could see in his life. The Chevalier de Quincy, who survived all his battles, wrote with enthusiasm when he recalled the sheer ominous beauty of it all: "People can tell me about concerts, plays, operas, pageants, in short the most beautiful and spectacular shows in the world, there is certainly none that can ravish one's eyes more than an army lined up in battle order waiting for the enemy, or marching to fight him."[11]

---

11  Charles Sevin, Marquis de Quincy, *Mémoires du Chevalier de Quincy*, Léon Lecestre, ed., (Paris: Renouard, 1898–1901), Vol. 3, p.136.

A battle line was not, however, an instantaneous affair that originated from the orders of one officer. The commanding generals decided on the general dispositions that were then put in place by many staff and regimental officers to place the regiments in their proper place and in battle lines. This could take all day. Once it was in place, it had to move in an orderly manner, and remain a coherent formation that could stand up well under the enemy's fire. Individual soldiers might panic (although it seems to have been quite rare) break rank and run, but would be stopped and even killed by a sergeant behind the rank. The whole ethos of combat was to fight, win, survive and at least fight well in defeat too. To run before the enemy – there was then no psychological understanding of battle trauma – was likely to guarantee death and eternal scorn from one's comrades and nation.

## Firepower

The accuracy of seventeenth and eighteenth century firearms has nothing in common with the precision and rapidity of portable weapons in our own twenty-first. A soldier armed with a matchlock musket might fire and reload in about a minute or more. Flintlock muskets might double this rate of fire, but it was the advent of the cartridge that speeded it up to a possible four to six shots a minute, but this was theoretical and for a well-trained soldier. This was mostly not the case and, during training drills at Strasbourg in 1703, it was noted that most soldiers turned their heads when firing. Since "nothing was so necessary as to accustom them to shooting" they would be required to shoot two or three times at every drill. However, it took many weeks of relentless drill to learn the manual of arms and master its many movements to attain a somewhat rapid rate of volleys. No man in battle could keep firing at such a rate for long: after about 30 shots, the black powder residue would clog up the musket's vent and barrel while the flint had to be replaced, all of which took time to clean and replace while under enemy fire.

As the muskets used were then quite inaccurate, soldiers did not aim at a somewhat precise target beyond about 60 metres. A musket's range might be approximately 260 metres, but this varied also and its effective range was perhaps about half that distance. As a line of infantry marched nearer to the enemy, the effectiveness of firepower increased, and telling results would be seen in the ranks. Volley fire by battalion, company or squad was considered the most effective. In this instance, steadiness was probably even more important than rapid fire. A good example is the performance of some French infantry at the 1704 battle of Blenheim. Five British battalions moved up to attack a French line of 4,000 infantrymen. The French did not fire until the British infantrymen were about 30 yards (27.4m) away. Their devastating volley instantly brought down some 800 redcoats, a third of their brigades, which meant something like 20 percent of the French rounds were effective. Another brigade came up in reinforcement and another salvo made a further 1,370 British casualties of about 17 percent effectiveness. As is well known, action in other parts of the battlefield went very badly for the French army and it was defeated, but this gives an idea of effectiveness of firepower in linear warfare.[12]

There was also much smoke from the musket firing, which soon covered the battlefield in a cloudy haze and indeed would negate visibility. The situation of a soldier in this hellish battle spot is actually reported by an officer, rather exceptionally as the obviously smoke-filled battlefields of the black powder musket period were so common that hardly any battle account mentions smoke obscuring everything; the same can be said of battle art with smoke conveniently looking like clouds at the sides. The officer noted that his soldiers in the midst of battle with heavy smoke all around and amongst them were very tense, cramped up together in the closed ranks, got in each other's way, could not hold up their musket until the order to fire came. '[In] serious affairs [engagements], the soldiers don't know what they are doing and cannot distinguish objects in the thick smoke…'[13]

The musket barrels being smoothbore, why did they not rifle them to obtain a more accurate shot? *Carabines*, as rifled firearms are called in French, were known and armed mostly elite cavalrymen. But rifles were troublesome and slow to load as well as being much more expensive. Their barrels were shorter so having bayonets was not an advantage in close combat and it seems the vast majority and possibly all rifles had no bayonets. Riflemen were thus at the mercy of a bayonet charge so that a unit so armed could not hold a position against a determined enemy. Overall, the efficiency of individual rifle shots could not equal the mass firepower of repeated volleys in a general engagement. At that time, battlefield success or failure depended largely on thousands of infantrymen marching in ranks giving and enduring a hailstorm of lead balls.

## Accoutrements

For much of the seventeenth century, soldiers had the buff bandolier slung over the left shoulder with the charges held by strings and a leather bag to hold bullets. It was described by Mallet as being three to four inches wide and two and a half feet long (presumably from the shoulder), with 12 powder charge containers suspended by cords from the shoulder belt. These bandoleers were generally carried by men armed with matchlock muskets, although those using flintlock muskets might have had them too, or else, a small bullet bag. There were powder horns and flasks, but some found that powder in a coat pocket was more handy even if more dangerous. But these were men used to dangerous situations. The buff leather shoulder belt was four to five inches wide and was slung over the right shoulder.

All this was changed by a royal order of 14 December 1683. The bandoleer was abolished for infantry musketeers and fusiliers who henceforth were

---

12  B.P. Hugues, *Firepower* (Staplehurst: Spellmount, 1974), p.81.
13  Bonnefoy, *Les armes de guerre portatives en France*, Vol. 1, p.151. Quoting an extract of a letter by Lt. Knoch of 15 May 1759 describing an action near Liège. The situation in battle was the same from the seventeenth century to the advent of smokeless powder in the later nineteenth century.

# THE ARMIES AND WARS OF THE SUN KING 1643–1715 VOLUME 2

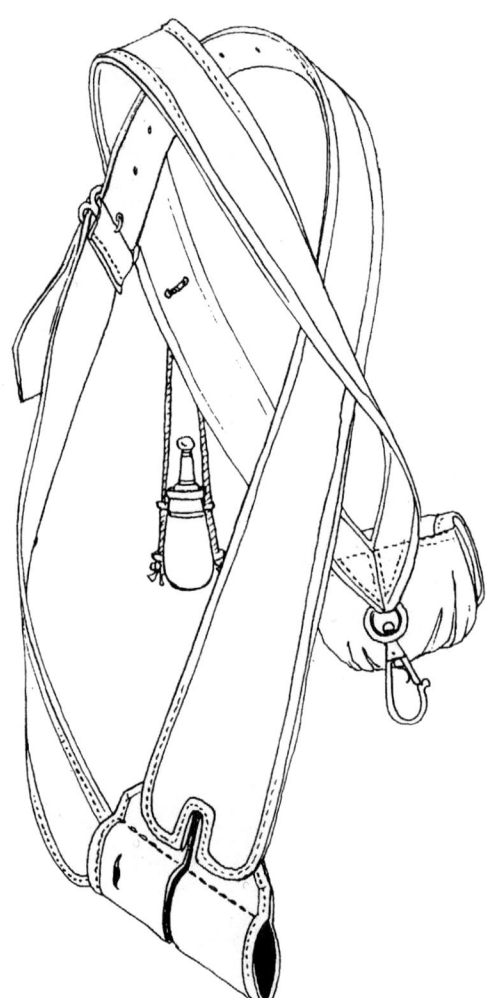

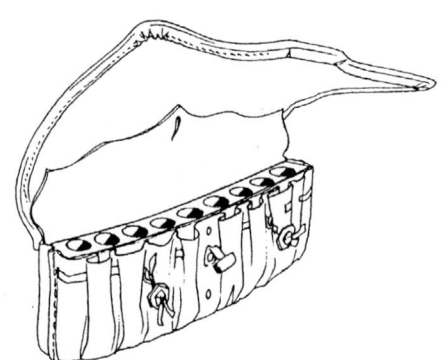

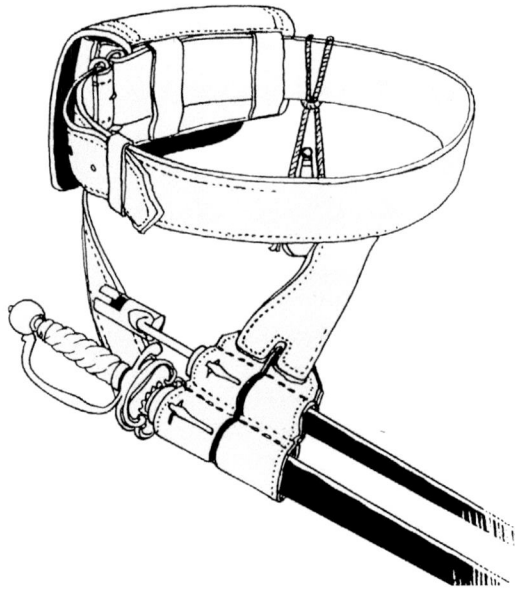

Above, left: accoutrements for fusiliers, 1670s and 1680s. Soldiers using flintlock muskets tended not to have charge bottles strung from their shoulder belts, but needed pouches for their flints and bullets. These pouches were initially a modest size. Drawing by Michel Pétard. (Private collection. Courtesy of the artist)

Top, right: detail of a back view of an infantryman, late seventeenth and early eighteenth centuries. It shows how the belt frogs were arranged to carry a plug bayonet with the sword. Reconstruction by Michel Pétard. Collection and photo: National Historic Sites, Parks Canada.

Right: infantry waist belt with sword, bayonet and cartridge box, early eighteenth century. The frog for the socket bayonet is parallel to the sword. The open cartridge box shows ts wooden block in its leather container, with two small bags in front for extra bullets and flints. Drawing by Michel Pétard. (Private collection. Courtesy of the artist)

# INFANTRY WEAPONS

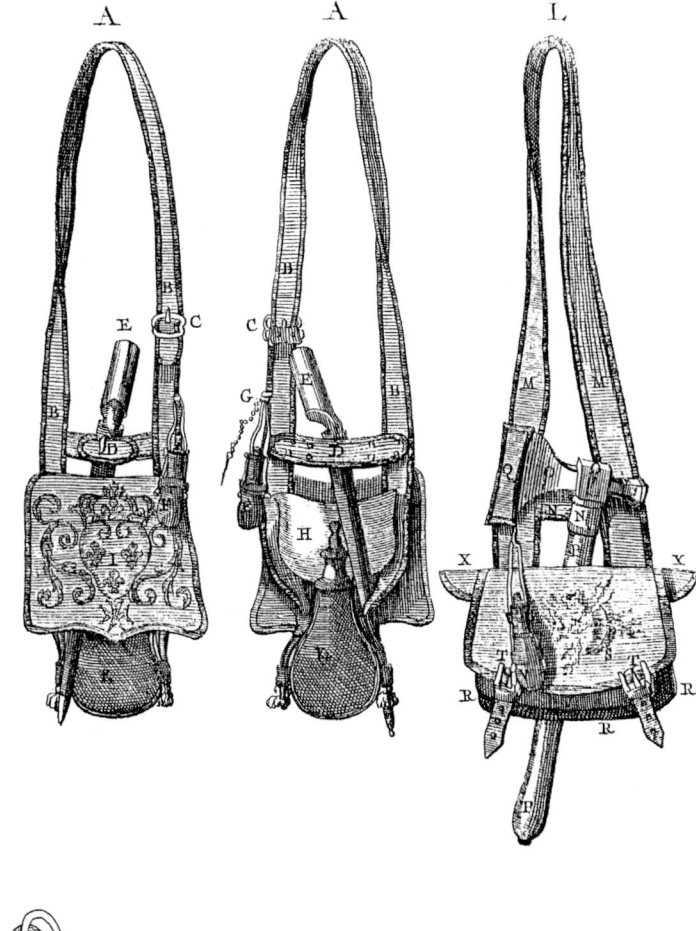

Right: infantry ammunition pouches, 1697. A: front and back views of fusilier's accoutrements. B and M: sling. C: buckle. E: socket bayonet. G: priming flask. L: grenadier's accoutrements. H: ammunition pouch. G: chain and pickers. I: flap cover of pouch. K: powder flasks. O: hatcher with hammer head. R: grenadier's pouch. T: buckles to close grenadier's pouch. X: "ears" of the pouch. "Each infantryman is issued a buff sling with an ammunition pouch covered with a Russia [leather] flap with a boiled leather powder flask with a wooden or spring stopper." Print after Saint-Rémy's *Mémoires d'artillerie*. (Author's photo)

Below: ammunition pouch, powder horn and leather powder flask, late seventeenth century. Reconstruction after period artwork and artefacts. Drawing by Michel Pétard. (Private collection. Courtesy of the artist)

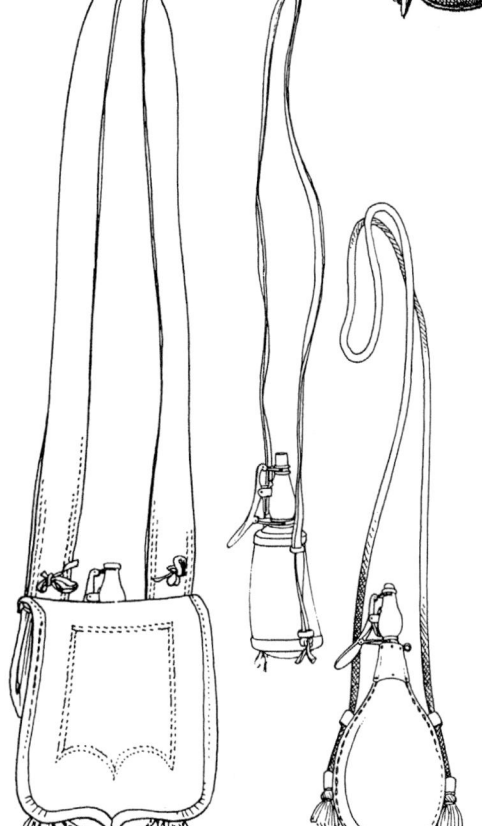

Above: officer's cartridge box, early eighteenth century. The wooden box was covered with buff velvet, its flap having a vermeil (a rich ruby red hue) metal plate embossed with trophies. Print in *La Giberne*, 1904. (Author's photo)

Infantrymen on sentry duty, late seventeenth century. This side view shows the musketeer's pouch with a socket bayonet attached. At night, the original caption reads, he "was not to be approached by anyone without shouting *qui va là* [who goes there] and if it happens there is no answer, he must shoot to alarm the guardhouse." The pikemen has his pike and the musketeer sentry had his match cord lighted. Print after Guérard. (Anne S.K. Brown Military Collection, Brown University Library, Providence, RI, USA. Author's photo)

each to carry enough powder to fire 30 shots, which came to about a pound. Soldiers were now to have a powder flask containing the pound of powder and a *fourniment* that then designated a leather bullet bag. It was often covered by a stiff leather flap sometimes engraved with the King's coat of arms. This item might also be called a *gibecière*. Even in French today, what those items were called can be confusing and several definitions are possible. The flask and the fourniment were carried by a buff belt slung over the left shoulder. A smaller flask called a *pulverin* was also seen; it contained fine powder and was used for priming the lock. This type of equipment gradually changed from the 1690s and into the early 1700s. The powder flasks, usually made of wood covered with dark leather, and containing a pound of powder were replaced by powder horns garnished with brass. These powder horns featured a brass thumb-activated mechanism which measured the amount of powder necessary for each charge. This horn had enough powder for about 30 to 40 shots and was carried by its own narrow buff belt slung over the left shoulder.[14]

From the 1690s, the cartridge was adopted. It consisted of a paper cylinder containing the bullet and the powder charge. Instead of using the powder horn to load each charge which took time, the soldier now would bite off a

---

14  Alain Manesson Mallet, *Les Travaux de Mars* (Paris, 1684), Vol. 3, p.18.

bit of paper from the cartridge with his teeth, pour a small amount of powder in the musket's pan, ram the rest of the cartridge down the musket's barrel with his ramrod and he was soon ready to fire. A reserve of cartridges thus increased the speed of fire as the charges were already prepared.

As a result, it was decided that all soldiers should be given *gargoussiers* instead of *fourniments*. This newly invented *gargoussier* was a ventral cartridge box held by the waistbelt. It consisted of a slightly curved wood block into which were bored holes for cartridges; not many holes as surviving specimens usually have nine. The block went into a buff leather container with two loops to slip it on the waistbelt. It was covered by a flap of leather. In front of the cartridge box, but invisible because hidden by the flap, were two small pouches of soft buff leather, one for flints, the other for extra bullets. This was not adopted overnight. It was less expensive and merely logical to let older accoutrements wear out in time; the very numerous number of infantrymen in the French armies also was a factor, but, by 1705–1710, most if not all soldiers had the new cartridge box.

## Weapons Into a New Century

As seen above, there were many rather latent changes between the 1640s and the 1690s. These came in small doses that nevertheless changed the very appearance of a battalion by the beginning of the eighteenth century: the pikes were gone, replaced by flintlock muskets with socket bayonets. Equipment had changed too. Some questioned the way officers and NCOs were armed on some fronts where new fighting conditions appeared, notably in mountains. There were many individual orders but no simple general instructions to guide officers so some were issued by area commanders. In June 1698, some older instructions were repeated and new ones added according Lieutenant General d'Artagnan's instructions. All captains and other officers were reminded to have uniform model spontoons 7½ feet (2.28m) high. All sergeant's halberds were of the same model and be 6½ feet (2.10m) high. All muskets were to have a leather cock cover, put on when the cock was down and resting and to which a narrow string attached it to the trigger guard. Bayonets were to be of the socket type. The text is rather unclear regarding bayonets, but seems to describe a long stem with a shorter blade, which would be as in Saint-Rémy's 1697 work (see illustration). Soldier's muskets were to be well polished and their sword hilts of brass except for the Swiss, who had them in iron.[15]

A decade later, in 1709, General Broglie, infantry inspector of the troops on the Italian border, brought out his own instructions, which were printed at Grenoble so they had a wide distribution. They give an idea in the evolution of infantry armament by the closing years of the War of the Spanish Succession. A somewhat surprising feature was that it was already

---

15 Instructions of 25 June 1698 by Lieutenant General d'Artaignan quoted in: *Carnet de La Sabretache*, December 2005, pp.136–137.

French infantry soldier having a glass of wine, early eighteenth century. Print after Watteau. (Anne S.K. Brown Military Collection, Brown University Library, Providence, RI, USA. Author's photo)

the practice "in this army" to arm officers with muskets rather than spontoons because "this armament is more convenient for service in the mountains." They also had a "uniform" cartridge pouch or box, a powder horn with a "silk cord of uniform colour" and a "steel bayonet shorter and more polished" than the soldier's. Their gorgets had to be clean and worn on duty. Half of the sergeants were armed with muskets like the officers, the others still carried halberds.

A soldier's musket barrel was not to be browned "on the pretext of safeguarding it, which is one [cause] of negligence and uncleanliness." Muskets were to have rings to attach slings of buff or Russia leather. The type of bayonet did not matter as long as it was "good and uniform in the regiment" and its scabbard made of good leather with brass hook and tip. The same was true for soldiers' swords. They further were to have a pouch with its belt to put in their powder flask made preferably of boiled leather, a cock cover, vent prickers with a thin chain, six flints and 20 rounds. A surprising item was that there were two rifles "to be the same length as [ordinary smoothbore] muskets" per company issued to veteran soldiers and best shots. These rifles were certainly for small parties skirmishing in the mountains at the Italian border.[16]

In all this, the King had an opinion too and "having been informed that the officers of his troops were armed differently depending on which country their regiments were serving, some having spontoons and others flintlock muskets with bayonet." As he wished that their weapons be "uniform" he ordered on 1 December 1710 that colonels, lieutenant colonels and captains be henceforth armed with spontoons while subaltern officers have muskets and bayonets throughout the army except for the guard regiments whose officers continued to have spontoons.[17]

---

16 Charles-Guillaume Broglie, 'Règlement pour les réparations des bataillons destinés à servir sur la frontière du Piémont', *Carnet de La Sabretache*, 1923, pp.496–302.
17 Sieur de Briquet, *Suplément au code militaire* (Paris, 1734), Vol. 4, pp.159–160.

# 11

# Uniforms, Colours and Music

## Uniforming the Infantry

In 1643, when Louis XIV became king, the French army did not have uniforms. At best, there might be uniformity amongst some troops with similar clothing, either as liveries for certain guard units, or because of a bulk supply provided for troops in the field in need. For instance, in 1628, several cities furnished 2,500 grey and 100 crimson red suits. In 1643, a company of French troops in Brisach was seen "marching two by two in one platoon, they all wore grey-black uniform clothing"; in 1657, the city of Paris supplied 1,600 suits consisting of lined *justeaucorps*-style coats with breeches, stocking, shoes and caps. Besides such exceptions, the usual practice was that soldiers enlisted wearing their own clothing. On service, shirts, shoes and stockings wore out after a campaign or two and needed replacement. In wartime, this might be done by pillaging, but in peacetime, it had to be bought. A pair of shoes would cost about three livres, which was beyond a private soldier's means, so an advance would be offered by his captain and, in time, all his soldiers would owe him money with interest, one sol per day being deducted from the soldier's pay.[1]

Without uniforms, soldiers resorted to such items as sashes for recognition on the battlefield. French soldiers traditionally had white sashes, the Spanish red, Austrians yellow and so on. Many soldiers had no sashes and there were times when they wore their (basically white) shirts over their coats during assaults or else tying something white to their hats. In 1652 during the Fronde, the *Grande Mademoiselle* ordered the troops of the princes led by Condé to wear small bunches of straw on their hats to distinguish "those [soldiers] who did not want to pass for *mazarins*" and they according had the straw at the battle of 2 July 1652 at the Porte Saint-Antoine in Paris. So, for their own distinction, the royal army's soldiers put white ribbons in their hats shortly thereafter to be henceforth distinguished as the King's troops.[2]

---

1  Henry Lehr, 'L'Uniforme de 1643 à 1645', *Le Passepoil*, 1934, p.72.
2  Susane, *Histoire de l'infanterie française*, Vol. 1, p. 184; *Mémoires de Valentin Conrart*, L.J.N. Monmerqué (ed.) (Paris: Foucault, 1826), pp.142, 333, 364–365.

# THE ARMIES AND WARS OF THE SUN KING 1643-1715 VOLUME 2

Officer of the Régiment du Roi, c. 1676. The Régiment du Roi was not part of the guard, but it was very prestigious because it was the Sun King's own model regiment. Its officers wore coats embroidered with gold and silver during the 1660s and 1670s. Print after Alfred de Marbot. (Canadian War Museum, Ottawa. Author's photo)

In the early 1660s several regiments devised ways to partially or wholly clothe their men and this implied that some uniformity was achieved if only because of buying in quantity. In general, grey or brown cloth seems to have been procured due to their more modest prices. So that the army would always be properly dressed, the King ordered on 14 May 1666 that the captains could keep taking a sol a day from their men's pay with the added provision that they would have to keep records of how the money was spent. A soldier was designated to keep the records to be reported and audited yearly; if in surplus, the money was paid back to the soldier or the debt risen if he had spent more. This basic system was used in the French army until 1886. It guaranteed money was available to clothe a regiment and commanders now started to think of having uniform colours for their units.[3]

In the summer of 1666, the King gathered some 20,000 troops in a temporary camp at Houilles, near Paris, so as to stage a grand parade. Captain Claude Severat was there with his company that belonged to the Lyonnois Regiment, which was commanded by members of the very wealthy and powerful Villeroi family. As early as 1664, Severat had outfitted his men "with long justeaucorps [long-skirted coats]" claiming to have been the first to do so, as well as providing hats, stockings and cravats. This was done again in 1665 to be reviewed by the Marquis de Villeroi. At this point, some of the clothing might have been of the same hues, but it was in 1666, when to be reviewed by the King, that Severat mentions that "we [had] made uniform coats of a good grey-white cloth, lined with a red Spanish cloth, red stockings, a buff bandolier [edged] with a big red fringe, a white hat plume with a large ponceau [red] ribbon at the hat and at the shoulder." The regiment then went to Saint-Sébastien, also near Paris, for another camp assembling about 30,000 troops, for which "we dressed the regiment from head to foot, all the officers in grey camelot cloth garnished with a gold lace, those of the captains worth 20 pistoles and those of the lieutenants 10 pistoles." Thus, there was rank distinction by this lace. There were "12 [officer-]cadets clothed in grey

---

3  Carnot, 'Deux documents sur l'origine de l'uniforme militaire', *Carnet de La Sabretache*, 1904, pp.578–579; Victor Belhomme, *Histoire de l'infanterie en France* (Paris: Lavauzelle, 1892), Vol. 2, pp.93–94, 127–128.

with a silver lace thereon, a laced hat with a white feather, and red ribbon, armed with a very gilded partisan." The sergeants wore "grey cloth [coats] lined with red with a silver lace everywhere." There were further "four pertuisaniers per company, dressed in green with a large aurore [orange] lace; our drummers were dressed the same." Green was the livery of the Villeroi family and although the Lyonnois Regiment was named after the city and area of the city of Lyon, royal permission had long been granted for the family's livery to be worn rather than the King's.[4]

At another review near Paris in 1668, the King wanted officers of the Régiment Du Roi to wear cuirasses with "coats embroidered with gold and silver." Early on, Louis XIV expressed his wish that officers should have the same uniform as their men, but never actually imposed it strictly although every officer knew that if it was a good idea, especially if the King was present at a review or for an inspection.[5]

The better quality dress, uniform or not, of an officer distinguished him from his men. His badge of authority was the crescent-shaped gorget worn below the neck when on duty. This was the visible symbol of his status as a commissioned officer in the King's army. There was not official model for gorgets and their shape evolved, becoming smaller by the end of the seventeenth century. The Chevalier de Guignard later noted that all "officers must wear when on duty … a gorget of brass, plain, without coats of arms, ciphers nor mottos, which they must wear under their cravats…", but there was not actually a prescribed model until 1767 in the French army. There were also some embossed with engraved trophies and coats of arms – those of the king were preferred – as well as plain ones seeming favoured from the eighteenth century, but not exclusively. An important aspect is that, traditionally, officers in French regiments always had gilded gorgets no matter what their unit's button and lace colour was, those in Swiss units had silvered gorgets and officers in German regiments

Officer's gorget, mid seventeenth century. Polished steel. The sole use of gilt gorgets for French officer appear to date from a decade later. (Philadelphia Museum of Fine Art. Author's photo)

A pair of soldier's shoes, late seventeenth to early eighteenth century. (Musée de l'Armée, Paris. Author's photo)

---

4   Carnot, 'Deux documents sur l'origine de l'uniforme militaire', *Carnet de La Sabretache*, 1904, pp.579–581.
5   Louis Vanson, 'Le régiment du Roi', *Carnet de La Sabretache*, 1897, p.675.

had polished steel gorgets. Other foreign regiments all seem to have had gilt like the French.[6]

Before 1660, ordering soldiers and officers to have certain fine details in their appearance and regarding what they wore would have provoked angry reaction, especially in French regiments. The King and Minister of War Louvois thought otherwise and their wishes were increasingly found to be a rather good idea, especially because of the order of 14 May 1666, so that more and more units were seen in uniform, and not just the royal guards. Liveries had been worn by some soldiers since the middle ages, notably those who were close to their noble commander such as drummers, but now this notion was integrated into a broader scheme. Most colonels could not afford dressing their whole regiment in their livery, but they could dress it with decent quality yet inexpensive natural wool that would be in varying shades of grey, grey-white or brown with drummers and, in some cases, NCOs and *pertuisaniers* in livery clothing or else in a better quality version of the soldiers' dress. The coat lining would sometimes be in a contrasting colour, such as red or blue, that made it more attractive especially when cuffs were turned up. Naturally, fashion took over and soldiers were soon seen with coloured ribbons on hats, coats and even garters. By 1673, the concept of uniformity seems to have been fairly commonplace. In March, Luxembourg wrote to Louvois that some troops had varied clothing noting that about half of his troop's clothing was still good "and if some were given to those [whose clothing] was worn out, these soldiers will look variously coloured, and it would be a villainous thing if the clothing was not identical."[7]

Fashion or not, some noble officers were simply against wearing uniforms, considering that they were being forced to wear a livery like their footmen. Yet this was a persistent royal wish from the mid 1660s that persisted during the whole reign. Those were not men who were inclined to wear any uniform, even less to be told how to dress their hair and how long it should be, and totally agonised by specifications about the size of their coat cuffs. Louis XIV was patient, but there were limits. The Marquis de Coëtquen, colonel of the infantry regiment of that name from 1697 and a proud member of Brittany's ancient nobility, although ordered by the King to wear the regimental uniform at a royal review, simply refused to do so. Seeing this, the angry Sun King told him in front of the troops that he was henceforth "broken" (*cassé*) from his command to which he replied: "Fortunately Sire, the pieces remain." It was an example of what could happen if the King's wishes were not attended to.[8]

Uniformity definitely had a good effect on esprit de corps and the interior economy of units since the men would be, on the whole, clothed properly

---

6   Guignard, *L'École de Mars*, Vol. 1, p.614. There were no specific officer's rank badges ordered in the French army until December 1762.

7   Service Historique de la Défense (SHD), AG, A1, Vol. 322, Luxembourg to Louvois, 31 March 1673. Louvois replied he was not issuing new clothing and recommended a serious mending of the uniforms.

8   Eugène Sue, *Histoire de la Marine française* (Paris, 1845), Vol. 2, p.147 after Mirabeau's memoirs. The King bore no grudges and later promoted Malo-Auguste de Coëtquen to general's rank; he was a brave officer and lost a leg at Malplaquet.

giving a smart and orderly appearance; it was a great and positive change from just a decade earlier. Louvois also thought it was a good way to identify and catch deserters. In terms of the national economy, it created a sizeable demand for all kinds of cloth in large quantities that, in turn, encouraged the creation of large-scale local production of cloth, especially in the provinces of Berry and Languedoc.

Once a uniform was chosen by a regiment, it was not always kept, but on the whole, a certain continuity may have taken place. So far however, material culture research has not yielded many descriptions of what uniform colours units actually wore. Not until the 1690s do some documents emerge that give descriptions of the dress of some units (see appendices). These are amazingly varied in some instance so it would be hasty to conclude that the hues and details of a regimental uniform known during 1690s would be the same 20 or 30 years earlier. Nevertheless, uniformity evolved in the last quarter of the seventeenth century from basically individual regimental uniforms to more permanent national army dress. In general, grey-white became the common colour for most line infantry regiments, usually distinguished by red or blue, but there were also other coat and distinctive colours recorded.

Foreign regiments were seemingly amongst the first to adopt uniform clothing. We know of the Douglas Scottish Regiment dressed in red lined with white in 1667 and Furstenberg's German Regiment in blue lined with yellow in 1669–1670. It has endlessly been repeated since the nineteenth century that the foreign regiments had blue coats for the Germans, red coats for the Swiss, brown for Italians and grey-white for others. Some add that this was made official during the 1680s. The seventeenth century evidence given in the uniform appendix below show some of these national foreign units indeed dressed in those colours, but some Swiss and Germans wore such hues as yellow and green with some Italians and Walloons were in blue or red. It is more correct to state that the blue for Germans, red for Swiss and so on became more commonplace from the early eighteenth century under Louis XV's reign and it was then that complete printed descriptions of the army appeared.[9]

There are very few certified surviving French army garments of that period. Some military coats seemingly of the 1680s, now preserved in the Royal Army Museum in Stockholm, Sweden, form probably the most important collection known of such items. A few are illustrated in this volume. These coats are traditionally said to have been sent from France to Sweden by Louis XIV; this is not formally certified by documents, but, besides "looking French", all are blue lined with red, which are the colours of the French royal livery as expressed by the King himself. It was certainly the perfect colour to choose for what appears to have been a useful diplomatic gift from Louis XIV to Charles XI.[10]

---

9    The first complete printed list appears to have been Lemau de la Jaisse's large poster-like *Carte générale du militaire de France* (Paris, 1730) followed, from 1733, by seven-yearly *Abrégés* that came in the form of small books.
10   Erik Bellander, *Dräkt ohh Uniform* (Stockolm: Norstedts, 1973), pp.144, 176, 591–592; Thomas Roth, 'The French Uniform Mystery', *Uniform* (Stockolm: Arméemuseum, 2010), pp.24–33; Bengt

A coat of a royal regiment, *c*. 1680s. Blue coat with red cuffs and lining, possibly for an enlisted man. Yellow metal buttons. The red material has faded. (Courtesy Royal Army Museum, Stockholm. AM.015470)

An all blue coat, possibly for a NCO, *c*. 1680s. Yellow or gold buttons, thing gold lace edging the cuffs and pockets. The lining may have been red but have now faded a buff hue. (Courtesy Royal Army Museum, Stockholm. AM.017538)

# UNIFORMS, COLOURS AND MUSIC

By the time of the grand 1698 camp at Compiègne, a lot had changed, which shows how far higher authority had succeeded in imposing its desires on such things as hairstyle or knee garters. On 25 June 1698, Lieutenant General d'Artagnan, director general of the infantry in Flanders issued the following instruction, summarised here, to the troops:[11]

> Officers will be dressed in the same colours as soldiers. Captains will have an inch wide of silver or gold lace edging, meaning one or the other [depending on the regiment's button colour], with gold or silver buttonholes and thread … The other officers will have the same dress except [for the lace] edging.

All cravats had to be tied the same way with two turns around the neck with the ends tucked under the waistcoat or coat. Stockings were to be worn uniformly with white or buff garters. Shoe buckles were to be uniform and cords would be issued for the men to "tie their hair behind." Hat brims were held up by retainers and the crown came down on the forehead within a "finger's width" of the eyes. The skirts of soldier's coats were not to go below the knees. Regiments that had waistcoats would wear their coat unbuttoned all the way down "but would always wear their waist belt over the coat."

For the September 1698 review at Compiègne, it was noted by an observer that "all the princes alternatively appeared at the head of their regiments in uniform" and the infantry was:

> … distinguished by different colours for the [coat] cloth, the cuffs, the waistcoats, the stockings and the ribbon that soldiers wore on the shoulder. It was the first time that one saw the whole infantry wearing waistcoats. Officers were also dressed according to the [uniform of their] corps. All the troops had hats edged with gold or silver, with cockades…[12]

An infantry officer, *c.* 1710. A fine view of a typical officer's dress in the early eighteenth century. From a 1710 print by Watteau. (Courtesy Rijksmuseum, Amsterdam. RP-P-OB-5433)

---

Hermansson, 'The Justeaucorps in the Royal Army Museum in Stockholm', *IAMAM Bayerisches Armeemuseum, Specialist symposium*, Ingolstadt, 21 to 25 May 1979. Some of the coats were almost certainly the inspiration for Swedish army uniforms from the late seventeenth century, notably the Model 1687 infantry coat. Later on, the origin of these garments was lost to the point that they were labelled "Old Pomeranian clothes" in 1759 with two even defined as "Russian" coat to quote the museum's label on these garments. Oral history, however, ought not be put aside because it is a form of documentation just as examining the artefacts themselves that are all in the colour of the royal livery of France, which is likely to not to have been by accident.

11 Quoted in: *Carnet de La Sabretache*, December 2005, pp.136–137.
12 Nodot, *La Rivale travestie ou les aventures…arrivées au camp de Compiègne* (Paris, 1699), n.p.

Broglie's 1709 instructions called for a simpler uniform "as much as possible" for captains and subaltern officers. Their uniform coat were not to have "any gold or silver thread buttons or buttonholes", like the sergeant's, but made of better quality cloth. The best buttons to have were those of silver or gold on wood because they were light in weight. Sergeants' coats were to have gold laces on the cuffs and their buttons be better than those of the soldiers. Their hats were laced with gold or silver lace. Drummers were dressed in the livery worn by their regiment and their drum belts and waist belts were had livery lace; they also were to have a linen smock and a linen drum cover to protect the coat and drum from excessive wear. Drum majors were to have "a few fine laces on their coat cuffs and pockets" to distinguish them. Soldiers were to be well dressed with good coats, waistcoat, breeches, stockings, shoes, two shirts, two cravats, gaiters and hats. The best hats had wide brims and the soldiers were not to take off the hooks and eyes to keep up the brims "as they often did"; soldier's hat lace was not mentioned in these instruction. Wool lace "a finger wide" [and presumably black] was provided to tie the hair. In mountainous countries, shoes soles were to be reinforced with nails to last longer.[13]

At that time there were severe supply shortages. Many infantrymen were wearing nearly worn out uniforms by 1709–1710. A British report noted that "the [French] Enemy is in extreme Want, insomuch that in several places their Leathern Shoes were taken from them in the winter and locked up till the opening of the Campaign, & wooden Shoes given them in the mean time…" The French infantry may have looked more ragged than formerly, but its worse trials of the War of Spanish Succession were behind them and, soon thereafter they persevered and triumphed wearing proudly their worn out or new uniforms because the shortages were only temporary as the allies then learned.[14]

## Colours

During the reign of Louis XIII and even before that time, an infantry regiment that had a white mestre de camp colour was one of the few old so-called "permanent" regiments designating those, such as the Gardes-Françaises or Picardie, that were not disbanded between wars. Henceforth, from 1661, the mestre de camp company would be known as the colonel's company and all such companies in all regiments would henceforth have a white colonel's colour (the British equivalent being the king's or queen's colour). It no longer indicated permanency of certain units, but announced that all regiments in the army were answerable to the King. The white colour was plain consisting of the white cross of France with white quarters in most

---

13 Charles-Guillaume Broglie, 'Règlement pour les réparations des bataillons destinés à servir sur la frontière du Piémont', *Carnet de La Sabretache*, 1923, pp.496–302.
14 *The Manuscripts of Marquess Townshend*, Eleventh Report, Appendix, Part IV, London, 1877, p.63, Stephen Poyniz to Thomas Ward, The Hague, 1 April 1710. He also mentioned that "The [allied] Magazins are ready and the [British] Army very well cloathed & recruited."

## UNIFORMS, COLOURS AND MUSIC

Left: infantry ensign, mid seventeenth century. Colour poles were then quite short and did not rest on the ground. Print after Collombon's *Trophée d'armes*, Lyon, 1650. (Author's photo)

Below: ensign, Dauphiné Regiment, late seventeenth to early eighteenth century. The uniform was a grey coat with blue cuffs and lining according to the 1692 and 1702 lists. Print after J.E. Hilpbert. (Courtesy Anne S.K. Brown Military Collection, Brown University Library, Providence, RI, USA)

Left: ensign holding a regimental colour of the Dauphin Regiment, late 1660s–1670s. The regiment initially dressed in grey with cuffs and stockings of different colours for its five squads according to Daniel's history. See colour plate section for the colour. Print after Philippoteaux. (Courtesy New York Public Library, New York City)

Regimental colour-pike's spear, late seventeenth and eighteenth centuries. This iron example was originally gilded. (Musée de l'Armée, Paris. Author's photo)

French regiments, but some had gold lilies and mottos thereon, for instance if honoured with the "royal" prefix. Foreign regiments tended to have more elaborate decorations such as figures or other devices painted on their white colours.

As a consequence, and from the 1660s onwards, the other colours carried in a regiment, the *drapeaux d'ordonnance* (the British equivalent being the regimental colours) became more permanent insofar as their design and hues displayed in their quarters. Up to the middle of the seventeenth century, there was one *drapeaux d'ordonnance* per company in French infantry regiments, but this decreased thereafter to three per battalion (including the colonel's colour in the first battalion). Nearly all regiments had the white cross, emblematic of France, with quarters having a multitude of designs in various colours (see illustrations for a sampling of the extraordinary variety that produced some masterpieces of flag design). No regiment was to have exactly the same regimental colour as another. Royal and provincially titled regiments had regimental colours that did not change thereafter. In gentlemen's and princes' regiments, the quarters were originally in the livery colour of their colonel and would change when another colonel took command and imposed his livery. This changed during the last third of the seventeenth century in that the colour's patterns remained the same when a new colonel was appointed. Foreign regiments generally followed basic French usage, but might also have exceptions such as some German units having three central lilies instead of the white cross.

While there seems to be many regimental colours illustrated in this book, there were many, many more including a vast number now unknown or uncertain. For older permanent regiments, regimental histories and traditions followed by nineteenth century historians and artists that attribute colours going back, in some cases like Picardie, to the sixteenth century using largely eighteenth-century sources. However, the few sources that exist that were compiled at the time when Louis XIV reigned were not widely known until the mid twentieth century, when French researchers became more aware of the Dutch trophy plates featuring captured colours and early eighteenth century compilations. Those reproduced here are simply given as a sampling of the extraordinary variety in attractive heraldic designs that was then achieved and remained unsurpassed thereafter. The descriptions vary and we have relied in particular on Charrié's, Fourré's and Hall's compilations that we consider the best recently published sources.[15]

---

15 Pierre Charrié, *Drapeaux et étendards du roi* (Paris: Léopard d'or, 1989); P. Fourré, *Trophées de la guerre de Succession d'Espagne 1700-1713* (Paris: Ch. Teranna, 1994); P. Fourré, *Les drapeaux de l'infanterie française sous Louis XIV 1638-1715* (Saint-Cloud: privately published typescript with drawings, 1977); Guignard, *L'École de Mars*, Vol. 1, p.736; Robert Hall, *Flags and Uniforms of the French Infantry 1688-1714* (Farnham, UK: Pike and Shot Society, 2002). See the annotated bibliography in Hall's study for details on du Vivier and other early sources.

For recognition in the very smoky battles of that era, all regiments in French service had a white cravat tied below the colour pole's pike. All colours had cords with tasselled ends, often of the colours of the quarters. The size of the colours varied. In the early seventeenth century, they might be between 250 and 300cm square. They were supposed to be square, but some were rather rectangular, 250 by 270cm for the Gardes-Suisses at the end of the seventeenth century; about 198cm for Dauphin in 1706 and 180cm square with a 34cm wide cross in *c*. 1710. The poles were still short in the seventeenth century and ensigns rested the lower end on their hip. The longer poles came in gradually, seemingly from the end of the seventeenth century and early eighteenth century when they were at about 360cm long including the spear. The spear head, which was about 20cm, might be of gilded iron (see illustration) or of a lily according to an order to make 14 colour poles, which tells us there was not a precisely fixed pattern.[16]

## Military Music and Early Infantry Bands

The association of music, armies and battles appears to go back to the earliest times. Drums and flutes are prehistoric and the Bible mentions that the walls of Jericho collapsed at the sound of trumpets. The Romans had great military parades to the sound of various instruments. This sort of display somewhat vanished during the Dark Ages in western Europe until the Crusades when Christian knights rediscovered instruments in the Middle East such as cymbals and elaborate kettle drums that are said, in conjunction with trumpets, to have had a positive effect on martial music. In the fifteenth century, the Swiss were the first to use portable drums to regulate marching in step. The Renaissance continued this trend with mounted troops adopting the trumpet while foot troops had drums and, from the 1530s, fifes and even bagpipes brought by Scots mercenaries were heard in French armies. From 1534, the usual practice was to have a drummer and a fifer in every infantry company. The evolution of infantry tactics stipulated that drums became important to signal movements on battlefields or during parades. Formations of musketeers and pikemen marched to the beat of the drum. Fifers became scarcer on the establishment, but did not disappear entirely.[17]

In the early seventeenth century, the Sieur de Praissac could write that the first duty of all drummers was to beat all orders such as the alarm, the march, the double step, *La Diane* (reveille) and others. Drum majors became common in regiments ranking as NCOs to look after the drummers and fifers who needed to be disciplined, trained and taught to march into battle. They all provided music, which was only accessible to ordinary people – including soldiers – in the company of persons who mastered various instruments such as lutes, violins and oboes. There were also Oriental influences to provide

---

16 Charrié, *Drapeaux et étendards du roi*, pp.57–58.
17 Thierry Bouzard, *Le tambour dans les armées du roi de France: partitions et usages* (ULCO: Boulogne-sur-Mer, 1983), n.p. Online at: <lasabretache.fr/wp-content/.../10/Le_tambour_dans_les_armees_du_roi_de_Fra.pdf>.

Top left: score of the *Marche des soldats de Turenne* (March of Turenne's Soldiers), mid seventeenth century. This march was composed for the troops by royal court composer Jean-Baptiste Lully, no doubt at the request of the King. Print from Faivre d'Arcier and Royé's 1895 *Historique du 37e regiment d'infanterie*. (Author's photo)

Top right: infantry drummer, 1670s and early 1680s. This print confirms that drummers often had more ornate clothing than private soldiers, being often decorated with lace and dressed in the hues of the colonel's livery. In Maneson Mallet's *Les travaux de Mars,* 1686 edition at The Hague. (Private collection. Author's photo)

Left: Infantry drummer, mid seventeenth century. The caption reads: "The drummer, necessary in the army." Print after Collombon's *Trophée d'armes*, Lyon, 1650. (Author's photo).

## UNIFORMS, COLOURS AND MUSIC

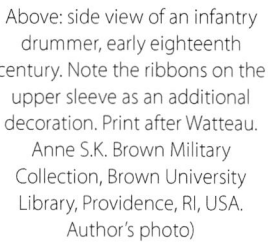

Above: side view of an infantry drummer, early eighteenth century. Note the ribbons on the upper sleeve as an additional decoration. Print after Watteau. Anne S.K. Brown Military Collection, Brown University Library, Providence, RI, USA. Author's photo)

Above: rear view of an eighteenth-century infantry drummer. A remarkably fine view showing the tasseled shoulder ribbons, the way drums were usually carried and a good view of the sword and its belt. Print after Watteau. (Anne S.K. Brown Military Collection, Brown University Library, Providence, RI, USA. Author's photo)

Left: Champagne Infantry Regiment, drum-major, early eighteenth century. The drummers of the Champagne Regiment wore the King's livery coat of blue lined with red, garnished with the King's grand livery lace. The drum major holds a long cane to conduct the musicians. It was, at that time, a simple, utilitarian object. The coat of its drum-major had, in addition, gold lace on the sleeve between the livery lace and edging the cuffs. Print after Lucien Rousselot. (Private collection. Author's photo)

Infantry fifer, mid seventeenth century. The caption reads: "The fifer, to rejoice the soldiers." Print after Collombon's *Trophée d'armes*, Lyon, 1650. (Author's photo)

certain sounds as well as to add an exotic aspect. Cavalry regiments sought to have kettle drums and some infantry formations had cymbals, sometimes as "jingling johnnies" when fixed to an ornate pole and, eventually, the ultimate *chic* was to have an African musician dressed in Oriental costume. Persons with good voices were sought and might form groups of singers. As it were, it encouraged soldiers to sing during long marches to the tunes of *Cadet Roussel* or *Malbrouk s'en va en guerre* (Marlborough goes to war) to name some still familiar in francophone countries.[18]

There were several ways to beat drums in the army – the Swiss, the German, the Irish, the Scots and the French styles were heard. In 1662, Clérambault's Regiment was marching with drums to its accustomed German style as was the German Alsace Regiment until 17 September 1663 when a royal order specified that drum beats would henceforth be in the French style for all units, be they French or foreign, notably for posting guards when serving together in garrisons. Otherwise, conforming to royal wishes, French regiments beat drums in the French style, the Swiss in the Swiss style and others in the German or Swiss styles noted the Duc de Villeroi in 1683. What these were like exactly is shrouded in mystery. Surviving partitions are rare and open to many interpretations. A 1666 note further reveals that the Lyonnois Regiment could drill *à la baguette* (to the tap of the drums) rather than by shouted commands, which must have been done in other regiments also.[19]

The Sun King understood the impressive psychological effect of combining uniformed soldiers marching in step with the sound of martial music. It struck people's imagination and sense of glory. Furthermore, he felt that it would be even grander if it was orderly and similar. In 1670, the beat of la générale (for the assembly of troops), almost certainly written by famed court composer Jean-Baptiste Lully, was introduced in March followed by a royal order on 10 July imposing it on the entire army. This was the first time uniform drumbeats were imposed by higher command and they became

---

18 The influence of Ottoman music in the West resulted in many marches. Although it concerns mainly compositions of the eighteenth and nineteenth centuries, *Invitation to the Seraglio: Period Dances, Marches and Occasional Pieces* by the London Academy of Ottoman Court Music, director Emre Araci (Warner Classics, CD2564 61472-2) has recorded an amazing 19 marches to orchestral music. Many forgotten traditional songs of Old France with a military theme are still widely sung in French Canada and are the subjects of countless recordings and books.

19 Bouzard, *Le tambour dans les armées du roi de France*, n.p.; Carnot, 'Deux documents sur l'origine de l'uniforme militaire', p.580.

quite important because they were henceforth also used to assemble urban civil populations all over the nation for the next two centuries. To achieve uniformity, the King further announced that the drum major of the Gardes-Françaises was being sent out "to instruct the drummers of the troops" as to the beats they would all play. To march and fight to the same drum commands throughout the largest army in Europe was thus achieved.[20]

The King had organised pageants in his youth and, in those, military drummers and fifers were joined by musicians of wind, string and reed instruments. Music now began to be noted on paper for the various players. To provide a fuller sound experience, Louis XIV did not hesitate to adjunct his court musicians to his guard's musicians so as to form something of an orchestra – the ancestor of our military bands. A certain sense of unity could be seen as both the guards and the King's musicians wore the same basic blue lined with red royal livery. Lully composed several pieces named marches for parading troops such as the Marche des soldats de Turenne and the Marche des Mousquetaires. So did François Couperin. These were heard at lavish festive or formal events and soon drew enthusiastic crowd to see the pageantry and hear the martial music. It was said that such grandeur had not been seen since the days of the Romans. In 1681, the oboes of the King's Musketeers were considered to have been "very satisfying" to the ears of Russian ambassadors. At the King's funeral on 23 September 1715, "kettledrums, trumpets, oboes [and] drums" were impressively heard in St Denis cathedral.[21]

All this pomp and circumstance was not only for performances by royal guard units. The grand nobles that "owned" some of the older regiments also pitched in, creating bands at their own cost. The popularity of martial music spread wider and soon influenced military ensembles, practices and music in other countries. By the late seventeenth century, trombones and clarinets had joined other instruments; the modern military band had come of age. It should be noted that, in the days of the Sun King, the rhythm was slow for drumbeats and for music. Quick steps came much later although, even nowadays, the French Foreign Legion has kept its slow marching rhythm.[22]

---

20  SHD, AG, A1, Vol. 636, Circulaire aux gouverneurs de la frontière, 18 March 1670, quoted in Bouzard, *Le tambour dans les armées du roi de France*, n.p.
21  *Mercure Galant*, May 1681, p. 314; October 1715, p.249.
22  André Corvisier et al, *Dictionnaire d'art et d'histoire militaires* (Paris: PUF, 1988), pp.601–604; *3 siècles de musique militaire* (Musidisc Europe LP 30 RC 788) has a few pieces of the Sun King's era played by the wind ensemble of the Leipzig Academy led by Captain Erich Seifert.

# 12

# Camping on Campaign

## The Sun King and his Army on Campaign

When a king went on a military campaign with his army, it created a peculiar situation insofar as the actual command of the forces and raised a myriad of other issues. With the Sun King on campaign, the notion of the royal presence took an even more complicated issue. In the sixteenth century and before, the King was the general leading the army in battle and his strategic and tactical choices were central to success or failure. King Henry IV was a good example of such a royal general. In the seventeenth century, the situation changed with royal rulers in several western European countries leaving the actual command to senior officers, some of which were far superior as effective field commanders than their crowned princes who nevertheless could be seen with all the trappings of supreme military authority in their official portraits.

Once the Sun King took effective and autocratic power in 1661, it became an absolute necessity that, when the ruler of Europe's most powerful kingdom travelled with his army, it be done with all the fully deployed possibilities of the age – the royal party had to be grand and overwhelmingly impressive with plenty of luxury, abundance and magnificence. Prestige, grandeur and propaganda demanded pomp that befitted a great king. There were hundreds of servants, pages and petty officials for food and drink, not just for the King, but for many, many dozens of guests and officers that were admitted to the royal compound. This would be guarded by hundreds of royal guardsmen to ensure the King's security.

Louis XIV liked very much the trappings of military command and understood far more than his contemporaries the power of positive propaganda that hailed him as a near-Olympian glorious French version of Mars, the God of war, who was ever victorious. If the King was present at an engagement, it had to be absolutely certain that it would be a victorious affair "won by the King" to feed the royal propaganda.

This naturally created an extra worry for the marshals and generals. Not only did they have to worry about their own performance facing the enemy, but the safety of the King with his ever-victorious image was a sacrosanct factor. Victorious battles had to be guaranteed. For an all-out engagement in the field, one had to invoke the doctrine of overwhelming superiority.

Tents of the French army's headquarters during the siege of Cambrai, 1677. This encampment is probably not the King's quarter, but it is certainly for senior officers and officials. The tents shown are of suitable quality. The King is seen at the centre. Detail from a print after van der Meulen. (Courtesy Anne S.K. Brown Military Collection, Brown University Library, Providence, RI, USA)

This had been possible in 1667–1668 and in the Dutch summer campaign of 1672 when even crossing the Rhine was not very risky. The French army had four to five soldiers to every Dutch soldier. By the autumn of 1672, the generals knew that help would eventually reach the Dutch and the score would be evened; thus future field engagements could spell disaster for the Sun King. He certainly understood this and was shrewd enough not to actually believe he was a great tactician. On the other hand, if an army besieging a fortress was much stronger than the defending garrison and if enough resources combined with the talents of a genial engineer such as Vauban were deployed, positive results were almost certain. And once the place was taken, propaganda could then announce that the besieged fortress was "taken by the King" for his glory. Therefore, both for the safety of the King and for a glorious outcome, laying siege to fortress cities was the best way to deal with the problem of having the King amongst his army. From 1673, the number and intensity of extensive siege operations multiplied (see map), many having the presence of the King.

Since the King had to be an Olympian figure of greatness, which appears to have been something especially dear to the Sun King, his camping gear was up to that lofty standard. Not only was he the ruler, he was there as the commander-in-chief. The logistical problems posed by the King's party, which was a huge and not very fast caravan involving a multitude of horses and wagons with hundreds of retainers and servants, perhaps 400, could be seen as more complicated than the army he was with. On the way to his destination and once on spot with an army for, say, a siege, it was frequent that the King would actually spend the night in a local nearby chateau, but there was also *le quartier du roi* (the King's quarter) that was a near sacred area reproducing as much as possible a royal palace. This area was closely guarded by troops of the royal guard and it often was surrounded by field fortifications; no one could enter it who was not authorised to do so. The King's quarter was not usually set up in the middle of a field as is sometimes shown in prints, but in areas with fruit trees and gardens that were much more agreeable. Within were many tents of outstanding luxury for various purposes. The three largest tents consisted of an anti-chamber tent ornamented with two golden suns, a dining tent and a guardsmen's tent, also decorated with two golden suns on each side, hands of justice and sceptres and golden lilies on the tent's material that was painted blue with gold highlights. There was a tent-chapel ornamented by a golden sun and surmounted by three gilded crosses where the King would hear mass every morning. Another luxurious tent was the one used as a reception hall for ambassadors. Apart from his protocolary morning *lever* (rising), meetings with officers and officials, parades, inspections and, if at a siege, tours of the trenches, the King's activity also involved a dinner whose service was as in a royal palace with a great choice of food and wine. Princes, generals and courtiers would dine with him with more familiarity than at court, although he sat in a chair and his guests had stools; Saint-Simon commented that apart from when he was with the army, the King "never ate with any man under any circumstance".

The tents consisting of the King's private apartments were actually portable wooden houses that reproduced the suitably luxurious interior decoration of Versailles when it was a small hunting lodge chateau. This consisted of the King's bedchamber, his office and his wardrobe with all suitable furniture. These structures were covered with richly decorated linen to look like tents although brass chimneys from the fireplaces emerged above.[1]

Grand nobles and senior officers and officials would go on campaign in grand style with at least several suitably appointed tents and numerous servants. They also had their personal guard companies for their security. Some of these high ranking officers were also colonels-in-chief of regiments and sometimes, their regiment was with their army on campaign. An example of belongings is given by those of Lieutenant General de Bouligneux killed at the siege of Verrua

---

1 Paul Bastier, 'Louis XV sur le front de la Guerre de Succession d'Autriche' at <*https://chartres.hypotheses.org/4927?*>. Much of the camping gear used by Louis XV consisted of reproductions of Louis XIV's equipment kept in the warehouses of the chateau of Vincennes. For grand nobles and senior officers and officials, the ambassador of Spain in France during the 1740s – a less ostentatious era than the Sun King's – mentioned 17 tents for him and his suite, which he considered average for persons of quality.

in Italy on 15 December 1704. An inventory of his belongings revealed he had, presumably in his tents, a bed covered with red and another with green, two tables, eight tablecloths, a dozen chairs and cooking instruments. There was a lot of silverware including several large serving dishes, 35 plates, forks, spoons and knives, salt, pepper and sugar containers, a coffee pot, a tea filter and six candle holders valued at 7,002 livres. His stable included 20 horses and seven mules. Besides his guardsmen, he had 23 servants to attend him. We might add that this was probably a very modest equipage; an order of 15 April 1707 restrained what was allowed to a lieutenant general to 40 horses with two or three carts for himself and his suite. Marshals would have had a larger suite. Be they mediocre or good commanders, they felt that it was important to show, in imitation of their royal master, that their position in society was enviable and superior to the many commoners who, then as now, envied their wealth and thus admired them for their financial ease forgetting that money has little to do with a general's success on the battlefield.[2]

There were exceptions to the above, perhaps many more than are recorded since the chroniclers were primarily dazzled by displays of riches and power that many senior officers wished to project. For all the baggage trains on campaign, one could also see the greatest marshal having and obviously enjoying a low-keyed lifestyle on campaign. Marshal Turenne like to roam around his men's camps in the evening to see how they were, if they had enough of the basic necessities, chit-chat a bit, which caused his soldiers to call him their "father" because they sensed he was one of them as much as one of the greatest generals of their times. In August 1705, the Duc de Vendôme was seen by Quincy in his camp at an evening meal with his brother after the battle of Cassano. "All they had to regale themselves was soldier's bread with a small piece of cheese; their table was a log with a bayonet planted in it into which a candle had been stuck" to provide some light.[3]

## The Infantry's Lodging

The great majority of regimental field officers – namely colonels, lieutenant colonels and majors – had more humble circumstances and were nevertheless lodged with suitable dignity. They usually had a rectangular canvas tent whose large size was not standard. It was covered by a marquise awning of blue and white canvas providing additional cover against sun or rain. Company officers had a tent much like those of the NCOs and private soldiers, measuring about 2m 30cm square. Unlike the men's, it was also covered by a marquise awning of blue and white canvas.[4]

---

2   F.B., 'L'équipage de champagne d'un lieutenant général (M. de Bouligneux) en 1704', *Carnet de La Sabretache*, 1901, pp.84–87.
3   Quincy, *Mémoires*, Vol. 2, p.122. We will give more details on Louis-Joseph de Bourbon, Duc de Vendôme in Volume 4; he led armies yet was from a 'bastard' royal blood line and thus could not be an officially recognised prince of the blood nor a marshal. As a result, he did not fit any category of senior officers officially listed.
4   Pierre Benigny, 'Campement', *Le Passepoil*, 1924, pp.47–48.

Above: the French army's camp at the siege of Douai, 1667. The tents and general aspect of the camp are not as neatly laid out as recommended in military manuals. Detail of a print after van der Meulen. (Courtesy Library and Archives Canada, Ottawa. NL15529)

Left: examples of field officers' (top) and regimental officers' (bottom) tents. Print after Pierre Benigny. *Le Passepoil*, 1924.

# CAMPING ON CAMPAIGN

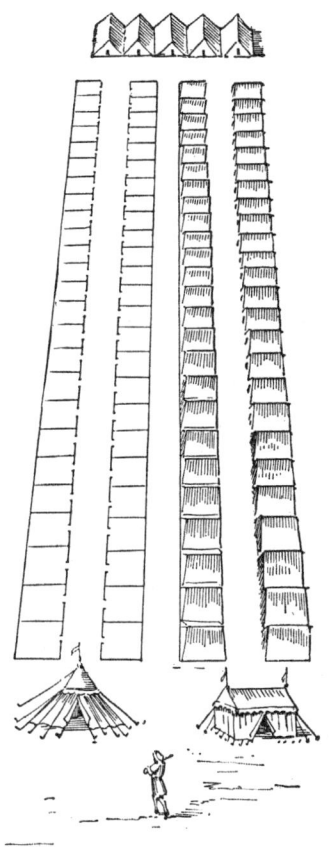

# THE ARMIES AND WARS OF THE SUN KING 1643–1715 VOLUME 2

Previous page, clockwise:

Nine infantry fusiliers sleeping in a tent, early eighteenth century. Eight of these rather cramped soldiers are more or less undressed, using their coat as a blanket with some wearing their hat as a night cap. The ninth fusilier (lower left) is sleeping all dressed, presumably ready to stand his turn with a night guard or in case of an alarm. Print after Watteau. (Private collection. Author's photo)

Tents neatly laid out for an infantry regiment on campaign, second half of the seventeenth century. One hundred enlisted men's tents are shown, which would shelter around 900 to 1,000 men. Print incorporating features in Mallet's 1672 **Les Travaux de Mars**. (Private collection. Author's photo)

An infantry regiment leaving its winter quarters, *c*. 1695. This remarkable print is a social comment showing what a burden quartering troops was for peasants. An officer notes that one of the peasant girls is pregnant; a soldier grabs pigeons, the host and his wife are pressured by two soldiers to give them food and wine are amongst the scenes shown. Print after Guérard. (Anne S.K. Brown Military Collection, Brown University Library, Providence, RI, USA. Author's photo)

Below: camp scene of troops on campaign, early eighteenth century. This print shows what is rarely mentioned in correspondence, namely the women and children who who were with their military mates and fathers sharing a hard life, exemplified here by the worn out tents and living out in the open. Detail of a 1710 plate after Watteau. (Courtesy Anne S.K. Brown Military Collection, Brown University Library, Providence, RI, USA)

Troops on a march, *c.* 1685–1690. The infantryman at left carries many pots and pans and might be a company or squad cook; his companion has a fur-covered knapsack. A right, what appears to be a fusilier since his shoulder belt supports a pouch. The waist-belt is invisible, but worn under the coat to support his typical soldier's sword. Detail from a painting of the period. (Musée Condé, Chantilly. Author's photo)

As for the men's tents, they were of canvas and might be somewhat more rectangular than those of company officers. They did not have the *marquise*, at least in theory, as some prints and paintings depict the tent's material as striped canvas. A battalion, in ideal circumstances camping in a flat field, would have its tents in rows of 25 tents close together forming "streets" in a tent regimental village that could contain about 900 men, assuming nine soldiers lodged in one tent. The field officers' and the company officers' tents were at either end.

## Rations

The infantryman's basic ration had been defined in 1636 and was basically renewed by the King's order of 12 November 1665. It did not substantially change thereafter. The private soldier was entitled to a daily ration of 2 pounds (978g) of bread, 1 pound (489g) of meat of either veal, beef, mutton or pork, and a pint (932ml) of wine or a pot of cider or one of beer. The variety depended on what was available where the soldiers happened to be. Another variation could be salted dry fish or a hard cheese to respect the lean (no meat) Friday in Catholic countries. In winter quarters, soldiers were fed by their inhabitant host and the cost of their food, which was calculated as the army ration, was deducted from their *taille* tax bill. Thus, inhabitants were surely stingy about what they provided. Soldiers who had a rank fared better. Their food was the same, but they had more. Sergeants had two rations. Second lieutenants had three, lieutenants four and captains six.[5]

---

5   Guignard, *L'École de* Mars, Vol. 1, pp.657–658; P. Eveno, 'L'alimentation conditionnée par la solde', *Carnet de La Sabretache*, December 2005, pp.205–207; Rousset, *Histoire de Louvois*, Vol. 1, pp.248–250.

Infantry marching, c. 1695. The original caption reads: "One of the great fatigues of the soldier when marching is to carry, besides his weapons, the tent, the pot of his chambrée, especially when it rains or is too hot. This [carrying] charge is done in turn. The name chambrée applies to five or six soldiers who share the same hut or barrack." Print after Guérard. (Anne S.K. Brown Military Collection, Brown University Library, Providence, RI, USA. Author's photo)

As can be seen in many contemporary prints, there was more variety in the food of the common soldiers than the prescribed bread and meat official ration. One notes the heads of chickens or ducks sticking out of haversacks or the whole fowl strung to some belt. These were not part of the rations so were likely "liberated" from some poor farmer by troops marching through or else seized from a stingy host when leaving winter quarters. Vegetables and fruit were to be bought when not hurriedly picked in a field and these would also have been available, along with more wine and something stronger like brandy, from sutlers following the regiments. They too had a tent or two identifiable by some sign hung on a tent pole with, perhaps, a folding table and, often, a sutler's or soldier's female companion looking after the business with a smile for all – an appreciated presence in a man's world. The famed *filles de mauvaisevie* (basically prostitutes) were not, in principle, tolerated in or near the regimental camps or quarters due to disciplinary problems they could cause (a topic we will examine in the next volumes). Those in camp were the accepted wives, and their children, who "followed the drum" with the loves of their lives in the days of the Sun King. It was a rough and often short life for all these humble people, soldiers and their dependents, but all shared the pageantry of war at one of its historical peaks as well as its horror, going places they would never otherwise see in the adventurous lives they sought.

# Appendix I

# French Length Measures and Currency Under Louis XIV

## Length Measures

Note that the French foot was not the same length as the English foot. The French 12 inches is longer and comes to 12.789 inch, English measure. Before 1668, there were several systems of measurement in France.

The official French length measures from 1668 to 1840 were:

    2 Miles make 1 Lieue = 3.898 km
    1,000 Toises make 1 Mile = 1.949 km (English mile = 1.61 km)
    3 Toise make 1 Perche = 5.847 m
    6 Pieds (feet) make 1 Toise = 1.949 m (English fathom = 1.83 m)
    12 Pouces (inches) make 1 Pied (foot) = 32,484 cm (English foot = 30.48 cm)
    12 Lignes (lines) make 1 Pouce (inch) = 2.707 cm (English inch = 2.54 cm)
    12 Points make one Ligne (line) = 2.256 mm
    1 Point = 0.188 mm

## Currency

One livre or livre tournois had 20 sols (occasionally called *sous*) and one sol had 12 deniers. This basic system, ideally in silver pieces, was equivalent to the pre-1971 currency used in Great Britain and parts of the British Commonwealth: 1 pound had 20 shillings and a shilling had 12 pence.

    From this basis, there was quite a bewildering number of currency variations in Ancien Régime France. The most important was the Louis d'or (the gold Louis). Introduced in 1640, its gold content provided an officially regulated high value pound against the basic silver tournois pound whose value fluctuated. It was an early form of the gold standard. For instance, to have one Louis d'or one would need:

1640: 10 livres
1652: 12 livres
1654: 10 livres
1656: 11 livres
1686: 11 livres, 10 sols
1687: 11 livres, 5 sols
1689: 11 livres, 12 sols
1700: 13 livres, 5 sols
1708: 12 livres, 15 sols
1709: 20 livres
1713: 14 livres
1715: 20 livres

Contemporary documents and later studies do not (or cannot) always make the difference between the ordinary livre tournois and the Louis d'or. Needless to add that troops were paid in the basic livre tournoi.

Besides and with the above, various species were also used more or less formally. Values expressed could fluctuate in livres tournois:

1 gold Guinée Portugaise (Portuguese guinea) was worth 48 livres
1 gold Pistole d'Espagne was worth 21 livres, 10 sols
1 silver Écu à Couronne or Gros Écu was worth 6 livres, 12 sols
1 silver Spanish piastre or dollar was worth about the same as the silver écu
1 silver Petit Louis or Petit Écu was worth 3 livres, 6 sols

## Appendix II

# Infantry Regiments 1643–1715

For maximum simplicity we list the regiments as follows:

Regimental name and date of creation are given for those raised from 14 May 1643 (date when Louis XIV becomes king), regimental name changes with date, disbandment or amalgamation date.

The great majority of units went by the names of their current colonel and these changed frequently. Dates are not shown when the unit existed after 1715. Thus Gramont raised before 1643 became Louvigny in 1665, Guiche in 1687, Coëtquen in 1696, Tourville in 1709 and served after 1715 under other names.

Units with provincial names such as Normandie or other permanent designations such as La Marine did not change names.

The great majority of the some 728 infantry regiments listed below took part in many battles and campaigns; just listing them all would require at least another volume. We have, however, listed in brackets after the current colonel's name, when applicable, names of certain battles that are relatively well known. We further add a few of the more uncommon and distant campaigns simply to show that some regiments served in unusual places. Spelling of names, which varies enormously in various sources, follow Susane's compilation.

## Existing on 14 May 1643 Under the Name of:

**Picardie** (Rocroi 1643, Dunes 1658, Lille 1667, Holland 1672, Maastricht 1673, Sicily 1675, Blenheim 1704, Ramillies 1706, Oudenarde 1708, Malplaquet 1709).

**Piémont** (Rocroi 1643, Dunes 1658, Hungary 1664, Holland 1672, Sicily 1675, Namur 1692, Neerwinden 1693, Torino 1706, Oudenarde 1708, Malplaquet 1709, Denain 1712).

**Navarre** (Holland 1672, Namur 1692, Blenheim 1704, Malplaquet 1709, Denain 1712).

**Champagne** (Lille 1667, Holland 1672, Sicily 1676, Namur and Steenkirk 1692, Blenheim 1704, Malplaquet 1709, Denain 1712).

**Normandie** (Holland 1672, Sicily 1676, Namur 1695, Torino 1706, Barcelona 1714).

**Nérestang, Saint-Mesme** 30 June 1645, **Silly** May 1657, **Castelnau** 1665 (Lille 1667, Holland 1672), **Bourbonnais** from 1 February 1673 (Senef 1674, Namur 1692, Neerwinden 1693, Blenheim 1704, Oudenarde 1708, Malplaquet 1709, Denain 1712).

**Rambures** (Rocroi 1643, Dunes 1658, Lille 1667, Senef 1674), **Feuquières** 4 August 1676 (Marsaglia 1693), **Leuville** 27 April 1700.

**Auvergne** (Lille 1667, Holland 1672, Namur and Steenkirk 1692, Marsaglia 1693, Torino 1706, Lerida 1707, Barcelona 1714).

**Sault** (Lille 1667, Holland 1672, Marsaglia 1693, Barcelona 1697), **Tessé** 17 October 1703 (Torino 1706, Toulon 1707), **Tallard** 30 November 1707.

**Vaubécourt**, **Espagny** January 1649 (Stenay 1654, Hungary 1664), **Bandeville** 1669 (, Holland 1672), **Vaubécourt** 18 February 1677 (Marsaglia 1693), **Nettancourt-Haussonville** 25 April 1695, **Mailly-La Houssaye** 3 August 1704 (Almanza and Lerida 1707), **Bueil-Racan** 11 March 1708, **La Brosse** 27 February 1712, **Boufflers-Rémiancourt** 14 November 1713.

**Hallwin, Orléans** 1647, **Languedoc-Orléans** 1648, disbanded 13 February 1660.

**Poudenx, Navailles** 4 February 1645, **Herbouville** July 1652, **Saint-Vallier** 1666 (Crete 1669), **Chateauneuf** 1671 (Holland 1672), **Artois** 1673 (Senef 1674, Namur 1692, Neerwinden 1693, Blenheim 1704, Barcelona 1714).

**Bussy-Lameth**, disbanded December 1658.

**Hôtel, Plessis-Praslin** 17 December 1650 (Stenay 1654, Dunes 1658, Lille 1667, Holland 1672), **Poitou** 31 August 1682 (Namur and Steenkirk 1692, Neerwinden 1693, Blenheim 1704, Oudenarde 1708, Malplaquet 1709, Denain 1712).

**Lyonnois** (Lille 1667, Holland 1672, Namur 1692, Neerwinden 1693, Torino 1706, Antibes and Toulon 1707, Oudenarde 1708, Malplaquet 1709, Denain 1712).

**Aiguebonne**, disbanded 1656.

# INFANTRY REGIMENTS 1643–1715

**Espagny**, into **Guyenne** January 1649.

**Carmain**, disbanded 1643.

**La Douze**, disbanded 1648.

**Vaillac**, disbanded 18 April 1661.

**Montausier**, **Crussol d'Uzès** 10 October 1665 (Holland 1672, Sicily 1675, Namur and Steenkirk 1692, Neerwinden 1693), **Antin** 3 December 1702, **Grondin** 19 December 1703 (Ramillies 1706, Oudenarde 1708, Malplaquet 1709), **La Gervasais** 26 July 1712

**Castel-Bayard**, into **Aunis**.

**La Suze** (joined Fronde 1649), disbanded 1653.

**Vidame d'Amiens** (Rocroi 1643), disbanded 1649.

**Annevoux**, **Conti** 4 June 1649, disbanded 20 January 1650.

**Tournon**, disbanded 1645.

**Ferrières**, disbanded 1647.

**Touraine**, **Amboise** 1650, **Kercado** 1653 (Stenay 1654), **Chambellay** 1654, **Montaigut** 1667 (Crete), **Touraine** 1673 (Marsaglia 1693, Barcelona 1697, Torino 1706, Toulon 1707, Malplaquet 1709).

**La Force Castelmoron**, **Orval** May 1646, **Cugnac** 27 January 1647, **Duras** 1650 often termed **Duras-Montmorency** (Dunes 1658), **Lorges** 8 November 1661, **Rauzan** 1665 (Lille 1667, Crete 1669), into **Duc d'Anjou** 20 January 1670.

**Turenne** (Stenay 1654, Dunes 1658, Hungary 1664, Lille 1667, Holland 1672), **Maine** 14 August 1675 (Namur and Steenkirk 1692, Portugal 1704, Almanza 1707, Denain 1712).

**Saint-Paul**, disbanded 1645.

**Ventadour**, disbanded 1645.

**Navailles**, **La Mothe** 20 April 1667 (Lille 1667, Holland 1672), disbanded for having badly defended Naarden, 4 October 1673.

**Mirepoix**, disbanded 1654.

Matignon, disbanded 1648.

Estrades, into **La Fare** 1648.

**Plessis-Bellière**, disbanded 1654.

**La Mailleraie** (Rocroi 1643), disbanded 1656.

**Bussy-Rabutin**, into **Mazarin-Français** 29 July 1656.

**La Tour, Schulemberg** 4 April 1652 (Lille 1667), disbanded 26 May 1668.

**Langeron**, disbanded 1653.

**Châtillon**, disbanded September 1650.

**Hauterive**, disbanded September 1650.

**Carces**, disbanded 1656.

**Nettancourt, Dampierres** 1652, **Humières** 1689, **Charost** 1702, **Béthune** 1709, **Saillant** 1712.

**Gramont, Louvigny** 1665 (Sicily 1675), **Guiche** 1687, **Coëtquen** 1696, **Tourville** 1709.

**Grancey** (Dunes 1658, Hungary 1664, Holland 1672, Marsaglia 1693), **La Chesnelaye** 1707 (Toulon 1707).

**Charost**, disbanded December 1658.

**Effiat**, disbanded 8 October 1643.

**Passage** (Stenay 1654, Dunes 1658), disbanded 20 July 1660.

**Tonneins, Montpouillan** 1644, disbanded 20 July 1660.

**Grandpré**, disbanded 1662.

**Saint-Aunetz**, disbanded 1648.

**Vervins** (Rocroi 1643), **Estrées** 11 April 1646, **Vervins** 1647, disbanded December 1658.

**Houdancourt**, disbanded 12 December 1659.

**Lambertye, Brinon** 3 January 1647, disbanded 20 July 1660.

# INFANTRY REGIMENTS 1643–1715

Courcelles, disbanded 17 June 1643.

Florainville, disbanded 8 October 1643.

Tavannes, disbanded 1648.

Le Ferron, into **Aiguebonne** and **Galères** 8 October 1643.

Rocquelaure, disbanded 12 April 1661.

**Douglas** (Scottish), (Dunes 1658, Flanders 1667, Holland 1672, Maastricht 1673), into the British army June 1678.

**La Mothe-Houdancourt**, **La Tour-Noaillac** 22 February 1647, disbanded 1658.

**Marchin**, **Launay-Gringenières** 18 May 1650, Marchin 1653, disbanded 1654.

Haucourt, disbanded September 1650.

**Bellebrune**, **Moret** and disbanded 1658.

Vandy, disbanded 20 July 1660.

Rébé, disbanded 12 December 1659.

**Huxelles** (Dunes 1658) into **Mazarin-Français** 11 February 1659, **La Reine** 12 March 1661 (Holland 1672, Senef 1674, Namur and Steenkirk 1692, Blenheim 1704, Torino 1706, Oudenarde 1708, Malplaquet 1709, Denain 1712).

**Schmidberg** (German), **Roqueservières** October 1643, **Schmidberg** 1644, disbanded 25 May 1651.

**Batilly** (German), **Watrouville** 1646, disbanded 1649.

Quincé (Rocroi 1643), disbanded 12 December 1659.

Biscaras, disbanded February 1644.

**Montpezat**, **Limousin** 15 June 1684.

**Bellefond**, **Noirmoutiers** 25 January 1645, disbanded 20 July 1660.

Roqueservières, into **Aiguebonne** and **Galères** 8 October 1643.

Aubeterre (Rocroi 1643), disbanded 12 December 1659.

Colonel's colour of the Bretagne infantry regiment, late seventeenth and early eighteenth century. Its white field had the coat of arms of the Duchy of Britanny with the motto *Potius mori quam foedari* (death rather than dishonour) in gold letters on a blue scroll. (Private collection. Author's photo)

**Bourgogne** (Stenay 1654), disbanded 12 December 1659.

**Castelnau**, into **Mazarin-Français** February 1644.

**Rantzaw** (German), **Royal-Allemand** 10 December 1644, disbanded 24 October 1648.

**Enghien** (joined the Fronde in 1649 with Prince Condé and rejoined the French royal army in 1659, Holland 1672, Senef 1674), redesignated **Bourbon** 28 December 1686 (Namur 1692, Bleinheim 1704, Torino 1706, Toulon 1707, Oudenarde 1708, Malplaquet 1709, Denain 1712).

**Bretagne**, into **Gevres** 10 August 1643.

**Dubuisson**, **Hocquincourt** 9 February 1652 (joined Condé and Fronde 1652), disbanded 1656.

**Miossens**, **Dunois** 1648, disbanded 1649.

**Clanleu**, disbanded February 1649.

**Périgord** (or possibly **Rasilly**), disbanded December 1658.

# INFANTRY REGIMENTS 1643–1715

Estavaillé (Swiss) (Rocroi 1643), **Molondin** 13 June 1648, disbanded 19 February 1654.

Coole (or **Coullon**) (Irish), into **Wall** 7 June 1645.

Fitzwilliam (Irish), disbanded November 1645.

Wall (Irish), **Castelnau-Mauvissière** 23 December 1650, disbanded 1663.

La Marine (Rocroi 1643, Stenay 1654, Holland 1672, Marsaglia 1693, Barcelona 1697, Torino 1706, Toulon 1707).

Noailles (Rocroi 1643), **Du Breuil** 1 February 1646, into **Vaisseaux-Mazarin** 1648.

Henrichemont, **Béthune** 1641, **Sully** 1649, **Béthune** 1655, disbanded 12 December 1659.

Boisdavid, disbanded 1644.

Conti, disbanded 4 June 1649.

Zullard (German) (Rocroi 1643), **Ravenel** 2 January 1647, disbanded 30 November 1652.

Roncherolles, disbanded 12 April 1661.

Boissy, disbanded 1645.

Melun, disbanded 1645.

Marolles, disbanded 1652.

Sénantes, disbanded 21 January 1644.

Galères, disbanded 1673.

Les Isles, disbanded 12 April 1661.

Havre de Grâce, disbanded 1645.

Béarn, **Toulongeon** 14 February 1644, disbanded 1648.

Poitou, transferred to the **French West India Company** in 1665.

Saintonge, **Albret** 1652, disbanded 1654.

Du Tot, disbanded late 1652.

**Nangis, La Tour-Rauquelaure** 24 October 1651, disbanded 12 December 1659.

**Feuquières**, disbanded December 1658.

**Guyenne** (joined Fronde 1651–1653), disbanded 20 July 1660.

**Espenan**, disbanded 6 August 1651.

**Estrées, Vardes** 19 June 1646, disbanded 20 July 1660.

**Villequier**, disbanded 1651.

**Sauveboeuf**, disbanded 1649.

**Castelan**, disbanded late 1644.

**Castreville**, disbanded 1657.

**Harcourt** (Crete 1669), disbanded 1672.

**Jonchères, La Ferté** 3 January 1647, disbanded 1657.

**La Couronne**, into **Duras** 1661.

**Montpeyroux**, disbanded 7 December 1659.

**Vaisseaux, Vaisseaux-Mazarin** 10 March 1644, **Vaisseaux-Candale** 1650, **Vaisseaux-Mazarin** 1658, **Vaisseaux-Provence** 1661, **Royal des Vaisseaux** 20 September 1669.

**Kaërgroët**, into **Mazarin-Français** 4 February 1644.

**Oëhm** (German), disbanded 1649.

**Kalrmbach** (German), disbanded 1648.

**Schombeck** (German), disbanded 2 October 1648.

**Kolhass** (German), **Broglio** 27 February 1654, into **Alsace** 12 December 1659.

**Saint-Preuil** (Rocroi 1643), **Gesvres** 1643, disbanded 1654.

**Courval, Mazencourt** 1650, **Hocquincourt** 6 May 1652, disbanded 12 December 1659.

**Fabert**, disbanded late 1650, re-raised 30 May 1652, disbanded December 1658.

**Watteville** (Swiss) (Rocroi 1643), disbanded 1652.

**Dauphiné**, disbanded 20 July 1660.

**Goësbriant**, destroyed at Rothwell in 1643.

**Maleyssie**, disbanded 1651.

**Metz**, disbanded 1658.

**La Rochette**, into **Galères** 11 October 1643.

**Averne**, **Tilladet** 14 January 1645, **Navailles** 11 March 1650, disbanded 1654.

**Wall** (Irish), into **Coole** 1645.

**La Feuillade**, disbanded 1643.

**Saligny**, disbanded 1649.

**Lesdiguières**, into **Sault** 20 November 1655.

**Lermont**, disbanded 1648.

**Monteclair**, disbanded 1650.

**Lannoy**, disbanded 1648.

**Caderousse**, disbanded 1645.

**Gonnor**, disbanded 8 October 1643.

**Rhan** (Swiss), **Lochmann** 1648, disbanded 19 March 1654.

**Rudella** (Swiss), **Praromann** 1642, disbanded 1653.

**Roll** (Swiss) (Rocroi 1643), **Sury** 1649, disbanded 1650.

**Am-Buchel** (Swiss), disbanded 1649.

**Mazarin-Italien** (Italian), **Anjou-Étranger** 24 April 1651, **Orléans** 12 April 1660.

**Grignols**, disbanded 8 October 1643.

**Cinq-Mars**, disbanded 8 October 1643.

**Laval**, disbanded 8 October 1643.

**Léglise**, disbanded 8 October 1643.

**Mignières**, disbanded 8 October 1643.

**Bridieu**, disbanded 1650.

**Palliers**, disbanded 1645.

**La Prée**, disbanded late 1643.

## Regiments Raised From 14 May 1643:

Being in the reign of Louis XIV, the date of the unit's creation is added.

**Reine-Mère** (Queen Mother) 25 June 1643 (Dunes 1658), **Artois** 1666 (Lille 1667, Holland 1672), **La Couronne** 1673 (Senef 1674, Namur 1692, Almanza 1707, Barcelona 1714).

**Comte d'Auvergne** 30 June 1643, **Duc d'Angoulême** 6 September 1644, disbanded 24 September 1650.

**Folleville** 9 July 1643, disbanded 12 December 1659.

**Schmidberg** (German) 26 December 1643, into **Roqueservières** 10 November 1644.

**Rattweil** (German) 22 December 1643, disbanded 2 October 1648.

**Flechstein** (German) 26 December 1643, disbanded 2 October 1648.

**Guy** (Swiss) 27 December 1643, disbanded 2 October 1648.

**Mazarin-Français** 4 February 1644, **Bretagne** 24 April 1651 (Stenay 1654, Dunes 1658, Holland 1672, Marsaglia 1693, Barcelona 1697, Torino 1706, Toulon 1707, Malplaquet 1709, Denain 1712).

**Carignan** (Piémont) 4 February 1644, **Carignan-Salières** 22 January 1659 (Canada 1665–1668, Holland 1672), **Soissons** 18 July 1676 (Sicily 1674–1675), **Perche** December 1690 (Marsaglia 1693, Torino 1706).

**Beaufort** April 1644, disbanded 2 October 1648.

**Anduze** April 1644, disbanded 1652.

# INFANTRY REGIMENTS 1643–1715

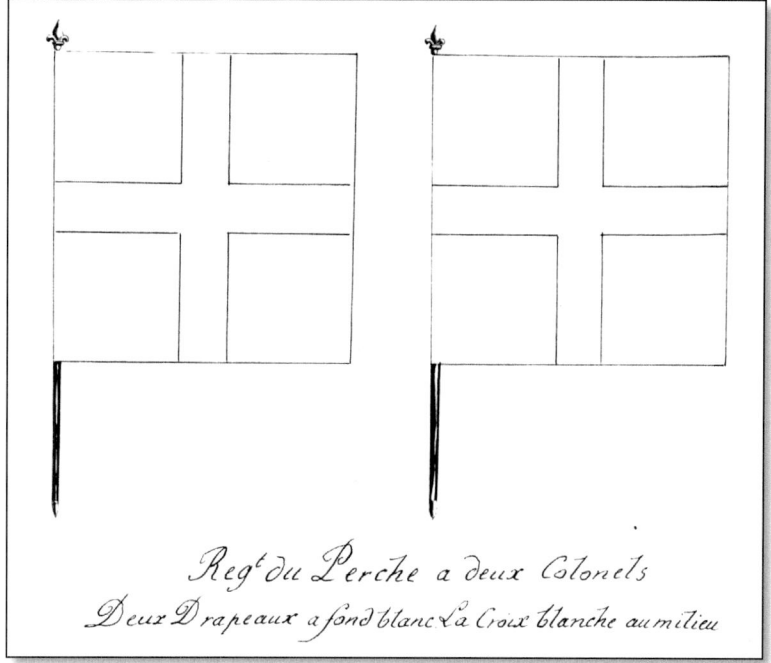

The two colonel's colours of the Carignan-Salières and later Perche regiments, 1659–1/18. Both were all white. This unique tradition went back to 1659 when the regiment of the Prince of Carignan and that of the Marquis de Sallières were merged; neither colonel was willing to give up his colour and so both colours were allowed. This went on after the regiment was named Soissons in 1676 and Perche in 1690 finally ending in 1718. (Du Vivier Ms copy. Jean et Raoul Brunon Collection. Author's photo)

**Frontenac** April 1644, disbanded late 1644.

**Guise** 6 June 1644, disbanded 12 December 1659.

**Ruvigny** 9 June 1644, disbanded late 1644.

**Condé** 11 June 1644 (joined Fronde end of 1649 and with Prince Condé until 7 November 1659 when reintegrated in the royal army. Holland 1672, Senef 1674, Marsaglia 1693, Blenheim 1704, Oudenarde 1708).

**Saint-Germain-Beaupré** 11 June 1644, disbanded 2 October 1648.

**Desmarets** 25 June 1644, disbanded late 1644.

**Cossigny** 25 June 1644, disbanded late 1644.

**Degli Oddi** (Italian) 12 July 1644, **Royal-Italien** May 1651, **Mazarin-Italien** 1652, disbanded 13 March 1661.

**Pontis** 18 August 1644, disbanded late 1644.

**Saint-Hurugues** 18 August 1644, **Linières** 26 April 1646, disbanded 1656.

**Bellemare** 18 August 1644, **Chouppes** 13 January 1646, disbanded 1655.

**Soiez** (German), into **Erlach** (German) 1648.

**Francières** 21 November 1641 (sometimes designated **Bassigny**), disbanded 2 October 1648.

**Altesse Royale** 20 December 1644, merged with **Royal** to form **du Roi** 13 February 1660, retitled **Royal** 21 May 1663.

**Mérinville** 6 January 1645, disbanded 24 November 1658.

**Chaussoy** 6 January 1645, disbanded late 1645.

**Calvières** 6 January 1645, disbanded 2 October 1648.

**Rhom** (Swiss) 6 January 1645, disbanded 24 October 1648.

**Ville** (Piémont) 12 April 1645, disbanded 21 July 1660.

**Mespieux** 12 April 1645, disbanded 2 October 1648.

**Palluau** 20 May 1645, into **Gassion** 20 October 1647.

**Vatimont** 29 July 1645, disbanded 1646.

**Bonickhausen** (German) 29 July 1645, disbanded 24 October 1648.

**Margraf** (German) 29 July 1645, **Raukoupk** 1646, disbanded 24 October 1648.

**Rokeby** (English) 18 November 1645, **Broglio** 8 July 1650, into **Gardes-Écossaises** and **Douglas** 16 December 1659.

**Tremblay** December 1645, unknown thereafter.

**Bournonville** (Walloon) 22 December 1645, disbanded 1647.

**La Vallière** 5 January 1646, disbanded 1647.

**Du Bouquet** 20 February 1646, disbanded 1651.

**Jonzac** 20 February 1646, 29 July 1645, disbanded December 1658.

**Priemski** (Polish) 27 February 1646, **Mazarin-Polonais** 22 February 1649, **Goltz** 15 February 1651, disbanded 1654.

**Platner** (Polish) 27 February 1646, disbanded 1654.

**Hôtel** 14 March 1646, **Créquy** 4 March 1655, disbanded 7 November 1659.

**Castelneau** 14 March 1646, disbanded late 1649.

# INFANTRY REGIMENTS 1643–1715

**Turin** 20 March 1646, disbanded 29 January 1657.

**La Braugelie** 23 May 1646, disbanded 12 December 1659.

**Saint-Amour** 23 May 1646, disbanded late 1646.

**La Roque** 23 May 1646, into **La Marine du Levant** 1648.

**La Grangerie** 23 May 1646, disbanded late 1646.

**Rogles** 23 May 1646, disbanded late 1646.

**La Marine du Levant** 17 June 1646, La Roque 21 April 1648, disbanded 1654.

**Laleu** 17 June 1646, Valois 1650, disbanded 1654.

**Flandres** 17 June 1646, Estrades 1649, disbanded December 1658.

**Aguilar** (Catalan) 6 January 1647, sometimes designated **Marguerit**, disbanded 20 July 1660.

**Sénister** (Catalan) 6 January 1647, **Moustaros** 1649, disbanded 1650.

**Ardenne** (Catalan) 6 January 1647, disbanded 1650.

**Gassion** 1 February 1647, **Palluau** 20 October 1647 (Dunes 1658), **Sourches** 24 April 1663 (Holland 1672), **Harcourt** 20 February 1675, Humières 17 March 1677, **La Châtre** 17 May 1684, **Saint-Sulpice** 1702, **Lannoy** 4 March 1708 (Malplaquet 1709), **Louvigny** 16 April 1712.

**Du Bosquet** 20 February 1647, disbanded 1651.

**Perrault** 27 February 1647, disbanded April 1654.

**Prince Rupert** (English) 14 March 1647, into **Rokerby** 12 November 1648.

**La Fare** 13 June 1647, disbanded 12 December 1659.

**Preston** (Irish) 18 June 1647, disbanded December 1661 or 1662.

**Muskerry** (Irish) 18 June or 15 August 1647, disbanded December 1661 or 1662.

**Duc d'Anjou** 9 July 1647, into **Anjou-étranger** 12 April 1661.

**La Motherie** 1 September 1647, disbanded December 1658.

**Modène** 1 September 1647, **La Guillotière** 31 March 1649, disbanded 12 December 1659.

**Erlach-français** 7 December 1647, disbanded 1654.

**Erlach-allemand** 7 December 1647, **Balthazard** 12 February 1650, into **Carignan-Salières** 1665.

**Baudard** (German) 7 December 1647, **Créquy** 30 April 1656, disbanded 7 November 1659.

**Cardinal de Sainte-Cécile** 3 January 1648, **La Fare** 1 September 1648, into the other **La Fare Regiment** March 1654.

**Pibrac** 13 January 1648, disbanded December 1651.

**Fabrègues** 13 January 1648, disbanded 1652.

**Piennes** 17 February 1648, disbanded 1652.

**Brouages** 6 June 1648, disbanded December 1651.

**Oléron** 6 June 1648, disbanded December 1651.

**Du Daugnon** 6 June 1648, disbanded December 1651.

**Amilly** 16 January 1649, disbanded December 1651.

**Courcelles** 16 January 1649, disbanded March 1649.

**Lavardin** 16 January 1649, disbanded March 1649.

**Gallerande** 16 January 1649, disbanded March 1649.

**Montasier** 17 January 1649, disbanded March 1649.

**Beaumont** 21 January 1649, disbanded April 1649.

**Marey** 24 January 1649, disbanded 20 January 1650.

**Candale** 10 February 1649, into **Vaisseaux** 1654.

**Paris** 10 February 1649, disbanded March 1649.

**Marsillac** 10 February 1649, disbanded 20 January 1650.

**Brie** 10 February 1649, disbanded 20 January 1650.

**Bar** 29 January 1649, disbanded 6 September 1653.

**Clermont** 20 Mars 1650, disbanded late 1650.

**Limosin** 16 June 1650, into **La Reine** 1661.

**Noailles** 25 June 1650, disbanded 1652.

**Du Breuil** 25 June 1650, disbanded late 1650.

**Périgueux** 25 June 1650, disbanded late 1650.

**Tilladet** 17 July 1650, disbanded August 1660.

**Saint-Géran Du Breuil** 27 July 1650, disbanded late 1650.

**Lévis** 27 July 1650, disbanded 2 January 1651.

**Berry** 27 July 1650, disbanded 1653.

**Hautefort** 4 August 1650, disbanded 1650.

**La Note** 5 September 1650, disbanded 1650.

**Mazon** 1650, disbanded 1650.

**Mancini** 1650, disbanded 1654.

**Tarente** 1650, disbanded 1650.

**Riberpré** 18 December 1650, into **Mazarin-Français** 11 February 1659.

**Vendôme** 25 February 1651 (Holland 1672, Marsaglia 1693, Barcelona 1697, Torino 1706, Oudenarde 1708, Denain 1712), **Duc de Berry** 2 July 1712.

**Mercoeur** 25 February 1651, into **Vendôme** 12 April 1661.

**Conti** 26 February 1651, disbanded 13 September 1651.

**La Ferté** 20 May 1651 (Hungary 1664, Lille 1667, Holland 1672), **La Sarre** February 1685 (Namur and Steenkirk 1692, Neerwinden 1693, Almanza and Toulon 1707, Malplaquet 1709).

**Estrades** 12 July 1651, disbanded 1661.

**Saint-Mégrin** 24 September 1651, disbanded late 1651.

Bourdeilles 24 September 1651, disbanded 28 December 1651.

Estissac 24 September 1651, disbanded 12 April 1661.

Rouillac 24 September 1651, disbanded 1655.

Gensac 24 September 1651, disbanded 1651.

Montendre 10 October 1651, disbanded August 1651.

Gardanne 10 October 1651, disbanded 1653.

Roannèz 2 November 1651, disbanded 1656.

Epernon 3 November 1651, disbanded 1653.

Mercoeur 10 December 1651, into **Vendôme** 12 April 1661.

Biron 26 December 1651, disbanded 1652.

La Mothe-Houdancourt 7 January 1652, disbanded 1656.

Menneville 17 February 1652, disbanded 1652.

Massiac 17 February 1652, disbanded 1652.

Maugiron 6 March 1652, disbanded 1652.

Fénelon 18 March 1652, disbanded 1653.

Bezançon 30 March 1652, disbanded 1652.

Montgobert 3 April 1652, disbanded August 1652.

Chastellier-Barlot 3 April 1652, disbanded 1652.

Albret 3 April 1652, disbanded 1654.

Clare 3 April 1652, disbanded 1652.

Richelieu 3 April 1652, disbanded 1653.

Isle-de-France 3 April 1652, disbanded 1653.

Degli Oddi (Italian) 21 May 1652, disbanded 1653.

Bougy 8 June 1652 (Stenay 1654), **Andonville** 31 December 1657, disbanded 12 December 1659.

# INFANTRY REGIMENTS 1643–1715

**Beauvau** 8 June 1652, **Nancré** 20 July 1657, disbanded 20 July 1660.

**Bourlemont** 8 June 1652 (Stenay 1654), disbanded 12 December 1659.

**La Salle** 25 July 1652, disbanded late 1652.

**Soyecourt** 5 August 1652, disbanded 12 December 1659.

**Carces** September 1652, disbanded late 1652.

**Entragues** September 1652, disbanded late 1652.

**Arpajon** 10 Octobre 1652, disbanded late 1652.

**Duc d'York** (Irish) 31 Octobre 1652, **Royal-Irlandais** 22 March 1657, into **Inchiquin** 1661 or disbanded 24 February 1664.

**Fusiliers d'Hocquincourt** 28 December 1652, disbanded 12 December 1659. This unit was the first in the French army to be completely armed with flintlock muskets as an experiment.

**Linières** 30 May 1653, disbanded 1656.

**Dillon** (Irish) 20 June 1653, disbanded 24 or 29 February 1664.

**Buttler** (Irish) 20 June 1653, into **Muskerry** July 1655.

**Glatz** (Irish) 20 June 1653, into **Royal-Irlandais** 6 January 1657.

**Campbell** (Scottish) 20 June 1653, into **Royal-Irlandais** 6 January 1657.

**Inschinkin** (or **Inchiquin**) (Irish) 20 June 1653, into **Royal-Irlandais** 6 January 1657.

**Fleissey** (Irish) 20 June 1653, into **Royal-Irlandais** 6 January 1657.

**O'Sullivan** (irish) 20 June 1653, into **Royal-Irlandais** 6 January 1657.

**Reynell** (English) 20 June 1653, into **Royal-Irlandais** 6 January 1657.

**Naper** (or **Napier**) (Irish) 20 June 1653, into **Royal-Irlandais** 6 January 1657.

**Digby** (Irish) 20 June 1653, into **Royal-Irlandais** 6 January 1657.

**Chaulnes** 15 July 1653, disbanded 12 December 1659.

**Virville** 15 July 1653, disbanded late 1653.

**Tornézy** 15 July 1653, disbanded late 1653.

**Saint-Luc** 15 July 1653, disbanded late 1653.

**Poyanne** 15 July 1653, disbanded 1654.

**La Rasle** 15 July 1653, disbanded late 1653.

**La Vogadera** (Piémont) 15 July 1653, disbanded 1655.

**Aletz** 15 July 1653, disbanded late 1653.

**Ehwolf** (Suisse) 15 July 1653, disbanded late 1653.

**Longueville** 15 July 1653, disbanded 1655.

**Canillac** 12 January 1654, disbanded 1655.

**Conti** 11 March 1654 (Flanders 1667, Candia 1669, Holland 1672, Senef 1674), disbanded 1698.

**Perne** 11 March 1654, disbanded late 1654.

**Lillebonne** 11 March 1654, disbanded 1658.

**Villette** 11 March 1654, disbanded late 1654.

**Salières** 11 March 1654, united with **Carignan** to form **Carignan-Salières** January 1659.

**Belzunce** 11 March 1654, disbanded 12 December 1659.

**Mazarin-Français** 21 October 1654, **La Fère** 1661 (Lille 1667, Holland 1672, Senef 1674, Namur and Steenkirk 1692, Torino 1706, Toulon 1707, Oudenarde 1708, Malplaquet 1709).

**La Porte** 19 April 1655, disbanded late 1655.

**Marins** 19 April 1655, disbanded late 1655.

**Roquebrune** 19 April 1655, disbanded late 1655.

**Royal** 20 January 1655, merged with **Altesse Royale** to form **du Roi** 13 February 1660, retitled **Royal** 21 May 1663 (Lille 1667, Holland 1672, Maastricht 1673, Namur and Steenkirk 1692, Blenheim 1704, Malplaquet 1709).

**Alsace** (German) 16 April 1656 (Lille 1667, Holland 1672, Senef 1674, Namur 1692, Barcelona 1697, Blenheim 1704, Ramillies 1706, Oudenarde 1708, Malplaquet 1709, Denain 1712).

**Bouillon** (Walloon) May 1656, disbanded late 1656.

**Illes** (Catalan) 4 July 1656, disbanded 20 July 1660.

**Valavoire** 6 January 1657, disbanded 12 December 1659.

**Royal-Irlandais** 6 January 1657, into **Duc d'York** (Irish) 22 March 1657 which then took the title of **Royal-Irlandais**, disbanded 24 February 1664.

**Prince de Hesse** (German) 20 February 1657, disbanded 20 July 1660.

**Prince de Salm** (German) 20 February 1657, disbanded 20 July 1660.

**Livery** 20 February 1657, disbanded late 1657.

**Richelieu** 20 February 1657, disbanded late 1657.

**Catalan-Mazarin** 25 May 1657, **Royal-Catalan** 13 March 1661, **Royal-Roussillon** 27 January 1667 (Lille 1667, Senef 1674, Neerwinden 1693, Oudenarde 1708, Malplaquet 1709, Denain 1712).

**Brégy** 25 May 1657, disbanded late 1657.

**Saint-Piez** 25 May 1657, disbanded 12 December 1659.

**Pfyffer** (Swiss) June 1657, disbanded 12 December 1659.

**Courten** (Swiss) June 1657, disbanded 12 December 1659.

**Schomberg** (German) 26 January 1658, June 1657, disbanded 24 October 1660.

**Humières** 26 January 1658, disbanded 20 July 1660.

**Prince Alméric** (Italian) 26 January 1658, disbanded 12 April 1661.

**Prince Alphonse** (Italian) 26 January 1658, disbanded 12 April 1661.

**Cosnac** February 1658, disbanded 12 December 1659.

**Württemberg** (German) August 1658, disbanded 20 July 1660.

**Ribepré** 4 December 1658, disbanded 12 December 1659.

**Broglio** 16 December 1659, disbanded June 1669.

**Le Roi** or **Du Roy** 2 January 1663 (Lille 1667, Holland 1672, Senef 1674, Namur 1692, Neerwinden 1693, Ramillies 1706, Oudenarde 1708, Malplaquet 1709, Denain 1712).

**Navires** formed in 1663 with men from **Galères** and **Isles**, transferred to the **French Company of the Indies** in 1664.

**Dauphin** 15 June 1667 (Holland 1672, Namur and Steenkirk 1692, Namur 1695, Blenheim 1704, Torino 1706).

**Jonzac** 12 July 1667 (Lille 1667, Holland 1672, Senef 1674), Sainte-Maure 1677, **Beauvoisis** 1685 (Namur 1692, Neerwinden 1693, Torino 1706, Toulon 1707, Barcelona 1714).

**Montpeyroux** 20 November 1667 (Crete 1669), **Rouergue** 1671 (Senef 1674, Marsaglia 1693, Torino 1706, Toulon 1707).

**Château-Thierry** 20 November 1667, **Saint-Léger** 1670, into **Bourgogne** 1671.

**Bourgogne** 1 March 1668 (Holland 1672, Torino 1706, Toulon 1707, Malplaquet 1709, Denain 1712).

**Duc d'Anjou** 19 December 1669, **Anjou** August 1671 (Holland 1672, Namur and Steenkirk 1692, Neerwinden 1693, Torino 1706, Toulon 1707, Barcelona 1714).

**Royal-Marine** 24 December 1669 (Holland 1672, Sicily 1676, Namur 1692, Torino 1706, Oudenarde 1708, Malplaquet 1709, Denain 1712).

**Amiral de France** 24 December 1669, **Vermandois** 1671 (Holland 1672, Senef 1674, Namur and Steenkirk 1692, Neerwinden 1693).

**Furstenberg** (German) 27 March 1670 (Holland 1672), **Greder** 3 September 1686 (Namur and Steenkirk 1692, Neerwinden 1693, Blenheim 1704, Oudenarde 1708, Malplaquet 1709, Denain 1712).

**Fusiliers du Roi** 4 February 1671, **Royal-Artillerie** 1693 (see Volume 4).

**Royal-Italien** (Italian) 27 March 1671 (Holland 1672, Senef 1674, Namur and Steenkirk 1692, Neerwinden 1693, Ramillies 1706, Oudenarde 1708, Malplaquet 1709, Denain 1712).

**Hamilton** (English or Scottish) 30 April 1671 (Holland 1672, Maastricht 1673), into **Furstenberg** 10 March 1678.

# INFANTRY REGIMENTS 1643–1715

**Carlisle** (English) 30 April 1671(Holland 1672), disbanded 10 March 1678.

**Churchill** (English) 30 April 1671 (Holland 1672), disbanded 10 March 1678.

**Dunkan** (English) 30 April 1671 (Holland 1672), disbanded 10 March 1678.

**Royal-Anglais** (English) 15 February 1672 (Holland 1672), disbanded 10 March 1678.

**Erlach** (Swiss) 17 February 1672 (Holland 1672, Senef 1674), **Manuel** September 1694 (Barcelona 1697), **Villars-Chandieu** 17 January 1701 (Ramillies 1706, Oudenarde 1708, Malplaquet 1709).

**Stuppa** (Swiss) 17 February 1672 (Holland 1672, Senef 1674, Namur and Steenkirk 1692, Neerwinden 1693), **Brendlé** 17 January 1701 (Toulon 1707, Oudenarde 1708, Malplaquet 1709, Denain 1712).

**Salis** (Swiss) 17 February 1672 (Senef 1674), **Porlier** October 1690 (Namur 1692), **Reynold** 30 September 1692 (Neerwinden 1693), **Castellas** 25 June 1702 (Ramillies 1706, Toulon 1707, Barcelona 1714) .

**Pfyffer** (Swiss) 17 February 1672 (Holland 1672, Senef 1674), **Hessy** 20 December 1689 (Marsaglia 1693, Almanza 1707, Denain 1712).

**Languedoc** 20 March 1672 (Namur and Steenkirk 1692, Blenheim 1704).

**Royal-Wallon** (Walloon) July 1673, disbanded 1678.

**Bouillon** (Walloon) July 1673, disbanded 1678.

**Vierzet** (Walloon) July 1673, disbanded 1678 (but probably actually after 1679).

**Huxelles** 30 October 1673, **Plessis-Bellières** 22 January 1675, **Montsoreau** 24 February 1692 (Marsaglia 1693, Barcelona 1697), **Vaudreuil** 26 October 1704, **Sourches** 5 September 1706 (Almanza 1707).

**Genevois** 28 November 1673, disbanded 1678.

**Greder** (Swiss) 5 December 1673 (Namur and Steenkirk 1692, Neerwinden 1693, Ramillies 1706), **Affry** 22 December 1714.

**Navailles** 19 February 1674, **Hamilton** January 1679, **Jarzé** 1685, **Médoc** 22 May 1691 (Marsaglia 1693, Barcelona 1697, Torino 1706, Toulon 1707, Almanza 1707).

**Albret** 1 March 1674, **Gandelus** 9 August 1678, **Clérambault** 19 April 1679 (Marsaglia 1693), **Mirabeau** 11 April 1697 (Torino 1706, Toulon 1707), **Gensac** 7 April 1711 (Denain 1712).

**Castries** 1 March 1674, **Morangiès** 16 April 1695, **Louvigny** 2 August 1705 (Torino 1706, Oudenarde 1708, Malplaquet 1709), **Bacqueville** 27 January 1711.

**Perri** (Corsican) 12 June 1674 (in French establishment but actually 9 March 1673) (Senef 1674, Sicily 1675–1678), into **Royal-Roussillon** 10 August 1682.

**Listenois** 9 August 1674, **Royal-Comtois** 1685 (Namur and Steenkirk 1692, Marsaglia 1693, Torino 1706, Denain 1712).

**Schomberg** 15 November 1674, **Larry** 4 January 1681, **Sceaux** 24 August 1688, **Blainville** 6 September 1689, **Maulévrier** 10 July 1690 (Namur and Steenkirk 1692, Neerwinden 1693), **Du Fort** February 1706 (Torino 1706, Almanza 1707), **Lyonne** 29 November 1710 (Denain 1712).

**Ducal** (Savoy) 26 November 1674, disbanded 11 January 1679.

**Savoie** (Savoy) 26 November 1674, disbanded 11 January 1679.

**Saluces** (Savoy) 26 November 1674, disbanded 11 January 1679.

**Provence** 4 December 1674 (Sicily 1675–1678, Namur and Steenkirk 1692, Neerwinden 1693, Blenheim 1704, Oudenarde 1708, Malplaquet 1709, Barcelona 1714).

**Zurlauben** (German) 1675, disbanded 1678.

**Vivonne** 23 January 1676 (Sicily 1676), **Thianges** 25 September 1688 (Steenkirk 1692, Neerwinden 1693), **Mortemart** 30 March 1702 (Sicily 1676; Oudenarde 1708, Malplaquet 1709), **Laval** 27 February 1712 (Denain 1712).

**Stuppa Jeune** (Swiss) 28 January 1677 (Sicily 1677, Steenkirk 1692), **Surbeck** 16 October 1692 (Neerwinden 1693, Denain 1712), **Hémel** 8 May 1714.

**Noailles** 22 February 1677, disbanded 15 February 1678.

**Piettemont** (Walloon) 22 February 1677, **Famechon** 1 November 1677 (Ireland 1689–1690, Marsaglia 1693), **Isenghein** 11 February 1697 (Blenheim 1704, Oudenarde 1708).

**Saint-Laurent** (Piémont) 8 December 1678, **Nice** 8 May 1691 (Namur and Steenkirk 1692, Neerwinden 1693, Blenheim 1704, Oudenarde 1708)

# INFANTRY REGIMENTS 1643–1715

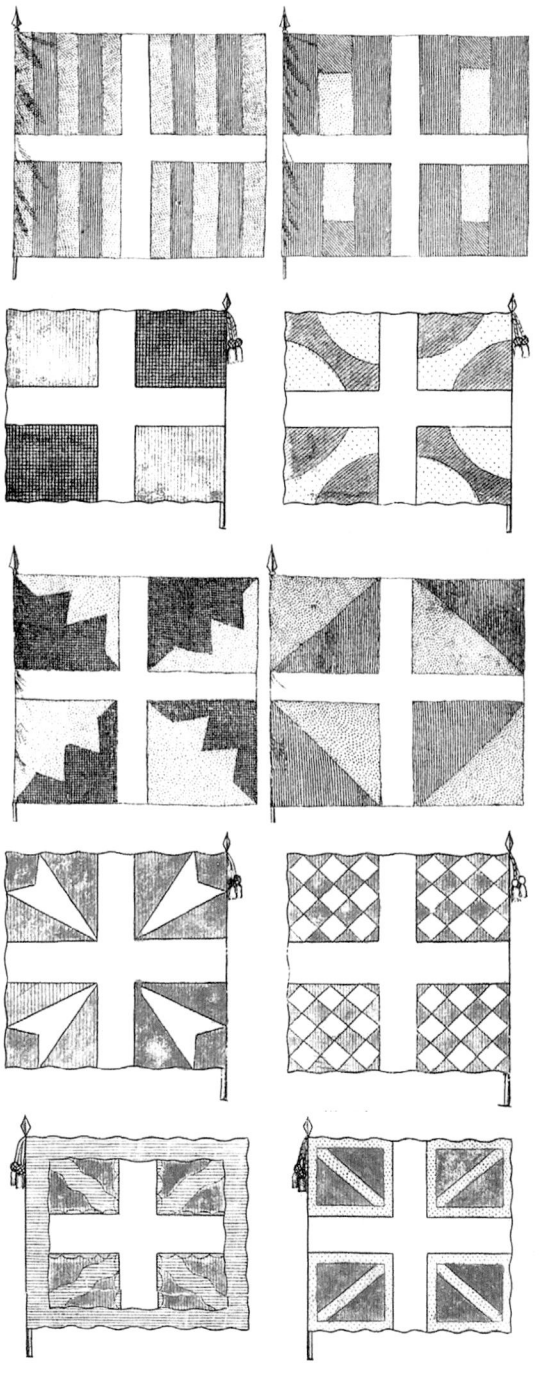

Regimental colours of the Béarn and Dauphiné regiments, early eighteenth century. Yellowish buff and red for Béarn; red, green and buff for Dauphiné. (Courtesy Rijksmuseum, Amsterdam. RP-P-OB-84.205)

Regimental colours of the La Sarre and (possibly) the Albaret regiments, early eighteenth century. Red and black for La Sarre; green and yellow for Albaret. (Courtesy Rijksmuseum, Amsterdam. RP-P-OB-83.399)

Regimental colours of the Vexin and Dampierre regiments, early eighteenth century. Black and yellow for Vexin; red and yellow or buff for Dampierre. (Courtesy Rijksmuseum, Amsterdam. RP-P-OB-84.205)

Regimental colours of the Chabrillant and Sanzey regiments, early eighteenth century. Both are white and red. (Courtesy Rijksmuseum, Amsterdam. RP-P-OB-83.399)

Regimental colours of the Nice (Italian) and Tavannes regiments, early eighteenth century. Blue and red for Nice; red and yellow for Tavannes. (Courtesy Rijksmuseum, Amsterdam. RP-P-OB-83.399)

**Konigsmark** (German) 10 August 1680, **Surbeck** 25 October 1686, **La Mark** 24 January 1693 (Marsaglia 1693, Ramillies 1706, Oudenarde 1708, Malplaquet 1709).

**Toulouse** 20 February 1684 (Namur and Steenkirk 1692, Neerwinden 1693, Blenheim 1704).

**Guyenne** 21 February 1684 (Blenheim 1704, Oudenarde 1708, Malplaquet 1709, Denain 1712).

**Lorraine** 21 February 1684 (Namur 1692, Marsaglia 1693, Blenheim 1704, Oudenarde 1708, Malplaquet 1709, Denain 1712).

**Lallement** (Walloon) June 1684, **Zurlauben** 14 April 1685 (Ireland 1690, Namur and Steenkirk 1692, Neerwinden 1693, Blenheim 1704), disbanded 21 September 1704.

**Flandre** 1 September 1684 (Marsaglia 1693, Torino 1706).

**Berry** 2 September 1684 (Marsaglia 1693, Naples 1702–1704, Torino 1706).

**Béarn** 2 September 1684 (Marsaglia 1693, Blenheim 1704, Oudenarde 1708, Malplaquet 1709, Denain 1712).

**Hainaut** 4 September 1684 (Namur 1695, Torino 1706, Denain 1712).

**Boulonnois** 5 September 1684 (Marsaglia 1693, Blenheim 1704, Oudenarde 1708, Malplaquet 1709, Denain 1712).

**Angoumois** 6 September 1684 (Torino 1706, Barcelona 1714).

**Périgord** 7 September 1684 (Namur 1692, Barcelona 1697, Torino 1706, Lerida 1707).

**Saintonge** 8 September 1684 (Blenheim 1704, Malplaquet 1709).

**Bigorre** 9 September 1684 (Marsaglia 1693, Lerida 1707).

**Forez** 10 September 1684 (Ireland 1689–1690, Torino 1706, Toulon 1707).

**Cambrésis** 11 September 1684 (Torino 1706, Denain 1712).

**Tournaisis** 12 September 1684 (Toulon 1707, Malplaquet 1709, Denain 1712).

**Foix** 13 September 1684 (Namur and Steenkirk 1692, Blenheim 1704, Malplaquet 1709).

**Bresse** 14 September 1684 (Marsaglia 1693, Torino 1706, Denain 1712).

# INFANTRY REGIMENTS 1643–1715

**La Marche** 15 September 1684 (Ireland 1690, Namur and Steenkirk 1692, Neerwinden 1693, Torino 1706, Toulon 1707, Barcelona 1714).

**Quercy** 16 September 1684 (Marsaglia 1693, Torino 1706, Toulon 1707, Barcelona 1714).

**Nivernais** 17 September 1684 (Namur 1692, Marsaglia 1693, Blenheim 1704, Oudenarde 1708, Malplaquet 1709, Denain 1712).

**Brie** 18 September 1684 (Torino 1706, Toulon 1707).

**Soissonnais** 19 September 1684 (Namur and Steenkirk 1692, Neerwinden 1693, Torino 1706, Toulon 1707).

**Isle-de-France** 20 September 1684 (Marsaglia 1693, Barcelona 1697, Torino 1706, Toulon 1707).

**Vexin** 21 September 1684 (Namur 1692, Torino 1706, Toulon 1707, Malplaquet 1709, Denain 1712).

**Aunis** 22 September 1684 (Namur and Steenkirk 1692, Blenheim 1704, Denain 1712).

**Beauce** 23 September 1684 (Oudenarde 1708).

**Dauphiné** 24 September 1684 (Marsaglia 1693, Torino 1706, Almanza 1707).

**Vivarais** 25 September 1684 (Marsaglia 1693, Torino 1706, Toulon 1707).

**Luxembourg** 26 September 1684 (Oudenarde 1708, Malplaquet 1709).

**Bassigny** 27 September 1684 (Marsaglia 1693, Torino 1706, Toulon 1707).

**Beaujolais** 16 June 1685 (Marsaglia 1693).

**Ponthieu** 16 June 1685 (Namur 1695).

**Catinat** 24 October 1688 (Marsaglia 1693), **Sillery** 24 March 1701 (Almanza 1707), **Châtelet-Lomont** 1707, disbanded 1715

**Bouffler** (Walloon) 24 October 1688 (Namur 1692), **Miromesnil** 1 October 1694, disbanded 16 November 1714.

**Solre** (Walloon) 24 October 1688 (Namur and Steenkirk 1692, Neerwinden 1693, Barcelona 1697, Torino 1706, Oudenarde 1708), **Croï-Solre** 20 March 1709 (Malplaquet 1709), **Beaufort** 1709.

**Robecque** (Walloon) 24 October 1688 (Marsaglia 1693, Blenheim 1704), **Saint-Vallier** 26 October 1704 (Ramillies 1706, Oudenarde 1708), disbanded 15 November 1714.

**Poitiers** (Walloon) 24 October 1688, **Croï-Solre** 25 July 1700, **Aunay** 31 August 1709, into **Maine** 15 November 1714.

**Mérode** 24 October 1688, **Tournon** 28 October 1690 (Ireland 1690), disbanded 30 December 1698.

**Bouillon** (Walloon) 24 October 1688, disbanded 30 December 1698.

**Monferrat** (Piémont) 24 October 1688, **Royal-Monferrat** 26 September 1690 (Marsaglia 1693), **Gardes du Duc de Mantoue** 17 September 1702 (Torino 1706), disbanded 9 October 1706.

**Savoie** (Piémont) 24 October 1688, **Royal-Savoie** 26 September 1690, disbanded 30 December 1698.

**La Marine de Piémont** 24 October 1688, into 26 September 1690.

**Aoste** (Piémont) 24 October 1688, into **Montroux** 26 September 1690.

**Nice** (Piémont) 24 October 1688, into **Montroux** 26 September 1690.

**Santena** (Piémont) 24 October 1688, **Lamar** 25 March 1691 (Namur and Steenkirk 1692), disbanded 9 January 1698.

**Cavoye** 1 January 1689, **Mouchy** c. 1696, disbanded 30 March 1698.

**La Ilhière** 1 January 1689, disbanded 15 July 1698.

**Herbouville** 1 January 1689 (Neerwinden 1693), disbanded 30 March 1698.

**La Garde** 1 January 1689, **Villiers** 1695 (Namur 1695), disbanded 30 March 1698.

**Montenay** 1 January 1689, disbanded 30 March 1698.

**Menou** 1 January 1689, disbanded 30 March 1698.

**La Châtre** 1 January 1689 (Neerwinden 1693), disbanded 30 March 1698.

**Villars** 1 January 1689 (Neerwinden 1693), disbanded 26 October 1698.

**Cottanges** 1 January 1689, disbanded 16 May 1698.

**Desmoulins** 1 January 1689, disbanded 30 December 1698.

# INFANTRY REGIMENTS 1643–1715

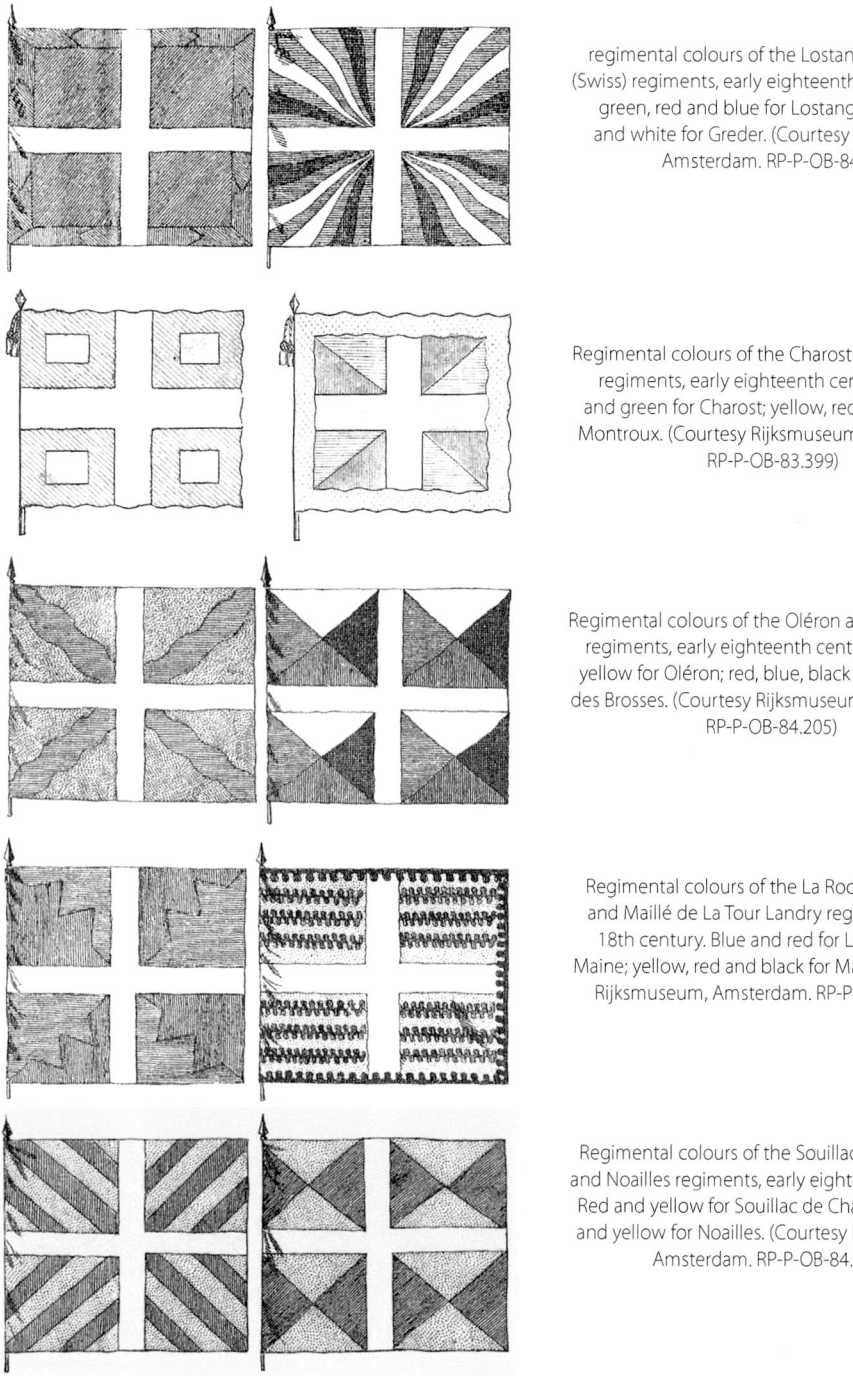

regimental colours of the Lostange and Greder (Swiss) regiments, early eighteenth century. Purple, green, red and blue for Lostange; blue, black and white for Greder. (Courtesy Rijksmuseum, Amsterdam. RP-P-OB-84.205)

Regimental colours of the Charost and Montroux regiments, early eighteenth century. White and green for Charost; yellow, red and blue for Montroux. (Courtesy Rijksmuseum, Amsterdam. RP-P-OB-83.399)

Regimental colours of the Oléron and des Brosses regiments, early eighteenth century. Blue and yellow for Oléron; red, blue, black and white for des Brosses. (Courtesy Rijksmuseum, Amsterdam. RP-P-OB-84.205)

Regimental colours of the La Roche du Maine and Maillé de La Tour Landry regiments, early 18th century. Blue and red for La Roche du Maine; yellow, red and black for Maillé. (Courtesy Rijksmuseum, Amsterdam. RP-P-OB-84.205)

Regimental colours of the Souillac de Châtillon and Noailles regiments, early eighteenth century. Red and yellow for Souillac de Châtillon; purple and yellow for Noailles. (Courtesy Rijksmuseum, Amsterdam. RP-P-OB-84.205)

**Aligny** 1 January 1689, disbanded 16 May 1698.

**Vaugrenant** 1 January 1689, disbanded 16 May 1698.

**Du Guast** 1 January 1689, Argenson 1695, disbanded 30 December 1698.

**Caixon** 1 January 1689 (Barcelona 1697), disbanded 16 May 1698.

**Poudeux** 1 January 1689, **La Bastide** 1692 (Barcelona 1697), disbanded 16 May 1698.

**Bonivatel** 1 January 1689, disbanded 16 May 1698.

**Boulins** 1 January 1689, disbanded 16 May 1698.

**Boissières** 1 January 1689, disbanded 30 December 1698.

**Noailles** 1 January 1689, into another regiment 1 October 1691.

**Saint-Jal** 1 January 1689, disbanded 30 March 1698.

**Dulac** 1 January 1689, disbanded 16 May 1698.

**Launay** 1 January 1689 (Neerwinden 1693), disbanded 30 March 1698.

**Fontenay** 1 January 1689, disbanded 30 March 1698.

**Lignery** 1 January 1689, disbanded 30 March 1698.

**Dupas** 1 January 1689, disbanded 30 March 1698.

**Lignières** 1 January 1689, disbanded 30 December 1698.

**Du Moulin** 1 January 1689, disbanded 30 December 1698.

**Belleisle** 1 January 1689, into **Dauphin** 30 December 1698.

**Berville** 1 January 1689, disbanded 16 May 1698.

**Destouches** 1 January 1689 (Barcelona 1697), disbanded 10 November 1698.

**Lostanges** 1 January 1689, disbanded 19 July 1698.

**Montendre** 1 January 1689, disbanded 16 May 1698.

**Cabanac** 1 January 1689 (Barcelona 1697), disbanded 16 May 1698.

**Milly** 1 January 1689, disbanded 16 May 1698.

# INFANTRY REGIMENTS 1643–1715

**Mirabeau** 1 January 1689, disbanded 30 March 1698.

**Tessé** 28 may 1689, Sanzay 17 October 1703 (Torino 1706, Barcelona 1714).

**Lorges** 28 May 1689, disbanded 1690.

**Gardes-irlandaises** (Irish) 9 October 1689 (Neerwinden 1693), disbanded 27 February 1698..

**Salis Jeune** (Swiss) 1 January 1690 (Namur 1692, Neerwinden 1693), **May 23** January 1702 (Ramillies 1706, Oudenarde 1708, Malplaquet 1709, Denain 1712), **Du Buisson** 28 May 1715.

**Courten** (Swiss) 6 February 1690 (Namur 1692, Neerwinden 1693, Barcelona 1714).

**Oberkann** (Swiss) 6 February 1690, **Polier** 13 June 1690, **Schellemberg** 6 November 1690 Namur 1692, Neerwinden 1693, Barcelona 1697), disbanded 18 January 1698.

**Yoël** (Danish) 1 March 1690, **Royal-Danois** (Neerwinden 1693, Barcelona 1697), disbanded 18 January 1698.

**Monnin** (Swiss) 14 March 1690 (Namur 1692), into **Courten** 18 January 1698.

**Dillon** (Irish) 18 June 1690 (Barcelona 1697), **Lack** 1702 (Almanza 1707, Barcelona 1714).

**O'Brien** (Irish) 18 June 1690 (Marsaglia 1693), **Lee** 18 November 1693, **Talbot** 25 August 1694, **Clare** 8 April 1696, **O'Brien** 11 August 1706.

**Mountcashel** (Irish) 18 June 1690, **Lee** 28 July 1694 (Blenheim 1704, Malplaquet 1709, Denain 1712, Barcelona 1714).

**Clare** (Irish) 16 June 1690 (Marsaglia 1693), **Lee** 18 November 1693, **Talbot** 25 August 1694, **Clare** 8 April 1696 (Blenheim 1704, Ramillies 1706), **O'Brien** 11 August 1706 (Malplaquet 1709).

**Leisler** (German) 1 August 1690, **Sparre** 29 October 1694 (Barcelona 1697, Malplaquet 1709), **Lenck** 10 March 1714.

**Thouy** (Piémont) 26 September 1690, disbanded 9 October 1706.

**Montroux** (Italian) 26 September 1690 (Neerwinden 1693, Blenheim 1704, Ramillies 1706, Oudenarde 1708, Malplaquet 1709), disbanded 15 July 1715.

**Perri** (Corsican) 26 September 1690 (Namur 1692 and Steenkirk, Neerwinden 1693, Blenheim 1704), disbanded 28 January 1715.

**Périgueux** 6 December 1690 (Neerwinden 1693), disbanded 30 December 1698.

**Gardes du Roy d'Angleterre** (Anglo-Irish), into French army September 1691 (Neerwinden 1693), into **Dorrington** (Irish) 26 February 1698.

**Dragons à pied de La Reine d'Angleterre** (Anglo-Irish), into French army September 1691 (Neerwinden 1693), into **Galmoy** (Irish) 26 February 1698.

**La Reine-irlandais** (Irish), into French army September 1691 (Marsaglia 1693, Barcelona 1697), into **Luttrel** (Irish) 27 February 1698.

**La Marine-irlandais** (Irish), into French army September 1691, into **Albemarle** (Irish) 27 February 1698.

**Dublin** (Irish), into French army September 1691, into **Albemarle** (Irish) 27 February 1698.

**Limerick** (Irish), into French army September 1691 (Marsaglia 1693), into **Berwick** (Irish) 27 February 1698.

**Athlone** (Irish), into French army September 1691 (Marsaglia 1693), into **Berwick** (Irish) 27 February 1698.

**Klincarthy** (Irish), into French army September 1691 (Barcelona 1697), into **Luttrel** (Irish) 27 February 1698.

**Charlemont** (Irish), into French army September 1691, into **Galmoy** (Irish) 27 February 1698.

**Noailles** 1 October 1691, **Beaufermés** 1704, **Brichambault** 1 December 1708 (Malplaquet 1709).

**Chartres** 14 November 1691 (Blenheim 1704, Ramillies 1706, Oudenarde 1708, Malplaquet 1709).

**Casal** (Piémont) 26 January 1692, disbanded 18 September 1695.

**Bernold** (German) 15 March 1692, into **Alsace** 17 March 1698.

**Bressey** 1 July 1692, disbanded 30 December 1698.

**Blésois** 4 October 1692 (Neerwinden 1693, Portugal 1704, Barcelona 1706, Almanza 1707, Barcelona 1714).

# INFANTRY REGIMENTS 1643-1715

Regimental colours of an unknown regiment and of the Picardie Regiment, early eighteenth century. Black and white for the unknown and red for Picardie. (Courtesy Rijksmuseum, Amsterdam. RP-P-OB-84.205)

Regimental colours of the Auxerrois and the Blaisois regiments, early eighteenth century. Both are blue, yellow and red. (Courtesy Rijksmuseum, Amsterdam. RP-P-OB-83.399)

**Gatinois** 4 October 1692 (Marsaglia 1693, Torino 1706, Toulon 1707, Barcelona 1714).

**Thiérache** 4 October 1692 (Marsaglia 1693, Torino 1706, Toulon 1707), into **Navarre** 7 October 1714.

**Barrois** 4 October 1692 (Barcelona 1697, Almanza and Lerida 1707), **Conti** 14 November 1713.

**Albigeois** 4 October 1692 (Marsaglia 1693, Torino 1706, Toulon 1707), disbanded 7 October 1714.

**Laonnois** 4 October 1692 (Blenheim 1704, Barcelona 1706, Almanza 1707), disbanded 20 September 1714.

**Auxerrois** 4 October 1692 (Blenheim 1704).

**Agénois** 4 October 1692 (Blenheim 1704, Ramillies 1706, Oudenarde 1708, Malplaquet 1709, Denain 1712).

**Charolois** 4 October 1692 (Almanza 1707), into **Lyonnois** 13 December 1714.

**Labour** 4 October 1692 (Torino 1706), into **Orléans** 7 October 1714.

**Bugey** 4 October 1692 (Torino 1706, Toulon 1707), into **Champagne** 7 October 1714.

**Santerre** 4 October 1692 (Blenheim 1704, Malplaquet 1709).

**Orléannois** 1 January 1693, disbanded 7 October 1714.

**Oléron** 2 January 1693 (Barcelona 1706, Lerida 1708, Barcelona 1714), disbanded 20 September 1714.

**Landes** 3 January 1693 (Ramillies 1706, Oudenarde 1708, Malplaquet 1709).

**Cotentin** 4 January 1693 (Torino 1706), disbanded 20 September 1714.

**Vosges** 5 January 1693 (Toulon 1707), disbanded 15 November 1714.

**Saint-Segond** (Italian) 24 February 1693 (Blenheim 1704), disbanded 22 January 1715.

**La Croix** 22 August 1695, disbanded 30 December 1698.

**Guiscard** 22 August 1695, disbanded 19 July 1698.

**Bretesche** 22 August 1695, disbanded 19 July 1698.

**Tessé** 22 August 1695, disbanded 1 September 1698.

**La Fare** 22 August 1695, disbanded 19 July 1698.

**Ximinès** 22 August 1695, disbanded 30 December 1698.

**Resnel** 1 November 1695, disbanded 30 December 1698.

**Villefort** 2 November 1695, into **Boulonnais** 30 December 1698.

**Bellafaire** 3 November 1695, disbanded 8 February 1699.

**Talende** 5 November 1695, into **Auvergne** 30 December 1698.

**Pons** 6 November 1695, disbanded 30 December 1698.

**De Laistre** 7 November 1695, disbanded 30 December 1698.

**Hautefort** 8 November 1695, into **La Couronne** 30 December 1698.

**Du Bièz** 9 November 1695, disbanded 9 November 1699.

**Trécesson** 11 November 1695, disbanded 19 July 1699.

**Sourches** 13 November 1695 (Barcelona 1697), disbanded 18 November 1698.

**Monchy** 14 November 1695, disbanded 10 March 1698.

**Courbé** 16 November 1695, disbanded 30 December 1698.

**La Mothe** 17 November 1695, into **Bourbon** 30 December 1698.

**Sanzay** 18 November 1695, into **Toulouse** 30 December 1698.

**Vidame d'Amien** 19 November 1695, disbanded 30 December 1698.

**Lesparre** 20 November 1695, disbanded 30 December 1698.

**Vallouze** 21 November 1695, into **Chartres** 19 July 1698.

**Soizy** 22 November 1695, disbanded 30 December 1698.

**Langlède** 23 November 1695, disbanded 30 December 1698.

**Montjoie** 24 November 1695, disbanded 30 December 1698.

**Beuzeville** 25 November 1695, disbanded 30 December 1698.

**Enonville** or **Esnouville** 26 November 1695, into **Picardie** 18 November 1698.

**Dunchaux** 27 November 1695, disbanded 30 December 1698.

**Broc** 28 November 1695, disbanded 30 December 1698.

**Varennes-Gournay** 29 November 1695, disbanded 30 December 1698.

**Stainville** 30 November 1695, disbanded 30 December 1698.

**Bueil** 1 December 1695, into **Normandie** 18 November 1698.

**Choisinet** 2 December 1695, into **Anjou** 15 November 1698.

**La Lande** 3 December 1695, disbanded 30 December 1698.

**Beaurepaire** 4 December 1695, disbanded 30 December 1698.

**Permangle** 5 December 1695, disbanded 13 November 1698.

**Siougeat** 6 December 1695, disbanded 18 November 1698.

**Bellefourièrre** 7 December 1695, disbanded 30 December 1698.

**Barville** 8 November 1695, disbanded 19 July 1698.

**Marillac** 9 December 1695, **Villemort** 28 April 1696, into **Champagne** 18 November 1698.

**Montalais** 10 December 1695, disbanded 30 November 1698.

**Conflans-Ménars** 11 December 1695, disbanded 18 November 1698.

**Brienne** 12 December 1695, disbanded 30 December 1698.

**Puynormand** 13 December 1695, into **Royal** 18 November 1698.

**Hossifaire** 14 December 1695, disbanded 18 November 1698.

**Maisoncelles** 15 December 1695, disbanded 18 November 1698.

**Serville** 16 December 1695, into **Champagne** 18 November 1698.

**Courville** 17 December 1695 (Barcelona 1697), into **Provence** 18 November 1698.

**Laigle** 18 December 1695, disbanded 18 November 1698.

**Lomagne** 19 December 1695, disbanded 26 November 1698.

**Sézanne** 20 December 1695, into **Royal-Marine** 30 December 1698.

**Damas** 21 December 1695, disbanded 30 December 1698.

**Chevalier de Damas** 22 December 1695, disbanded 8 February 1699.

**Gallard** 23 December 1695, disbanded 18 November 1698.

**Pézeux** 24 December 1695, disbanded 30 December 1698.

**La Force** 25 December 1695, disbanded 30 December 1698.

**Marignane** 26 December 1695, into **Champagne** 1698.

**Carrion-Nisas** 19 September 1696 (Barcelona 1697), disbanded 30 December 1698.

**Artagnan** 22 January 1697, disbanded 30 December 1698.

**Dorrington** (Irish) 27 February 1698 (Blenheim 1704, Malplaquet 1709, Denain 1712).

**Luttrel** (Irish) 27 February 1698, **Bourke** 18 June 1699 (Torino 1706, Barcelona 1714), **Wauchop** 20 March 1715, into Spanish army 8 June 1715.

**Albemarle** (Irish) 27 February 1698, **Fitz-Gérald** 10 February 1703 (Torino 1706, Oudenarde 1708), **O'Donnell** 7 August 1708 (Denain 1712), into **Clare** 6 February 1715.

# INFANTRY REGIMENTS 1643–1715

**Berwick** (Irish) 27 February 1698 (Torino 1706, Almanza 1707, Barcelona 1714).

**Galmoy** (Irish) 27 February 1698 (Torino 1706, Barcelona 1714), disbanded 30 January 1715.

**Sanguin** 6 February 1701, **Courrières** 1702, converted to garrison companies in 1706.

**Montendre** 6 February 1701, **Berthelot de Rebourseau 9** November 1702, **Esgrigny** 25 December 1704 (Torino 1706, Toulon 1707, Barcelona 1714), into **Bourbonnais** 30 July 1715.

**Pézeux** 21 September 1701, **Lafons de La Ferté** 5 Octobre 1702, disbanded 15 August 1714.

**Montpeyroux** 21 December 1701, **Montarois** 1702, **Châtillon** 1704, taken prisoner at Piannezza 1706.

**Bouzols** 29 December 1701, **Caumont-La Force** 1705 (Barcelona 1706 and 1714), **Lassay** 1714, disbanded 1715.

**Durfort-Boissière** 1 January 1702 (Torino 1706), disbanded 16 January 1714.

**La Faille** (Walloon) 2 January 1702, disbanded 1709.

**Bryas** (Walloon) 3 January 1702, **Croï** 1703, **Bournonville** 1703, disbanded 1709.

**Bandeville** 4 January 1702, destroyed at Blenheim 1704.

**Chabrillant** 5 January 1702, destroyed at Blenheim 1704.

**Albaret** 6 January 1702, destroyed at Blenheim 1704.

**Siougeat** 7 January 1702, destroyed at Torino 1706.

**Fourqueveaux** 8 January 1702, **Sourches** 17 October 1703, destroyed at Ramillies 1706.

**Marillac** 9 January 1702, into **Picardie** 31 December 1713.

**Lassay** 11 January 1702 (Blenheim 1704), **La Mothe d'Hugues** 26 April 1710 (Denain 1712), disbanded 30 October 1714.

**Gassion** 12 January 1702 (Oudenarde 1708), into **Navarre** 1714.

**Marignane** 14 January 1702, **Serville** 1705, **Beaujeu** 16 January 1709, disbanded 1714.

**Montboissier** 16 January 1702 (Blenheim 1704), **Longuerue** 18 April 1710, disbanded 13 December 1713.

**Franquières** 18 January 1702 (Blenheim 1704), disbanded 1714.

**La Londe** 18 January 1702, **Franclieu** 4 February 1706, disbanded 1714.

**Saint-Germain-Beaupré** 18 January 1702, into **Picardie** 24 January 1714.

**La Cru** 20 March 1702, **Caraman** 1705, disbanded 1714.

**Broglie** 22 March 1702, **Froulay** April 1703 (Torino 1706), **Tiraqueau** 1711, disbanded 1714.

**Brancas** 22 March 1702, Oyse 13 July 1709, **Labadie** 7 September 1711, disbanded 1715.

**Saint-Aulaire** 22 March 1702, **Châteauneuf** 4 August 1706 (Malplaquet), **Montviel** 1 October 1709 (Denain 1712), disbanded 13 December 1713.

**Roze** 26 April 1702, **Provenchère** 1704, **Ussy** 19 January 1706, into **Champagne** 21 January 1714.

**Nuaillé** 26 April 1702 (Oudenarde 1708), into **Piémont** 20 September 1714.

**Choisinet** 7 May 1702, **Cordes** 1705 (Toulon 1707), **Villeneuve** 1710, **Caylus-Rouairoux**, disbanded 30 July 1715.

**Guitaud** 7 May 1702, **Marloup de Charnailles** 25 August 1706, into **Poitou** 17 January 1714.

**Villenouvet** 7 May 1702, **La Fons** 19 January 1706, **Matha** 1710, disbanded 1714.

**Des Clos** 7 May 1702, **Nupcès** 1705, **Lespinay** 1711, disbanded 1714.

**Turbilly** 7 May 1702, into **Tallard** 20 September 1714.

**La Farre-Soustelle** 7 May 1702 (Torino 1706, Denain 1712), disbanded 7 October 1714.

**Vivours** 7 May 1702, **Briouze** 1705, **Vasières** 1713, disbanded 1715.

**Des Feugerez** 7 May 1702, **Giradin de Vauvray** 8 August 1706, **Barbaçon** 10 April 1707, into **Boufflers** 28 May 1714.

**Silly** 7 May 1702 (Blenheim 1704), **Maillé** 1705, disbanded 1714.

**Richebourg** 7 May 1702, **Barville** 1704 (Toulon 1707), **Riberac** 1710 (Barcelona 1714), disbanded 1714.

**Blacons** 7 May 1702, into **Auvergne** 12 November 1714.

**Varennes-Gournay** 13 May 1703, **Entragues** 13 May 1703 (Ramillies 1706), into **Boufflers** 12 November 1714.

**Tarnault** 14 May 1702, **Boissieux** 16 February 1707 (Toulon 1707), disbanded 10 December 1714.

**Louvignies** 14 May 1702, **Siffrédy** 16 April 1712, disbanded 1714.

**Tavannes** 14 May 1702, **Thomassin de Saint-Paul** 23 January 1707, **La Roque** 27 July 1709, disbanded 1714.

**Lannoy** 14 May 1702 (Barcelona 1706), into **Piémont** 1714.

**Martel** 14 May 1702, **Laubanie** 3 May 1710, into **Royal** 2 June 1714.

**Roussilles** 14 May 1702, into **Normandie** 20 November 1714.

**Monfort** 14 May 1702, **Arville** 3 February 1706, **Duprat** 1708, **Soupa** 1710, disbanded 1714.

**La Grise** 20 May 1702, **Montesson** 20 December 1706, disbanded 16 January 1714.

**Froulay** 21 May 1702, **Létorières** 7 March 1711, disbanded 1714.

**Saint-Simon** 21 May 1702, **Voluire** 30 January 1711, **Varennes-Kergoson**, disbanded 1714.

**Laval** 14 June 1702, **Sennectère** 1705, into **Boufflers** 12 November 1714.

**Castelet** 5 July 1702, into **La Gervasais** 21 January 1714.

**Conflans-Ménars** 5 July 1702 (Oudenarde 1708), **Astour** 1 December 1708, **Hernoton** 1711, disbanded 31 December 1713.

**Ourches** 5 July 1702, **Boulay** 1705, **Eppeville** 25 October 1710, into **La Reine** 1 February 1715.

**Scève** 12 July 1702, **Choiseul-Stainville** 1702, **Choiseul-Meuse** 1703, **Choiseul-Francières** 1703, **Murat** 1705, disbanded 1714.

**Lannion** 25 July 1702, disbanded 31 December 1713.

**Laigle** 25 July 1702, disbanded 1714.

**Chevalier de Damas** 25 July 1702 (Torino 1706, Lerida 1708), **Vallouze** 10 July 1708 (Barcelona 1714), into **Royal-Vaisseaux** 30 July 1715.

**Bellafaire** 25 July 1702 (Portugal 1704), **Tessé** 30 August 1705 (Barcelona 1706, Almanza 1707), **Bulkely** 11 May 1707, **Bochet** 23 May 1709, disbanded 1714.

**Enonville** 25 July 1702, **Livry** 21 November 1703 (Blenheim 1704), **Belzunce** 17 September 1704 (Denain 1712), **La Planche** August 1712, disbanded 1714.

**Du Moulin** (or **Marsilly**) 25 July 1702 (Torino 1706, Toulon 1707), **Bellisle** 28 October 1710 (Denain 1712), into **Touraine** 12 November 1714.

**Destouches** 25 July 1702, **Montmorency-La Neuville** 19 November 1702 (Toulon 1707, Barcelona 1714), into **Tallard** 30 July 1715.

**Lostanges** 25 July 1702 (Ramillies 1706), **Rasilly** June 1707, disbanded 1714.

**Talendes** 25 July 1702, **Duchay** June 1705, **Arcy** 1709 (Barcelona 1714), disbanded January 1715.

**Du Bièz** 25 July 1702 (Ramillies 1706, Oudenarde 1708), **Flamarens** June 1710, disbanded 1714.

**Trécesson** 25 July 1702, disbanded 3 February 1715.

**La Mothe** 25 July 1702, **Artagnan** 10 December 1709, disbanded 1714.

**Sanzay** 25 July 1702, **Sourches** 17 October 1703, **Choiseul-Beaupré** 5 September 1706, into **Boufflers** 19 January 1714.

**Menou** 25 July 1702 (Torino 1706), disbanded 21 December 1713.

**Tournon** 25 July 1702 (Barcelona 1706), **Payssac** 2 April 1709, into **Dauphin** 14 January 1714.

**La Mothe-Houdancourt** 25 July 1702 (Blenheim 1704, Ramillies 1706, Oudenarde 1708, Malplaquet 1709), **Ghistelles** 1709, **Perthuis** 20 February 1712, disbanded 1714.

**Gensac** 25 July 1702, **Piffonel** 1711, disbanded 1714.

**Saint-Evremont** 3 September 1702, disbanded May 1713.

**Guines** 3 September 1702, **Dampierre** 24 May 1705, into **La Gervasais** 20 March 1714.

**Chalmazel** 3 September 1702, into **Picardie** 7 October 1714.

**Castéja** 3 September 1702, **Saint-Léger** 1709, disbanded 8 January 1713.

**Coëtanfau** 3 September 1702, **Roure** 18 April 1706, into **Champagne** 20 March 1714.

**Poyanne** 3 September 1702, disbanded 1714.

**Savigny** 3 September 1702, **Boisset de Geaix** 1708, **Bérard** 28 April 1711, disbanded 1714.

**Francheville** 3 September 1702, **Rochefort** 1709, **Beauficel** 1712, disbanded 1714.

**Broissia** 3 September 1702, disbanded 1714.

**Maisonthiers** 3 September 1702, into **Navarre** 21 January 1714.

**Pujols** 3 September 1702, **Puységur** 1706, **Léotaud** 1708, **Valory** 21 November 1712, disbanded 21 January 1714.

**Doigny** 3 September 1702, **Thil** 30 April 1704, disbanded 1714.

**La Raimbaudière** 3 September 1702, into **Boufflers** 21 January 1714.

**Carné** 3 September 1702, **Hoccart** 20 January 1708, into **Navarre** 21 January 1714.

**Hérouville** 3 September 1702, **Conflans-Saint-Rémy** 20 January 1710, into **Tallard** 17 January 1714.

**Desmarets** 3 September 1702, **Verseilles** 1708, disbanded 1714.

**Caupos** 3 September 1702, disbanded 1714.

**Clermont** 3 September 1702, **Phélippes de la Houssaye** 14 January 1705, **Vassan** 8 April, into **Royal** 31 December 1713.

**Boufflers-Rémiancourt** 3 September 1702 (Malplaquet 1709), **Choiseul** 21 January 1710, disbanded 1714.

**Artagnan** 3 September 1702, into **Tallard** 17 January 1714.

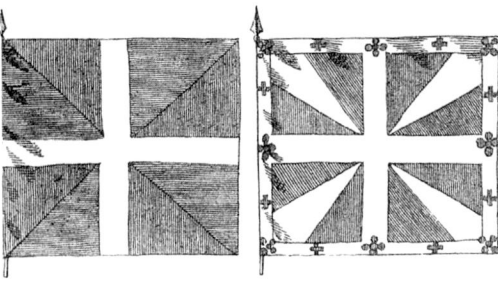

Regimental colours of the Perche and the Boufflers regiments, early eighteenth century. Both are blue, yellow and red. (Courtesy Rijksmuseum, Amsterdam. RP-P-OB-83.399)

**Valouze** 3 September 1702, **Grosbois** 1705, **Valence** 7 April 1708, disbanded 1714.

**Permangle** 3 September 1702, **Maulmont** 12 November 1708, disbanded 1714.

**Pfyffer** (Swiss) 15 September 1702 (Ramillies 1706, Oudenarde 1708, Denain 1712), disbanded 11 February 1715 (except for two companies that remained independent).

**Vigier** (Swiss) 15 September 1702, disbanded 11 February 1715.

**Rozières** 8 October 1702, Chevron 1707, **Bonnières** 1712, disbanded 13 December 1713.

**Pisançon** 3 December 1702, **La Villemeneust** 1707, disbanded 1714.

**La Rochedumaine** 3 December 1702, **Desangles** 20 July 1707, into **Royal** 31 December 1713.

**Aubigné** 10 December 1702, **Nogaret** 11 February 1706, disbanded 7 October 1714.

**Vaudreuil** 10 December 1702, **Brancas-Courbon** 24 September 1705, **Lostanges-Béduer** 29 November 1710, disbanded 13 December 1713.

**Montluc** 10 December 1702, **La Rivière-Castéras** 20 February 1707, into **Royal** 31 December 1713.

**Des Prez** 10 December 1702, **Rohan** 1710, disbanded 1714.

**Bornemont** 10 December 1702, **Beaujeu** 16 February 1709, disbanded 1714.

**Perthuis** 10 December 1702, **Morogues** 1708, **Bourg** 1710, disbanded 1714.

**Des Brosses** 10 December 1702, **Ormoy** 1711, disbanded 1714.

**Arigny** 10 December 1702, **Aubusson** 1706, **Varennes-Gournay** 11 January 1708, disbanded 1714.

**Houdelot** 10 December 1702, disbanded 1714.

**Lachau-Montauban** 10 December 1702, into **Tallard** 22 May 1714.

**Saint-Gery** (or **Saingery**), *c*. 1702, led by Marquis de Saint-Gery as per 1705 clothing bill, at Dunkirk 1705, possibly into **Brancas** 1705.

**Lestrange**, 1702, led by Joseph, Marquis de Lestrange as per 1703 clothing bill.

**La Feuillade** 1 January 1704 (Torino 1706), into **La Marine** 1714.

**Tessé** 7 March 1704, disbanded 25 January 1705.

**Montanègre** (Piémont) 1 June 1704, disbanded March 1705.

**Châteaubriand**, *c*. 1704. raised by Marquis de la Verrie Châteaubriand as per clothing bill of 15 February 1704, disbanded *c*. 1714.

**Reding** (German) 3 March 1705 (Barcelona 1706), **Lomagne** late 1706, **Reding** 16 February 1707 (Almanza 1707, Barcelona 1714), into **Royal-Bavière** 10 June 1715.

**Beltrambi** (Italian) 20 May 1705, disbanded 9 October 1706.

**Rangoni** (Italian) 15 September 1705, disbanded 9 October 1706.

**Fusiliers des Montagnes** 15 November 1705, disbanded 13 December 1713.

**Ségur** 15 December 1705, **Danois** September 1709 (Barcelona 1714), disbanded 31 July 1715.

**Noë** 1 January 1706 (Barcelona 1714), into **La Marine** and **Anjou** 29 July 1715.

**Thorigny** 1 January 1706, **Chambaud** 1706, 2nd battalion disbanded December 1711 and 1st battalion December 1713.

**Enghien**, 1 February 1706.

**Jaucourt** 2 February 1706, **Mancini** February 1708, **Chastes** 16 May 1709, **Clermont-Montoison** 15 April 1710, into **La Marine** 1714.

**Duc de Noailles** 2 February 1706, **La Baume** 1713, disbanded 18 March 1714.

**Maréchal de Noailles** 3 February 1706, **Bouhyer** 26 February 1709, into **Dauphin** 21 January 1714.

**Chamilly** 3 February 1706, **Mornac** 13 July 1707, into **Lyonnois** 19 January 1714.

**Grignan** 3 February 1706, **Bellaffaire** 5 January 1707 (Almanza 1707, Barcelona 1714), into **La Marine** 27 August 1715.

**Boufflers** 3 February 1706 (Oudenarde 1708, Malplaquet 1709), **Bombelles** 24 October 1711 (Denain 1712), into **Royal** 4 October 1714.

**Villequier** 3 February 1706, **Le Tellier** 1709, **La Motte** 1712, disbanded 31 December 1713.

**Clairfontaine** 4 February 1706, **Talleyrand** 1712 (Barcelona 1714), **Maulévrier** 1714, disbanded 30 January 1715.

**Romainval** 4 February 1706, **Cormis** 1712, disbanded 1714.

**Conflans** 4 February 1706, **Laval** 1709, **Ruys** 1712, disbanded May 1713.

**Urban** 4 February 1706, **Ambres** 1710, **Guignonville** 1712, disbanded 1714.

**Bragny** 4 February 1706, **Vieillevigne** 1707, **Grandlieu** 1708, **Arros** 3 September 1710, **Des Hayes** 20 February 1712, disbanded 1714.

**Choisel** 4 February 1706, **Houdetot** August 1712, disbanded 1714.

**Kaërgroët** 4 February 1706, **Sebbeville** 27 March 1708, into **Touraine** 19 January 1714.

**La Londe** 4 February 1706, into **Champagne** 19 January 1714.

**Bruslart** 4 February 1706, **Goëllo** 1712, disbanded 31 December 1713.

**Bourdonné** 4 February 1706, **Champigny** 1707, **Castelnau** 1712, disbanded 1714.

**Comte d'Houdetot** 4 February 1706, **Caylus** August 1712, disbanded 1714.

**Saillant** 4 February 1706, **Ussel** 2 April 1712, disbanded 1714.

**Villelongue** 4 February 1706, **Montreau** 1710, into **Condé** 1 January 1714.

**Baumelay** 4 February 1706, **Mouchan** 11 May 1707, **Damas** 10 July 1708, **Houdetot** August 1712 (Barcelona 1714), **Guerchy** 1714, disbanded 30 January 1715.

**Gramont** 4 February 1706, **Scèves** 1709, into **Flandres** 1714.

# INFANTRY REGIMENTS 1643–1715

**Montsoreau** 4 February 1706, **Houdetot** August 1712, into **Touraine** 14 January 1714.

**Ablois de Vieuville** 4 February 1706, disbanded 13 December 1713.

**Pont-du-Château** 4 February 1706, **Léon** 1710, disbanded 30 January 1715.

**Peyrela** (Walloon) 1 February 1707, transferred from the Spanish to the French army, **Storff** 1710, disbanded 1712.

**Pantoka** (Walloon) 1 February 1707, transferred from the Spanish to the French army, **Bylandt** 1709, disbanded 1712.

**Weinly** (Walloon) 1 February 1707, transferred from the Spanish to the French army, **Hamat** 1709, disbanded 1712.

**Rheingraf** (German) 1 February 1707, transferred from the Spanish to the French army, **Houdenhoé** 1708, disbanded 1712.

**Nassau** (German) 1 February 1707, transferred from the Spanish to the French army, **Trefferd** 1709, **Uhland** 1710, disbanded 1712.

**Albergotti** (Italian) 1 February 1707, transferred from the Spanish to the French army, **Letterio** 1711, disbanded 1712.

**Grimaldi** (Italian) 1 February 1707, transferred to the French army, **Caëtano** 1711, disbanded 1712.

**Los Rios** (Spanish) 1 February 1707, transferred from the Spanish to the French army, **Las Sierras** 1710, **Léon** 1711, disbanded 1712.

**Machieno** (Spanish) 1 February 1707, transferred from the Spanish to the French army, **Villesca** 1711, disbanded 1712.

**Sohé** (Walloon) 1 February 1707, transferred from the Spanish to the French army, **Mignons** 1709, **Kerkem** 1711, probably disbanded 1712.

**Assigny** 1 February 1707, transferred from the Spanish to the French army, **Scépeaux** 1708, disbanded 1712.

**Canillac** 1 February 1707, transferred from the Spanish to the French army, **Bellesuvée** 1708, **Feuquières** 1710, disbanded 1712.

**Pratamamo** (Italian) 1 February 1707, transferred from the Spanish to the French army, **Caraffa** 31 August 1711, disbanded 1712.

**Evoly** (Walloon) 1 February 1707, transferred to the French army, **Bacher** 1709, **Coupigny** 1710, disbanded 1712.

**Marimont** (Walloon) 1 February 1707, transferred to the French army, **Bouré** 1710, disbanded 1712.

**Ruppelmonde** (Walloon) 1 February 1707, transferred to the French army, **Bournonville** 1711, disbanded 1712.

**Poléon** (Walloon) 1 February 1707, transferred to the French army, disbanded 1714.

**Royal-Bavière** (German) 1 January 1709.

# Appendix III

# Uniforms

In this series, we strive to have a visual idea of what the Sun King's soldiers looked like and favour contemporary sources from publications and archives. Some are evoked above and we further present our translation of some of the main documents on this topic, namely the lists of 1692, 1698 and 1702. These are followed by various notes from correspondence and clothing bills from 1667 to 1711. On the whole, these are the main contemporary sources known on uniforms of the Sun King's infantry.[1]

### A)
État Général des Troupes de France ... 1692[2]

| Uniform | Coat | Cuffs and Lining |
|---|---|---|
| Picardie | grey | grey |
| Champagne | grey | grey |
| Navarre | grey | grey (...) |
| Vaubécourt | grey | grey |
| Le Roy | grey | blue (...) |
| Poitou | grey | blue (...) |
| Dauphin | grey | blue (...) |
| Le Maine | grey | (...) |
| La Reine | grey | red (...) |
| Les Vaisseaux | grey | blue(...) |
| Royal la Marine | grey | blue |

---

1 We cannot refrain from advising interested readers to be careful of interpretations, notably as found in Lienhart and Humbert, *Les Uniformes de l'Armée française depuis 1690* (Liepzig, 1897–1903) as well as descriptions given in Susane, *Histoire de l'infanterie française* which are rather weak and confused in Louis XIV's reign. The plates illustrating these works, even those by such a master as Philippoteaux, should also be considered with some scrutiny. On the other hand, we are pleased to print in our series the more plausible ones that are now largely forgotten and should not be.
2 BMG, Manuscrit A1b 1626 nicknamed "Tiroirs de Louis XIV".

| | | |
|---|---|---|
| Vermandois | grey | red (…) |
| Provence | brown | red (…) |
| Lorraine | grey-white | red |
| Toulouse | grey | blue (…) |
| Saintonge | grey | blue (…) |
| Dauphiné | grey | blue (…) |
| Aunis | grey | red (…) |
| Soissonois | grey | blue (…) |
| Ponthieu | grey | Brown (*feuille morte*) (…) |
| Humières | grey | red |
| Guiche | grey | yellow (…) |

**Foreign Infantry**

| | | |
|---|---|---|
| Zurlauben (German) | blue | red |
| Famechon (Walloon) | red | blue |
| [Royal-]Roussillon (Catalan/Spanish) | red | red |
| Erlach (Swiss) | blue | red |
| Stuppa (Swiss) | blue | red |
| Stuppa jeune (Swiss) | blue | red |
| Salis (Swiss) | red | green |
| Pfyffer (Swiss) | yellow | red |
| Greder (Swiss) | red | green (…) |
| Saint-Laurent (Nice/Italian) | blue | red |
| Royal-Italien (Italian) | brown (*minime*) | red |
| Porlier (Swiss) | blue | red |
| Hessy (Swiss) | blue | red |
| Reynold (Swiss)* | red | yellow |
| Monnin (Swiss) | blue | red |
| Courten (Swiss) | yellow | red |
| Schellemberg (Swiss) | green | red |
| Greder (German) | blue | yellow |
| Surbeck (German) | yellow | red |
| Joule (German)** | blue | red (…) |
| Royal-Montferrat (Piémont/Italian) | grey | yellow |
| Solre (Walloon) | grey | green (…) |
| Lamar (Piémont/Italian) | grey | blue |
| Montroux (Italian) | red | blue |
| Perri (Corsican/Italian) | grey | green (…) |
| Dubuisson (Swiss)*** | red | green |
| Lassala (Swiss)*** | red | yellow |
| Aygre (Swiss)*** | red | blue (…) |

\*      '1/4 C[ompagn]ie' (quarter company)
\*\*     Possibly Yoël Danish.
\*\*\*    'C[ompagn]ie fr[anche]' (Independent company)

B)

**Instructions to infantry regiments regarding the upcoming camp at Compiègne, spring and summer of 1698.**[3]

Minister of War Barbezieux to inspectors of infantry, 29 March 1698. 'You will explain that the King's intention is not to dress soldiers anew, unless it is the year when regiments must be clothed, or else that they are under extreme necessity, nor that captains spend more … that the King wishes only that the officers be uniformly clothed, that is to say with cloth of the same colour to that worn by the soldiers.'

Same to same, 11 April 1698. "… that at the Camp at Compiègne the infantry officers all wear uniform coats, that the captains must have a [gold or silver] lace edging and that the subalterns must not have it …"

Same to same, June 1698. "… the King has been informed that there are regiments in which officers are dressed in red or in blue, while the soldiers are in grey. His Majesty, not wanting to suffer this deformity in his troops, orders you to warn them, that he desires that they be clothed of the uniform coat of the same colour of the regiment in which they are."

C)

**Description of French infantry at Compiègne in the *Mercure Galant*, September 1698.**

The Infantry is distinguished … by the [coat] cuffs, the waistcoats, the stockings and the ribbons on the shoulder. All officers are dressed in a good grey cloth with buttons and buttonholes and a gold or silver edge on the cuffs of the [same] colour as those of their soldiers. The drums of the regiments that bear the names of provinces have the livery of the King, and the others those of the colonels whose regiments bear their names.

The du Roy Regiment is dressed in grey [coats] with blue cuffs and waistcoats, and orange [*feuille morte*] buttonhole lace on the coat; Officers have gold [lace].

Greder (German) has blue [coats] lined with yellow, with a white [lace] edging, blue waistcoats & pewter buttons.

---

3   AG, Guerre A1, Vol. 1439, Barbezieux to inspectors of infantry, 29 March, 11 April and June 1698.

The La Reine Regiment has grey [coats], lined with red with blue waistcoats, pewter buttons and red ribbons on the shoulder. The Drummers have the Queen's livery and the colours are black [and green].

Navarre has all grey [coats] without coloured cuffs, brass buttons and red waistcoats.

Languedoc has blue cuffs, yellow buttons, and an orange [*feuille morte*] edging lace, and red and orange ribbons.

Picardie has all grey [coats], without [coloured] cuffs and has red waistcoats and red ribbons.

Royal-Italien is dressed in brown with yellow waistcoats and ribbons of the same colour.

Dauphin has grey [coats]with blue cuffs and waistcoats, blue stockings and red ribbons.

Maine wears grey with blue cuffs.

Bourbonnois [is] all [in] grey.

The La Couronne and Toulouse [regiments] wear grey with blue cuffs.

Lee (Irish) has red [coats] with green cuffs, red waistcoats and white buttonhole lace.

Royal-Roussillon wears red with red waistcoats.

Crussol wears grey with red waistcoats, red and white ribbons.

Lyonnois wears grey with red waistcoats and [coat] cuffs.

Rouergue also has red cuffs.

D)

**Description of French infantry at Compiègne, 1698 by L.F. Corfey.**[4]

**Picardie:** white coat, white cuffs, red waistcoat, white stockings.
**Navarre:** white coat, white cuffs, red waistcoat, white stockings.
**Bourbonnois:** white coat, white cuffs, red waistcoat, red stockings.
**Du Roy:** white coat, blue cuffs, orange waistcoat [actually meaning blue

---

4   Lambert Friedrich Corfey, 'Reisetagebuch 1698–1700', ed. Helmut Lahrkamp, *Quellen und forschungen zur geschichte der stadt Münster*, new series, Vol. 9 (1977).

waistcoat with orange buttonhole lace], blue stockings.
**Lyonnois:** white coat, red cuffs, green waistcoat, red stockings.
**Dauphin infantry:** white coat, blue cuffs, blue waistcoat, blue stockings.
**Crussol:** white coat, white cuffs, red waistcoat, red stockings.
**Anjou:** white coat, blue cuffs, blue waistcoat, blue stockings.
**Maine:** white coat, blue cuffs, blue waistcoat, blue stockings.
**Humières:** white coat, red cuffs, red waistcoat, red stockings.
**La Reine:** white coat, red cuffs, blue waistcoat, red stockings.
**La Couronne:** white coat, blue cuffs, blue waistcoat, blue stockings.
**Chartres:** white coat, red cuffs, yellow waistcoat, red stockings.
**Royal-Roussillon:** red coat, red cuffs, red waistcoat, white stockings.
**Rouergue:** white coat, red cuffs, red waistcoat, red stockings.
**Vermandois:** white coat, red cuffs, blue waistcoat, red stockings.
**Greder (German):** blue coat, yellow cuffs, blue waistcoat, red stockings.
**Royal-Italien (Italian):** brown coat, red cuffs, yellow waistcoat, white stockings.
**Languedoc:** white coat, blue cuffs, blue waistcoat, red stockings.
**Stuppa (Swiss):** red coat, blue cuffs, orange waistcoat, blue stockings.
**Toulouse:** white coat, blue cuffs, blue waistcoat, blue stockings.
**Lee (Irish):** red coat, green cuffs, green waistcoat, white stockings.
**Poitou:** white coat, blue cuffs, blue waistcoat, blue stockings.
**Coëtquen:** white coat, red cuffs, yellow waistcoat, red stockings.

E)

État des Troupes de France en l'année 1702[5]

| Uniform | Coat | Cuffs and Lining |
| --- | --- | --- |
| Navarre | grey | grey |
| Champagne | grey | grey |
| Piémont | grey | grey (…) |
| Auvergne | grey | grey (…) |
| Du Roy | grey | blue (…) |
| Poitou | grey | blue (…) |
| Dauphin | grey | blue |
| Crussol | grey | grey (…) |
| Anjou | grey | blue |
| Du Maine | grey | |
| Humières | grey | red (…) |
| La Reine | grey | red (…) |
| Royal des Vaisseaux | grey | blue (…) |
| La Couronne | grey | grey (…) |
| Royal-Roussillon (Catalan) | red | red (…) |

---

5  BMG, Manuscript A1b 1626 nicknamed 'Tiroirs de Louis XIV'.

| Regiment | Coat | Facing |
|---|---|---|
| Royal la Marine | grey | blue |
| Vermandois | grey | red (…) |
| Stuppa (Swiss) | blue | red |
| Reynold (Swiss) | red | yellow |
| Hessy (Swiss) | blue | red (…) |
| Royal-Italien (Italian) | brown (*minime*) | red (…) |
| Provence | brown | red |
| Zurlauben (German) | blue | red (…) |
| Greder (Swiss) | red | green (…) |
| Greder (German) | blue | yellow |
| Surbeck (German) | yellow | red |
| Toulouse | grey | blue (…) |
| Lorraine | grey | green (…) |
| Saintonge | grey | blue (…) |
| Soissonois | grey | blue (…) |
| Aunis | grey | red (…) |
| Dauphiné | grey | blue (…) |
| Ponthieu | grey | brown (*feuille morte*) (…) |
| Solre (Walloon) | grey | green (…) |
| Salis (Swiss) | red | green (…) |
| Montroux (Italian) | red | blue (…) |
| Perri (Corsican/Italian) | grey | green (…) |

F)

**Notes on infantry uniforms, 1667–1711**

The following notes are from reproductions or transcriptions of contemporary documents. This is certainly not exhaustive and we are certain there are many more in obscure or forgotten publications as well as yet to be discovered in archives. As it is, many clothing bills have been published notably in Robert Hall's work on the *Flags and Uniforms of French Infantry under Louis XIV 1688–1714*, in which readers wishing more details will find them in the original French. We have summarised the main features of all documents in this appendix. The sources are given below.[6]

---

6   *Calendar of State Papers*, (London: HMSO, 1866), Vol. 219, pp.506, 522; SHD, AG, Guerre A1, Vol. 621, Louvois to Le Tellier, Saint-Germains, 11 May 1670; *Mercure Hollandois*, 1672, p.281; SHD, AG, Guerre A1, Vol. 621, Louvois to Zurlauben, Saint-Germains, 11 May 1679; SHD, AG, Guerre A1, Vol. 623, Louvois to Lallemand, Saint-Germains, 24 August 1679; *Mercure Galant*, December 1686, pp.189–190; SHD, AG, Guerre A1, Vol. 781, Louvois to Zurlauben, Versailles, 3 March 1687; *Mercure Galant*, October 1688, pp.212–213; Albert Callet, *Le Régiment de Bugey* (n.d, n.p.), p.416; La Sabretache, No. 417 (1958) pp.517–518; Roger Drouault, *L'habillement et l'équipement du régiment de Saint-Germain-Beaupré de 1702 à 1714* (Limoges: Ducourtieux & Gout, 1909); SHD, AG, A1, 1895, Traité fait entre Mr. le Comte de Seve…21 April 1703; SHD, AG, A1, 1896, Nous … Marquis de Monluc …18 March 1703; SHD, AG, A1, 1690, Comte de La Fare, Mémoire des habits … 24 October 1703; SHD, AG, A1, 1834, Marquis de Maillé clothing bill 4 February 1705. Jean Chagniot, *Paris et l'armée au XVIIIe siècle* (Paris: Economica, 1985), pp.270–271; Robert Hall, *Flags and Uniforms of French Infantry under Louis XIV 1688–1714* (Farnham, UK: The Pike and Shot Society, 2004), pp.46–138.

Douglas (Scottish), 1667. A note and a warrant of 3 October 1667 allowed the export of 5,000 yards or red cloth and 6,500 yards of white cloth for 15 companies of 100 men each.

Douglas or Hamilton's (Scottish), 1672. The Scottish companies in Maseyck, Netherlands, had 80 to 90 men each "clothed in red."

Furstenberg's German Regiment was raised from 2 February 1668 by Landgrave Wilhelm Egon von Fustemberg and came into French service on 27 March 1670. In May 1670, it was reported "all dressed in blue cloth [coats] lined with yellow."

Famechon's Regiment, 1679. Received in 1679 "red coats lined with blue" to last two years.

Vierzet's (Walloon) Regiment, 1679. Received from May 1679 coats that were "*feuille morte* [a shade of brown] lined with blue" sent to Perpignan; also advised by Louvois on 24 August 1679 that since "your soldiers have *feuille morte* coats, it would be well that officers have this colour with silver buttons so the regiment will have the same dress."

Bassigny, 1686. "All soldiers had new gold laced hats. Their bandoliers, waist belts and powder flask cords were also very clean; everything garnished by many ribbons of the colour of fire [red] and white. Their swords were all similar and all officers had very rich coats and equally ornamented."

Zurlauben's (Walloon) Regiment, 1687. "… His Majesty has ordered me to let you know that it wishes that in the future, the regiment you command be dressed in blue lined with amaranth [wine red]."

Vivonne, 1688. "…the colours had his [Marshal and Duc de Vivonne] coat of arms, which the King had allowed as well as the drummers wearing his livery."

Troops at the surrender of Bonn on Saturday 15 October 1689. The allied infantry lined up in two lines at the gate of *l'Étoile* (the star), "The Brandenburg Guards in a blue livery on foot … the Dutch Regiment of General Delwig and that of Lunenburg in Dutch service, all dressed in red … the regiments of General Major Schlangenberg and of General Major Lanoy, dressed in white …" and the French troops paraded out "… in this manner. A kettledrummer marched at the head, beating on his drums…then five trumpeters. They had liveries of red, ornamented with gold … dragoons in a green livery … an infantry battalion … [with] three white, black and red colours … a battalion of infantry … [with] three colours of black, white and yellow … another battalion… [with] three colours of black, white and red … the last battalion … three colours with white and red *lames* [literally blades–possibly meaning triangles] … a regiment of dragoons … [bearing] two green standards…finally a company of Germans with a white colour … List of the [French] troop in the garrison that came out … la Varenne [cavalry], 141 horse, one kettledrummer, six trumpeters and two standards …" Infantry: Marquis de Grange battalion, 237 men; Marquis de Castre, 275 men; a company of gunners, 33 men; Pionfi (or Pionsi), 336 men; Provence, 344 men; Bourbon, 203 men; Vendôme, 238 men; Poitou, 244 men; Asfeld Dragoons, 352 men; companies of Furstenberg's guards, 53 men; infantry and cavalry near the baggage, 1,137 men; 1,500 men remain in the city sick or wounded as per: *Mercure Galant*, November 1689.

Bugey, 1692. Grey-white coat, maroon brown cuffs.

Orléanois, 1699. Grey-white coat and blue cuffs, lining and blue breeches, brass buttons, royal livery for drummers. Officers had the same uniform but with gold buttons and buttonholes with gold edging lace on coat and waistcoat, black beaver hat with white plume, blue stockings.

Chamilly, 1699. Uniform unknown, but livery was scarlet with silver lace "three fingers wide" on all seams edge with green velvet lace half a finger wide bordered by a silver lace two fingers wide, all that lace covered the coat, green waistcoat and breeches laced silver, hat with white plume and silver lace as per April 1699 *Mercure Galant*.

Orléans, 1700. Grey-white coat, lining, waistcoat and breeches, scarlet cuffs, red breeches for sergeants.

Bouzols, 1701. Grey-white lined grey-white, red cuffs, waistcoat and stockings, grey-white breeches, brass buttons, false gold hat lace; drummers had buff (*isabelle*) coats, red cuffs, waistcoat and breeches.

Brancas Infantry Regiment 6 May 1702. 481 grey-white cloth coats with half-scarlet cuffs and grey lining, grey-white breeches; 26 sergeants grey-white cloth coats with scarlet cuffs and grey lining, grey-white breeches; 13 drummers Damascus colour coats, yellow cuffs and grey lining, grey-white breeches; 3 dozen buttons per coat.

Francheville, 1702. Grey-white lined grey-white, red cuffs, blue waistcoat, breeches and stockings, pewter buttons, false silver hat lace. Drummers, red coat lined blue with blue cuffs, livery lace, blue waistcoats, breeches and stockings, pewter buttons, false silver hat lace.

Saint-Aulaire, 1702. Grey-white coat and lining, red cuffs, grey-white breeches. Sergeants, grey-white coat lined grey-white, half scarlet cuffs. Officers had scarlet coat lining, scarlet waistcoat and breeches. Drummers, red coat with green lining.

Martel, 1702. Grey-white lined grey-white, red cuffs, grey-white breeches, red stockings, pewter buttons, hats with false silver lace. Sergeants, scarlet cuffs and stockings, silver laced hats. Drummers, scarlet coat, yellow lining, yellow and crimson livery lace.

# UNIFORMS

Castelet, 1702. Grey-white coat lined grey-white, blue cuff cuffs, waistcoat, breeches and stockings, brass buttons, false gold lace edging hats. Drummers, red with blue cuffs, lining, waistcoat, breeches and stockings, brass buttons, livery lace, false gold lace edging hats.

Richebourg, 1702. Grey-white coat lined grey-white, red cuffs, waistcoat and stockings, grey-white breeches, brass buttons, false gold lace edging hats, 494 red and buff aiguillettes to put on soldier's shoulders. Drummers, buff (*isabelle*) lined red, red cuffs, waistcoat and stockings, grey-white breeches, brass buttons, false gold lace edging hats.

Bouzols, 1702. Grey-white coat lined grey-white, red cuffs, waistcoat and stockings, grey-white breeches, brass buttons, false gold hat lace. Drummers, buff (*isabelle*) coat, red cuffs, grey-white breeches.

Des Clos, 1702. Grey-white coat lined grey-white, red cuffs, green waistcoat, grey-white breeches, red stockings, brass buttons, false gold hat lace. Drummers, green lined red, demi-violet waistcoat, grey-white breeches, red stockings, brass buttons, false gold hat lace.

Tavannes, 1702. Grey-white coat lined grey-white, red cuffs, waistcoat and stockings, grey-white breeches, brass buttons, false gold hat lace. Drummers, red lined with yellow, yellow cuffs, red waistcoat, breeches and stockings, brass buttons, false gold hat lace.

Carné, 1702. Grey-white coat and lining, red cuffs and waistcoat, grey-white breeches, red stockings, brass button, false gold lace on hats. Drummers, red coat with yellow lining and cuffs, red waistcoat, grey-white breeches, red stockings, brass button, false gold lace on hats.

Rozières, 1702 and 1710. Grey-white coat and lining, red cuffs, green waistcoat, grey-white breeches, red stockings, brass button, false gold lace on hats. Drummers, red coat with green cuffs and lining, green waistcoat, grey-white breeches, livery lace, brass button, false gold lace on hats.

Broissia, 1702. Grey-white coat and lining, red cuffs and stockings, grey-white breeches, brass button, false gold lace on hats. Drummers, yellow coat with blue cuffs and lining, livery lace, brass button, false gold laced hats.

Oysonville (or Oissonville), 1702. Grey-white coat and lining, red cuffs, waistcoat and stockings, grey-white breeches, brass button, false gold laced hats. Drummers, white with red cuffs and lining, red waistcoat and stockings, livery lace, brass button, false gold laced hats.

Vermandois, 1702. Grey-white serge coats with scarlet cuffs, blue waistcoats, grey-white breeches, scarlet stockings, brass buttons (36 per coat and 36 per waistcoat) and false gold lace for hats; drummers had blue coats with scarlet cuffs and lining, scarlet stockings, false gold lace for hats; sergeants had possibly grey-with coats lined grey-white with scarlet cuffs, blue waistcoats, grey-white breeches, scarlet stockings, gold buttons and gold laced hats; Officers had grey-white coats for captains and lieutenants, scarlet coat cuffs and lining, scarlet waistcoats and breeches, gilded buttons.

La Feuillade, 1703. Grey-white coat and lining, red cuffs and stockings, grey-white breeches, pewter button, false silver laced hats. Sergeants, 26 aiguillettes. Drummers, buff (*ventre de biche*) coat lined with yellow, livery lace, pewter button, false silver laced hats.

La Rochethulon des Prez, 1703. Grey-white coat and lining, red cuffs and stockings, grey-white breeches, brass button, false gold lace on hats. Drummers, Green coat with buff (*isabelle*) cuffs and lining, livery lace.

Saint-Germain-Beaupré, 1703. Grey-white coat, blue cuffs, lining, waistcoat, breeches and stockings, brass buttons, false gold hat lace. Sergeants, fine gold hat lace. Drummers, buff (*isabelle*) coat, blue lining, livery lace.

Scève (or Seve), 21 April 1703. grey-white coat and lining, red cuffs, grey-white breeches, red stockings, brass button, false gold lace on hats.

Curzay (or Cursay), 1703. Grey-white coat lined grey-white, red waistcoat, grey-white breeches and stockings, pewter buttons. Sergeants, red cuffs. Drummers, *gay* green coat, orange (*aurore*) cuffs and lining, pewter buttons, livery lace, 28 crosses for drummers (worn on coat's chest and back).

Laval, 1703. Grey-white coat and lining, scarlet cuffs, brass buttons, grey-white breeches, red stockings, false gold lace edging hats. Drummers, scarlet(?) coat with green(?) lining, orange (*aurore*) cuffs, green waistcoat and breeches, livery lace, red stockings, brass buttons.

Clermont, 1703. Grey-white coat and lining, false gold lace edging hats. Drummers, orange (*aurore*) cloth, crimson and white livery lace.

Montluc, 18 March 1703. Grey-white coat, red cuffs and stockings, yellow metal flat buttons, false gold hat lace. Drummers, red coat with yellow cuffs, broad silk lace, drums painted in old with coat of arms of the Marquis de Montluc.

Montboissier, 1703. Grey-white coat and breeches, blue cuffs and breeches, pewter buttons..

Lestrange, 1703. Grey-white coat lined grey-white, red cuffs and stockings, grey-white breeches, pewter buttons, false silver hat lace. Drummers, white coat with green cuffs and lining, livery lace, pewter buttons, false silver hat lace.

La Fare-Soustelle (also La Farre), 24 October 1703. Sergeants, three ounces of gold thread for three waistcoats.

Zurlauben (Walloon) 1703. Officers had blue cloth with blue lining cloth, enlisted men also blue cloth with blue serge for lining. For drummers, fifers and hautbois, *pourpre cramoisi* (purple crimson) cloth with blue serge.

Sillery, December 1703. Grey-white coat and lining, red cuffs, red waistcoat, grey-white breeches, brass buttons, false gold hat lace.

D'Aubigné de Tigny, 26 March 1704. Grey-white coat with grey-white lining, red waistcoat, grey-white breeches, brass buttons, false gold hat lace. Drummers, green cloth and pinkish buff (*couleur de chair*) cloth, livery lace.

Maillé de la Tour-Landry, 29 February 1704, 14 March 1705 and 30 May 1706. Grey-white coat and lining, cuffs red, red waistcoat, brass buttons. Sergeants, grey-white coat lined red, red cuffs, brass buttons. Officers, grey-white coat, red lining, black velvet cuffs, gold buttons, gold lace. Drummers, red coat with yellow cuffs and lining, livery lace (red, black and yellow silk), crosses for drummers (worn on coat's chest and back).

Mortemart, 1704. Grey-white coat lined with grey-white, scarlet serge (presumably for) cuffs, scarlet breeches, white and yellow metal buttons (mixed); drummers had buff (*isabelle*) coats with scarlet cuffs and lining (livery of the Duc de Mortemart).

Forez, 1704. Grey-white coat lined with grey-white, scarlet cuffs, waistcoats and stockings, grey-white breeches, brass buttons and false gold hat lace; drummers had blue coats with scarlet cuffs and lining laced with the king's small livery lace; gold buttons and hat lace for officers.

Voluire, 9 November 1705. Grey-white coat with blue cuffs, lining, waistcoat, breeches and stockings, "gold or silver" buttons and hat lace. Officers, gold buttons and hat lace.

Châtillon (or Souillac de Châtillon), 1705. Grey-white coat with grey-white lining, blue cuffs, waistcoat and stockings, grey-white waistcoat, pewter buttons.

Murat, *c.* 1705. Grey-white coat and lining, red cuffs, yellow waistcoat, grey-white breeches, red stockings, brass buttons, hats edged with false gold lace. Sergeants, half scarlet cuffs, waistcoats, breeches and stockings, brass buttons. Drummers, yellow coat, red cuffs, yellow waistcoat, grey-white breeches, red stockings, brass buttons, hats edged with false gold lace.

Saint-Gery, 1705. Grey white coat, blue cuffs lining, waistcoat, breeches and stockings, brass buttons, false gold hat lace. Drummers, half scarlet lined with blue, livery lace.

Provenchère, 1705. Grey-white coat and lining, red cuffs and waistcoat, false gold hat lace. Drummers, red coat, scarlet cuffs.

Phélippes de la Houssaye, 9 December 1705. Grey-white coat, red waistcoat. Sergeants, 26 gold lace for hats.

Vivarais, 15 December 1705 and 5 March 1706. Grey-white coat lined grey-white, red cuffs, waistcoat and stockings, grey-white breeches, brass buttons, false gold laced hats. Sergeants, red breeches, gold hat lace.

Thorigny, 1706. Grey-white coat with scarlet cuffs and lining, red waistcoat, grey-white breeches, brass buttons, scarlet stockings, false gold hat lace. Sergeant, gold lace. Drummers, scarlet coat, blue cuffs and lining, blue waistcoat, grey-white breeches, scarlet stockings, brass buttons, livery lace and gold lace for drum major.

Kaërgroët (also Kergroadec, and Quergroades), 20 March 1706. Grey-white coat lined grey-white, blue cuffs, blue waistcoat, breeches and stocking, brass buttons, false gold laced hats. Drummers, buff (*isabelle*) coat, blue cuffs, waistcoat, breeches and stocking, livery lace, brass buttons, false gold-laced hats.

Saillant, 1706. Grey-white coat lined blue, blue cuffs, blue waistcoat front, breeches and stocking, brass buttons, false gold laced hats. Drummer, coat blue, lined with blue, royal livery lace, brass buttons, false gold-laced hats.

Clairefontaine, 1706. Grey-White coat and lining, red cuffs, waistcoat, breeches and stockings, brass buttons and false gold hat lace; drummers seemingly had scarlet coats lined with scarlet, brass buttons.

Thomassin de Saint-Paul, 1707. Grey-white coat lined grey-white, red stockings, pewter buttons in 1707 but brass in 1708, false gold hat lace.

Boufflers, 1707. Grey-white coat lined grey-white, scarlet cuffs, red waistcoats, brass buttons, grey-white breeches, red stockings, false gold hat lace. Sergeants, gold lace.

Briouze, 1707. Grey-white coat and lining, red cuffs, red waistcoat, breeches and stocking, pewter buttons, laced hats. Sergeants, silver lace for edging hats and cuffs and probably half scarlet stockings.

Nivernais, 1707. Grey-white cloth, red cloth [probably for cuffs], breeches cut and sown.

Auxerrois, 1707. Grey-white cloth, red cloth [probably for cuffs and waistcoat], raw serge to make breeches, silver cuff and hat lace for sergeants.

Franclieu, 1707–1708. Grey-white coat lined with grey-white, red cuffs, blue waistcoat and breeches, pewter buttons and false river hat lace. Drummers, buff (*isabelle*) coat with blue cuffs and lining, black velvet livery lace, pewter buttons and false silver hat lace.

# UNIFORMS

Du Bièz, 1708. Grey-white coat lined grey-white, red cuffs, grey-white breeches, red stockings, pewter buttons, false silver hat lace. Sergeants, silver lace at cuffs and edging hats. Drummers, yellow coat with red cuffs and lining, black and white livery lace, pewter buttons, false silver hat lace.

Ussy, 1708. Grey-white coat lined grey-white, grey-white brass buttons. Drummers, green coat with orange (*aurore*) cuffs and lining, 26 crosses for drummers (worn on coat's chest and back).

Miromesnil, 1711. Grey-white coat lined with serge, knit wool breeches, red stockings, false gold hat lace, gold for sergeants, red sabre knot for grenadiers, red powder flask cord or strap.

Auxerrois, 1711. Grey-white coat lined with grey-white serge, red cuffs and waistcoat, grey-white breeches, royal livery for drummers, gold buttons for officers.

Appendix IV

# The Dutch Army

When Louis was born in 1638, the army of the Netherlands was arguably one of the finest in Europe. It was not a large army, but its professionalism was outstanding and it was also one the best armed forces in Europe. After the 1648 end of the Thirty Years' War, the Netherlands enjoyed a period of peace and prosperity, but the government neglected considerably the army. The results were seen during the 1672 French invasion when what Dutch army there was mostly collapsed. But it was not destroyed. It had retreated behind the water line although disorganised and unpaid. The new ruler, William of Orange, proved equal to the task of reorganising the army. He rallied all he could, the unoccupied parts of the country contributed the funds and, with his officers, built up over the years a Dutch army that was still modest in size at about 25,000 men, but once again a serious fighting force. It could not be much more since the logistics of the Dutch could not support and feed a stronger army. Over the next years and decades, the army was reorganised partly by adopting many practices in Louis XIV's army, although logistics were largely left to the private sector instead of the bureaucracy and this proved effective for the Netherlands, which was a world banking and business centre. The professional corps of the Dutch army were highly regarded, notably engineers. William of Orange was a competent general and so were other high ranking officer, for instance Coehorn, but no outstanding tactician emerged.

The size of the army grew and the Netherlands were also able to pay for contingents of foreign allied "Subsidie-troepen" (subsidised troops) to Germans states such as Brandenburg, Hesse-Kassel, Brunswick and other as well as to Sweden and Denmark when they were allies. In 1689, these troops amounted to 16,664 men in a Dutch force of 66,878 men and, in 1702, some 16,662 men in an army of 78,905 men. The army rose to 108,469 men in 1710 of which 77, 300 were Dutch soldiers. There were also foreign mercenary troops, notably the infantry regiments of the Scot's Brigade that were reorganised in 1674. In 1676, Watteville's Swiss Regiment entered Dutch service and heralded more Swiss regiments coming into the Netherland's service; there were seven by 1702 totalling about 14,000 men.

## THE DUTCH ARMY

Dutch troops in the roads of the Texel, 1671. This detail from a painting by Ludolf Bakhuysen shows a party of soldiers with officers. Most musketeers in the middle ground still wear steel helmets; there details are indistinct but some have blue coat, others brown. A sergeant (at left) wears a blue coat, a hat and has a wide buff bandolier. The officer with the lady in the foreground dons a black coat and breeches, buff stockings, blue bunches of ribbon at his hat and garters, a gold-embroidered crimson bandolier holding a gilt-hilted sword and an orange sash. (Courtesy Rijksmuseum, Amsterdam, SK-A-8)

Infantry officer of the Dutch army, c. 1695. Grey coat and breeches, red cuffs and lining, white stockings, orange sash, black hat with red and white plumes, gild sword guard. From a period magic lantern slide. (Rijksmuseum, Amsterdam. Author's photo)

# THE ARMIES AND WARS OF THE SUN KING 1643–1715 VOLUME 2

Guards of Stadholder William of Orange, c. 1695. The company of Swiss halberdsmen was called the Cent-Suisses, like those of Louis XIV, and were also dressed in sixteenth-century style. Their costume was red with capes of the same colour eded with blue and yellow, some with the badge of the Dutch lion and had black velvet caps; their halberd had large red tassels. The Garde du Corps initially wore blue in 1672 with embroidered coat of arms and ciphers later changed to red uniforms lined blue with silver lace and rode white horses. Sketch by Jan Hoynk van Papendrecht. (Courtesy Anne S.K. Brown Military Collection, Brown University Library, Providence, RI, USA)

# THE DUTCH ARMY

Cavalry formed a relatively modest part of the army at about 2,600 troopers in 1671, 3,633 troopers and 2,148 dragoons in 1715. In 1677–1678, the army was divided into 57 infantry regiments and 27 cavalry and dragoon units including the guards.

Dutch troops were present in many battles during this period. Those in their own country from 1672 and also in Flanders and Germany alongside the allies during the last quarter of the seventeenth century. Some of the main engagements were Senef, Cassel, Saint-Denis, Walcourt, Fleurus, Steenkirk, Neerwinden and Namur. In the War for Spanish Succession, Dutch troops were mostly in Flanders and Germany fighting in myriad of sieges and battles such as Bonn, Blenheim, Ramillies, Oudenarde, Ghent, Malplaquet, Denain and Le Quesnoy. Dutch troops were also sent to Spain and took part in the capture of Gibraltar and battles and sieges such as Ciudad Rodrigo, Barcelona, Alcantara, Almanza and Villa Viciosa. Not all were victories, but on the whole, Dutch troops fought with distinction and tenacity. The Netherlands also had militia companies organised in across the country, those in towns being often remarkably well appointed.

From the time of William of Orange, the previously neglected Dutch army was re-equipped with modern weapons and uniforms were gradually adopted. By the mid 1670s, it could match anything in the Sun King's army. Uniforms were mostly grey with linings and cuffs of different colours such as red for the Van Wijnbergen Regiment in 1690 or blue for the Saint-Amand Regiment; some wore blue coats such as the guards and some cavalry or red for the Scot's Brigade, whose Ramsay's Regiment had white lining in 1690 and its Darlymple's Regiment dressed in red coats with yellow lining complete with mitre-shaped fusilier caps whose fronts were embroidered with lions rampant at either side of a rock with the motto: "Firm". The guards somewhat emulated those of the Sun King with a mounted Gardes-du-Corps and Cent-Suisses, also armed with halberd and wearing the peculiar "ancient Swiss" costume, but in a red livery.[1]

Militiaman of Gravenhage, late seventeenth century. His firearm is the slightly older, but still lethal matchlock musket. Print after Daniel Marot. (Courtesy Rijksmuseum, Amsterdam. RP-P-OB-82.943)

---

1 James Ferguson, *Papers illustrating the history of the Scots Brigade in the service of the United Netherlands 1572–1782* (Edinburgh: University Press, 1899), Vol. 1; Olaf van Nimwegen, *The Dutch Army and the Military Revolutions 1588–1688* (Woodbridge, UK: Boydell, 2006); Bruno Mugnai, *Wars and Soldiers in the Early Reign of Louis XIV. Volume 1 – The Army of the United Provinces of the Netherlands, 1660–1687* (Warwick, UK: Helion, 2018); H. Ringoir, *De Nederlandse Infanterie* (Bussum: Dishoeck, 1968); P. Forbes Wels, *De Nederlandse Cavalerie* (Bussum: Dishoeck, 1963).

# Colour Plate Commentaries

## Plate 1 (L–R)

### Conti Regiment, *pertuisanier, c.* 1660–1670
Before 1670, many, perhaps all, infantry regiments had soldiers tasked with certain particular duties who were armed with partisans, hence their names. They wore the livery of their colonel, in this case, that of the princely and powerful family of Conti that, naturally, had its own regiments of infantry and cavalry. This Conti Regiment was raised in 1654 after the Fronde civil war and went on to serve in the 1667–1668 Flanders and Franche-Comté *Blitzkriegs*, the rather desperate siege of Candia in Crete and other campaigns later on. The Conti livery was yellow lined with blue lining and velvet cuffs, silver buttons and lace.

### Lyonnois, sergeant, 1666
The Lyonnois Regiment, although it had a geographical name referring to the city of Lyon and its area, was really a unit largely controlled and sponsored by the powerful grand noble Villeroi family. It was one of the first units to wear uniforms described in a 1666 parade as being grey-white with red lining and presumably cuffs to the coat, red stockings, dark red ribbons on the shoulder and at the hat that also had a white plume. Sergeants also wore grey-white lined with red, their coats being laced with silver "everywhere". The King was impressed, which must have been the wish of the Duke of Villeroi.

### La Reine Regiment, drummer, *c.* 1661–1675
This regiment, which had been Mazarin-Français, became La Reine – the Queen's – following the passing of Cardinal Mazarin in 1661. The drummers of the regiment thus wore from then onwards the Queen's livery, which was the opposite of the King's (which was blue lined red). The Queen's was red lined with blue with blue and white livery lace. The Queen's coat of arms was that of France paired with those of Navarre and this would have been painted on the red drum case.

COLOUR PLATE COMMENTARIES

# Plate 2

### Douglas Scottish Regiment, fusilier, 1672
In 1667, this unit was sent a shipment of red and white cloth to make uniforms. In 1672, Scots soldiers were seen in the Netherlands wearing red coats and, in 1684 after the regiment had gone into British service, it was reported in red coats with white cuffs. This soldier is armed with the frowned upon, but not completely disallowed. flintlock musket. Four infantrymen per company were allowed to have them as well as grenadiers from 1670. The equipment could have been the standard bandolier with the charges or, perhaps more likely, a pouch to keep the powder, bullets and flints.

### Infantry musketeer back view, c. 1673–1680
This equipment seen in this back view of a soldier armed with a matchlock musket was common to most French infantrymen during the 1670s. They had the buff leather bandoliers, one to hold the sword and the other devoted to the muskets ammunition: the powder bottles, the pouch for bullets, and a powder flask or horn.

### Vierzet Walloon Regiment, field officer, 1679
The Sun King wished that officers wear uniforms of the same colour as their soldiers. Some 1679 correspondence confirms this when Minister of War Louvois mentioned that the officers of the Vierzet Walloon Regiment should wear its *feuille morte* (dead leaf brown) lined with blue uniforms embellished with silver buttons. Field officers would almost certainly add liberal amounts of silver lace as was the fashion.

# Plate 3

### Condé Infantry Regiment, drummer, c. 1685–1695
Drummers of this regiment wore the livery of the princes of Condé. This consisted of an *isabelle* (yellowish or pale buff) coat lined and cuffed with red, and garnished with red velvet lace. Paintings at the Condé Museum in Chantilly show Prince Condé's guards and servants wearing this livery with gold buttons, red ribbons and silver hat lace. A drummer would have had red stockings and his drum case painted *isabelle* with the prince's coat of arms surrounded by trophies. On regimental drums, these last would have included small regimental colours (blue and *isabelle* quarters) on both sides. The drum collar was likely *isabelle* edged with red velvet lace.

### Stuppa Swiss Regiment, fusilier, c. 1690–1695
There were two Stuppa regiments in the French army's foreign establishment, old Stuppa raised in 1672 and young Stuppa that was organised in 1677. In 1692, both were described with blue coats with red cuffs and lining as were Erlach, Monin, Porlier and Hessy. The other six Swiss regiments had yellow, red or green coats. Other details are not given, but some soldiers may have had the "points" attached to the garters, a fashion amongst the Swiss.

**Montroux Italian Regiment, sergeant, c. 1690–1702**
Raised in 1690, this Italian regiment is reported wearing red with blue cuffs and coat lining in 1692 and again in 1702. We show other garments as being red, but there is no certainty regarding these and they could have been blue or some blue and some red or even other colours. We have shown the buttons as gold mainly because the regimental colours of blue and red have a gold border. This more interestingly shows that a foreign Italian unit, too, could wear a red coat if it chose.

## Plate 4

**Rouergue Regiment, fusilier, c. 1695–1700**
His uniform and equipment is typical of many regiments at the end of the seventeenth century. Flintlock muskets were carried by about half of the men in the army in the early 1690s and gradually became the only type of weapon arming soldiers by the beginning of the eighteenth century. The grey-white coat with red cuffs, waistcoat and stockings were noted in 1698.

**La Mark German Regiment, fusilier, c. 1702**
This regiment mostly served in Italy during the 1690's and in Flanders during the War of Spanish Succession. It had a yellow coat in the 1692 list when named Surbeck and yellow was still worn in 1702 when it was called La Mark although still called by its old name in that document. The La Mark family livery was white with black cuffs with lace of the same colour, which would have been worn by its drummers and trabans.

**Orléonnais Regiment, officer, 1699**
Raised in 1693, this regiment first served in Flanders and in Italy during the early 1700s. This officer wears the uniform that was provided in 1699 according to a clothing contract consisting of a grey-white coat with blue cuffs, lining, waistcoat, breeches and stockings, gold buttons and lace.

## Plate 5

**Royal-Roussillon Regiment, fusilier, early eighteenth century**
This regiment served with distinction in many campaigns during the reign of Louis XIV. It was originally on the foreign establishment until 1659 when Roussillon became part of France. It was reported as having an all red uniform in 1692 and was seen wearing red with white stockings at Compiègne in 1698 and listed as wearing that red uniform four years later and it probably wore that colour until the reign of Louis XV when it changed to grey-white with blue.

**Viverais Regiment, sergeant, c. 1705**
This regiment, raised in 1684, was serving in northern Italy when the illustrated uniform was made in 1705. It consisted of a grey-white uniform